EMPOWERING PROGRESS.

For over 200 years, Citi's mission has been to
enable growth and progress for our clients and
the communities we serve. That's why, as a
long-standing supporter, we salute the Foreign
Policy Association and its vital role as a catalyst
for change.

citi
Welcome what's next

GREAT DECISIONS 2020

GREAT DECISIONS IS A TRADEMARK OF THE FOREIGN POLICY ASSOCIATION.

© COPYRIGHT 2020 BY FOREIGN POLICY ASSOCIATION, INC., 551 FIFTH AVENUE, NEW YORK, NEW YORK 10176.

All rights reserved.

No part of this book may be reproduced in any form, or by any means, without permission in writing from the publisher.

PRINTED IN THE UNITED STATES OF AMERICA BY DARTMOUTH PRINTING COMPANY, HANOVER, NH.

LIBRARY OF CONGRESS CONTROL NUMBER: 2019950253

ISBN: 978-0-87124-267-9

Researched as of November 18, 2019.

The authors are responsible for factual accuracy and for the views expressed.

FPA itself takes no position on issues of U.S. foreign policy.

The Foreign Policy Association has moved office!

Our new address is:
551 Fifth Avenue, Suite 3000, New York, NY 10176.

The Valor of Knowledge

*J*ohn F. Kennedy observed that the ignorance of one voter in a democracy impairs the security of all. While President Kennedy was indulging in hyperbole, there is little doubt that leaders who make bad foreign policy decisions often trigger costly, long-term consequences for the polity as a whole.

In the course of the Foreign Policy Association's daunting first century, millions of Americans have worked with FPA to seek a more profound understanding of world affairs. The common purpose bringing us together has not been to impose a particular view but to consider and weigh many views. At the heart of this citizen effort lies the conviction that America must continue to frame its policies by the processes of democracy. Even the best policy cannot be sustained unless the public, whose interest it ultimately must serve, approves of the policy.

At FPA, we do not believe that global issues are too complex for citizens to understand if clearly briefed. Not to a limited circle, therefore, but to all, FPA extends an open invitation to join in a collective dialogue on our future in an interdependent world.

On the local news, an emergency room physician at Mount Sinai Hospital in New York City recently told the interviewer in a story on global pandemics, "I have to keep abreast of world news to do my job." This is no less true for those in education, business, banking, law; indeed, almost every profession. It is also true, if we are to be good citizens. Every generation has to exercise the responsibilities of citizenship by staying informed. This is key to sustaining our democracy.

In this election season, we would do well to heed the warning of President Franklin D. Roosevelt: "Democracy cannot succeed unless those who express their choice are prepared to choose wisely. The real safeguard of democracy, therefore, is education." And Thomas Jefferson: "Educate and inform the whole mass of the people...they are the only sure reliance for the preservation of our liberty."

In addition to being informed, Jefferson believed that citizens in a democracy had to be virtuous: "The minds of the people are to be informed by education of what is right and of what is wrong; to be encouraged in habits of virtue and to be deterred from those of vice...These are the inculcations necessary to render the people a sure basis for the structure and order of government." A virtuous society would escape corruption, an affliction endemic to many governments and one that undermines trust, which is at the very foundation of good governance.

Jefferson's views on inclusive governance represent a radical departure from the way elites conducted themselves in the past and continue to do so in many parts of the world. The edification of the masses necessarily dilutes power concentrated among the few. The Founding Fathers were prepared to subsume their own interests to the good of the Nation.

John Meacham writes in his magisterial book, *The Soul of America; The Battle for our Better Angels*, that "to know what has come before is to be armed against despair." Arthur Schlesinger, Jr., observed:

> *"History is to the nation much as memory is to the individual. The individual who loses his memory doesn't know where he came from or where he's going and he becomes dislocated and disoriented. Similarly, a nation that forgets its history is disabled in dealing with the present and the future."*

The neglect of history has incalculable consequences. That significant numbers of millennials favor leadership by a strongman is a tragic example of a lapse of knowledge of history.

Our schools must be held accountable for their deficiencies in teaching history, civics and global studies (HCGS). While we have initiatives to encourage education in math and science (STEM), as well as standardized testing that rewards schools that teach subjects like literature well, there is no system in place to incent schools to put more emphasis on HCGS. This is inexcusable, resulting in graduates who cannot differentiate democracy from dictatorship; who overlook that the United States Constitution comprises some of the most exceptional rules of government ever written; and who cannot even place America on a world map.

It is high time, in the words of FPA Director Peter F. Krogh, that we replace the valor of ignorance with the valor of knowledge.

Noel V. Lateef
President and Chief Executive Officer
Foreign Policy Association

Climate change and the global order
by Ronald J. Bee

A man rides riding a tricycle with plastic bottles to be recycled on a day of heavy pollution on December 1, 2015, in Beijing, China. China's capital and many cities in the northern part of the country recorded the worst smog of the year with air quality devices in some areas unable to read such high levels of pollutants. (LINTAO ZHANG/GETTY IMAGES)

In the August 2019 Special Report of *Scientific American*, the lead story "Sea Change: The Contest to Control the Fast-Melting Arctic," describes how nation-states have positioned themselves to exploit resources in the rapidly thawing north. Twelve years earlier on August 2, 2007, three Russian explorers descended 4,300 meters in a small submarine at the North Pole to claim new territory and planted a titanium national flag. When the submersible surfaced and the Russians boarded their nuclear-powered ice-breaker, President Vladimir Putin phoned the ship to offer his congratulations. While setting the flag amounted to a political stunt to bolster Russian morale during a worldwide recession, it also signaled a new era of competition between states more focused on acquiring national resources than cooperating to counter the international effects of climate change.

Since 2006, Russia and three additional Arctic coastal states—Norway, Denmark (because it owns Greenland), and Canada—have all filed overlapping claims to the seabed floor with the international Commission on the Limits of the Continental Shelf (CLCS). The CLCS facilitates the implementation of the UN Convention on the Law of the Sea, which establishes the outer limits of the continental shelf beyond 200 miles. The U.S., the fifth nation with arctic coastline, in Alaska, will present its pitch in 2022, expected to overlie

RONALD J. BEE *is the Director of the Hansen Leadership Institute at the University of San Diego. He lectures in international relations at the Oxford Study Abroad Program in Oxford, UK, and has served as the co-director of the University of California Roger Revelle Program on Climate Science and Policy*

Canada's claims. On August 20, 2019, President Donald Trump cancelled a trip to Denmark because Danish Prime Minister Mette Fredericksen refused to discuss selling Greenland to the U.S.

As President Putin expands military bases across Russia's long Arctic shoreline, the North Atlantic Treaty Organization (NATO) has responded by reinforcing its northern militaries, fearing that Russia might just take the seabed like it annexed Crimea, Ukraine, in 2014. In May 2019, U.S. Secretary of State Mike Pompeo, at an Arctic Council meeting in Finland, argued that Russia has acted aggressively and that China should be watched carefully, too, since it has helped finance Russia's natural gas storage tanks in the Arctic. The meeting ended without a declaration of cooperation for the first time in 23 years, casting a black cloud over future boundary negotiations.

In a special issue of National Geographic, *The Artic is Heating Up*, the magazine juxtaposes a "new cold war—as the ice melts, old rivals scramble for position" vs. "the carbon threat—thawing tundra will speed up global warming." In 2018, 879 unique ships sailed into the Arctic sea, nearly a 60% increase from 2012. The thawing of the permafrost will expose vast pools of methane, the article argues, which "could pump billions of additional tons of methane and carbon dioxide into the atmosphere every year—a threat that has yet to be fully accounted for in climate models."

Beyond geopolitics and the big Arctic thaw, what's at stake economically? In 2008, a U.S. Geological Survey study opined that the thick sediment of the Arctic may hold 30% of the world's undiscovered natural gas, 13% of its oil, valuable iron deposits and rare earth minerals. With the melting ice of the Arctic Ocean, shipping lanes could open up to tap into and exploit these resources.

On a global scale, the Arctic may represent a "canary in a coal mine" for the erosion of the global order's attempts to contain climate change. Have national politics and economic nationalism poisoned international agreements to reduce global temperatures? Climate accords such as the Rio Climate Convention of 1992 and the Paris Climate Agreement of 2015 may have become as imperiled as the coastal populations threatened by the rising seas. *Foreign Policy* has argued that "Rising Tides Will Sink Global Order" and that "global warming will produce national extinctions and international insurgencies—and change everything you think you know about foreign policy."

Are we really destined for such climate-induced chaos? A raucous December 2018 Conference of the Parties (COP) meeting in Katowice, Poland, suggests yes, we are, at least politically. Nations gathered to advance implementation of the Paris Climate Agreement. That did not happen. Why? Because of at least three reasons:

1. Oil and gas producers—the United States, Saudi Arabia, Kuwait and Russia—blocked recognition of the apocalyptic conclusions of the UN Intergovernmental Panel on Climate Change (IPCC) report which concluded that states must take "unprecedented" action to contain global greenhouse gas emissions. If emissions do not plateau within 12 years, scientists predict an increase of 1.5 degree Celsius in temperature, bringing with it catastrophic sea-level rise and other damaging effects;

2. Brazil, scheduled to host the next annual COP meeting, withdrew its sponsorship. Newly elected President Jair Bolsanaro, a climate change skeptic, and nick-named by some as "Trump of the Tropics," cancelled the summit. His foreign minister, Ernesto Araujo, went so far as to call the movement to reduce global warming a "plot by Marxists to stifle the economic growth of capitalist democracies while lifting China"; and

3. Poland and the U.S. went so far as to reaffirm their commitments to use

coal to fuel their economies. China, the world's third largest holder of coal deposits after the U.S. and Russia, under its international Belt and Road Initiative (BRI), has begun building more than 300 coal plants in places like Turkey, Vietnam, Indonesia, Bangladesh, Pakistan, Egypt, and the Philippines.

In the U.S., the polarization of domestic politics in an election year has clouded the climate debate. On February 7, 2019, Democratic Representative Alexandria Ocasio-Cortez (D-NY) and Senator Ed Markey (D-MA) introduced House Resolution 109 (HR 109), calling for the Federal Government to create a "Green New Deal" (GND) to overhaul if not eliminate the fossil fuel economy. The GND has two separate proposals: the "Green" plan on climate and energy aims to replace the energy grid with renewable fuels, a zero emissions transportation system, and retrofit all U.S. buildings to become non-carbon energy efficient; the "New Deal" plan calls for an extensive set of federal social programs including universal health coverage, a federally guaranteed jobs program, guaranteed housing, food security, and free college tuition. The New Deal portion also pays homage President Franklin D. Roosevelt's depression-era program (1933–36) that invested heavily in public works projects, financial reforms, and regulations.

Regarding climate, HR 109 goes as far as to state, "A changing climate is causing sea levels to rise and an increase in wildfires, severe storms, droughts, and other extreme weather events that threaten human life, healthy communities, and critical infrastructure." It argues further that "human activity is the dominant cause of climate change in the past century," and that the United States, having emitted 20% of global greenhouse emissions through 2014, has a duty to "take a leading role in reducing emissions through economic transformation."

The Trump administration has derided the GND while endorsing the "fracking revolution" that has reestablished the U.S. as the leader in global oil and gas production, created more jobs,

Before you read, download the companion **Glossary** that includes definitions, a guide to acronyms and abbreviations used in the article, and other material. Go to **www.fpa.org/great_decisions** and select a topic in the Resources section. (Top Right)

and reenergized the American economy. Economic growth and more jobs, the president's argument goes, neither comes from federal programs nor handouts; it comes from the private sector and market-driven forces. He further asserts that the exorbitant cost of a GND would bankrupt the federal government. The American Action Forum, for example, estimated the cost of GND between 53 and 92 trillion dollars, without adding the cost of free college tuition.

The issue of climate change has become mired in an American clash of fears over the extremes of "socialism" vs. "capitalism." For Trump supporters, green new dealers just want to tax and spend, stifle economic growth, erode the American way of life, and end the lowest unemployment rate since the 1960s. The president would argue the GND represents more of a socialist movement masquerading as science. For the green new dealers, the president's energy policies represents yet another capitalist chapter where the wealthy keep getting wealthier on the backs of the poor while pollution destroys the planet. They would rebalance the scales of environmental and social degradation by having the U.S. overhaul its economic system, dump fossil fuels, and redistribute wealth.

One should not underestimate that such extreme political claims aim more to shake up the political climate and attract voters in the 2020 elections than to conduct an honest assessment of the longer-term consequences of global environmental degradation. In the process, Congress has become a stagnant pool passing very few laws. House democrats have spent more time on impeachment proceedings than on funding the federal government.

Such "politics as usual" at local and national levels has direct consequences for the conduct of foreign relations. When economic national interests line up against UN warnings about climate, the global order usually loses to shorter-term political-economic imperatives. Can national economies accommodate a diversity of renewable and nonrenewable energy supplies? Or should they move forward solely with the fos-

sil fuels that continue producing wealth and economic development? How long can the earth accommodate rising C02 levels?

On September 23, 2019, UN Secretary General Antonio Guterres cast his vote by opening a "Climate Action Summit" to declare an international climate emergency. A summit document proclaimed, "Global emissions are reaching record levels and show no signs of peaking. The last four years were the four hottest on record, and winter temperatures in the Arctic have risen by 3 degrees Celsius since 1990. Sea levels are rising, coral reefs are dying, and we are starting to see the life-threatening impact of climate change on health, through air pollution, heat waves, and risks to food security." Secretary General Guterres called on all leaders to arrive with "concrete, realistic plans" to reduce greenhouse gas emissions by 45% over the next decade and to achieve net-zero emissions by 2050.

Greta Thunberg, a 16-year-old Swedish climate activist, addressed the summit, chiding leaders to act: "You have stolen my dreams and my childhood with your empty words….Entire ecosystems are collapsing. We are in the beginning of a mass extinction and all you can talk about is money and fairy

tales of eternal economic growth. How dare you!"

The climate summit targets have their origins in the 2015 Paris Agreement, which calls for global temperature target of below 2 degrees Celsius warming above preindustrial conditions. The accord requires each state commit to a "nationally determined contribution" (NDC) to achieve this goal. Parties must file annual progress reports on their pledged emission reductions—which so far have not been met.

On June 1, 2017, President Donald Trump announced his decision to withdraw from the Obama-era agreement, citing it "disadvantages the United States to the exclusive benefit of other countries, leaving American workers—who I love—and taxpayers to absorb the cost in terms of lost jobs, lower wages, shuttered factories, and vastly diminished economic production." Noting that China and India did not have to make reductions, the president claimed he would renegotiate the deal at a later date. That will have to wait until after the 2020 election. Under Article 28 of the Paris Climate Agreement, the U.S. cannot withdraw from the accord before November 4, 2020—one day after Americans go to the polls.

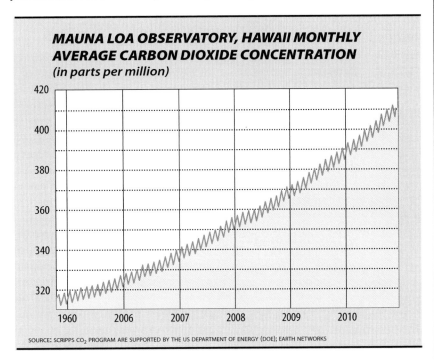

MAUNA LOA OBSERVATORY, HAWAII MONTHLY AVERAGE CARBON DIOXIDE CONCENTRATION
(in parts per million)

SOURCE: SCRIPPS CO₂ PROGRAM ARE SUPPORTED BY THE US DEPARTMENT OF ENERGY (DOE); EARTH NETWORKS

The science: a large-scale geophysical experiment

In 1957, Dr. Roger Revelle, Director of the Scripps Institution of Oceanography (SIO), and Dr. Hans Seuss at UC San Diego, published a study in the journal *Tellus* that suggested humankind, since the industrial age (1760–1840), had been transferring vast stores of carbon from the earth to the atmosphere via the burning of coal, oil, and gas. Our reliance on "fossil fuels" amounted to a "large-scale geophysical experiment of a kind that could not have happened in the past nor be reproduced in the future. Within a few centuries we are returning to the atmosphere and oceans the concentrated organic carbon stored in sedimentary rocks over hundreds of millions of years."

This seminal article on climate change went on to conclude that "This experiment, if adequately documented, may yield a far-reaching insight into the processes determining weather and climate." To document carbon's natural processes and everyday human influences on climate, however, scientists would need to measure carbon dioxide (CO_2)—the main carbon by-product of burning fossil fuels—in the atmosphere. Dr. Revelle worked with a colleague at SIO, Dr. Charles David Keeling, since 1956 to measure CO_2 in the atmosphere in Mauna Loa Observatory, Hawaii. They chose Mauna Loa as a monitoring site because of its distance from major continents to calculate global averages, and its altitude above the inversion layer where most local effects exist.

Keeling ran the Scripps CO_2 program until his death in 2005. Keeling's son Ralph F. Keeling now runs the program at SIO with the National Oceanic and Atmospheric Association (NOAA). NOAA focuses on tracking the conditions of the oceans, major waterways and the atmosphere. The Keeling Curve, as now known, represents the longest continuous measurement of CO_2 in the atmosphere. The jagged saw-tooth nature of the curve simply indicates natural growth cycles of plants (spring and fall). Plants grow via photosynthesis in the spring by absorbing CO_2 from the atmosphere and levels then decline. Then plants die or leaves fall and decompose in the autumn releasing CO_2 back into the atmosphere and levels then rise. The overall trend in CO_2 increases also mirrors median temperature rise, thus raising the question to what degree have human activities on earth also contributed to rising CO_2 and temperature levels.

The Global Change Research Act of 1990 mandated NOAA to conduct a U.S. Global Change Research Program (USGCRP) and to deliver a national assessment every four years to analyze the current trends in global change on a U.S. local, state, and national basis. In their Fourth National Climate Assessment, they concluded "Coastal communities and the ecosystems that support them are increasingly threatened by the impacts of climate change. Without significant reductions in global greenhouse gas emissions and regional adaptation measures, many coastal regions will be transformed by the later part of this century…many communities are expected to suffer financial impacts as chronic high-tide flooding leads to higher costs and lower property values."

Globally, according to Jeff Goodell, a contributing editor at *Rolling Stone* and author of 2017 book *The Water Will Come: Rising Seas, Sinking Cities, and the Remaking of the Civilized World*, "about 145 million people live three feet or less above the current sea level. As the waters rise, millions of these people will be displaced, many of them in poor countries, creating generations of climate refugees that will make today's Syrian war refugee crisis look like a high school drama production."

The term "global warming" first appeared in the 1975 paper in *Science* by Wallace Broecker entitled, "Climate Change: Are we on the Brink of Pronounced Global Warming?" Broecker asserted that by early in the 21st century, we "will have driven the mean planetary temperature beyond the limits experienced during the last 1000 years." In 1979 a National Academy of Science Study first use the term "climate changes" to describe what will happen if carbon dioxide continues to increase in the atmosphere.

Today, in common parlance, on internet sites, and the news media often use the terms global warming and climate change interchangeably. Scientists prefer the term climate change. According to NASA, global warming means the increase in the earth's average temperature due to rising levels of greenhouse gases. Climate change refers to a long-term change in the earth's climate, or of a particular region on earth. Put another way, global warming indicates surface temperature increases, and climate change includes global warming and everything else that affects climate due to the increase of greenhouse gases.

Greenhouse gases trap heat in the atmosphere. They include carbon dioxide (82%), methane (10%), nitrous oxide (6%) and fluorinated gases (3%).

The global climate has always changed from pre-human history to the present day, as has the earth's seasonal

Dr. Roger Revelle, head of the Scripps
(FRITZ GORO/THE LIFE PICTURE COLLECTION/ GETTY IMAGES)

Global CO$_2$ Emissions by Country, 2014

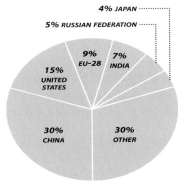

SOURCE: Boden, T.A., Marland, G., And Andres, R.J. (2017). National CO$_2$ Emissions from Fossil-fuel Burning, Cement Manufacture, And Gas Flaring: 1751-2014, Carbon Dioxide Information Analysis Center, Oak Ridge National Laboratory, U.S. Department of Energy.

carbon cycle that shuffles between the land, oceans, and sky. We had an ice age that began 2.4 million years ago and ended 11,500 thousand years ago However, with our human population now approaching 8 billion people and growing, our continued reliance on the combustion engine in cars and trucks, use of fossil fuels to heat and cool buildings, keep the lights on, run factories let alone our myriad appliances, our cumulative "carbon footprint" logically has become much heavier.

Elizabeth Kolbert, award-winning science writer for the *New Yorker*, and author of *The Sixth Extinction: An Unnatural History*, has noted "Since the start of the industrial revolution, humans have burned through enough fossil fuels—coal, oil and natural gas—to add some 365 billion metric tons of carbon to the atmosphere. Deforestation has contributed another 180 billion tons. Each year we throw up another 9 billion tons or so, and amount that has been increasing by as much as six percent annually. As a result of all this, the concentration of carbon dioxide in the air today—a little over 400 parts per million—is higher than at any other point in the last eight hundred thousand years."

Jeff Goodell explained the difficulty for humans to psychologically confront something that has not yet happened: "We have evolved to defend ourselves from a guy with a knife or an animal with big teeth, but we are not wired to make decisions about barely perceptible threats that gradually accelerate over time. We're not so different from the proverbial frog that boils to death in a pot of slowly warming water."

Not everyone, however, believes in eventual climate doomsday for frogs in pots or humans in sports utility vehicles. John Coleman has countered, "As the founder of the Weather Channel and a six-decade veteran TV news weatherman, I know a great deal about this topic. We meteorologists are well aware of how limited our ability is to predict the weather. Our predictions become dramatically less reliable as they extend out into the future. When we try to predict just a few weeks into the future our predictions become increasingly inaccurate. Yet the "climate change" establishment that now dominates the UN bureaucracy and our own government science establishment claim that they can predict the temperature of the Earth decades into the future. Their global warming scare is not driven by science; it is now being driven by politics."

By 1988, the growing body of scientific data on climate change led to the creation of the Inter-Governmental Panel on Climate Change (IPCC) by the World Meteorological Organization (WMO) and the United Nations Environmental Program (UNEP). The IPCC has assessed peer-reviewed and non-peer reviewed research published

about climate change with an objective, scientifically based mandate to evaluate the natural, political and economic risks of increasing greenhouse gases. Its reports heavily influenced the passing of the Rio Climate Convention of

Secretary General António Guterres speaks at the Opening Ceremony of the 2019 Climate Action Summit. (ARIANA LINDQUIST/UN PHOTO)

Global Order Climate Talks 1992–2019

1992 THE RIO EARTH SUMMIT creates the UN Framework Convention on Climate Change (UNFCCC) which aims to prevent "dangerous" interference in the climate system. The UNFCCC does not legally bind signatories to reduce emissions but requires meetings called Conference of the Parties (COP) to happen. As of 2019, 197 countries have ratified the treaty, including the U.S.

1995 FIRST UNFCCC MEETING takes place in Berlin (COP1), which creates the "Berlin Mandate" that aims to set legally binding mandates and timetables upon signatories to reduce greenhouse gas emissions. The U.S. pushes back against these requirements.

1997 KYOTO PROTOCOL creates the first legally-binding climate treaty in Japan (COP3). It calls for reducing emissions to 5% below 1990 levels and sets up a monitoring system to track progress. The Protocol also creates a carbon market for countries to trade emissions and support sustainable development, a system known as "cap and trade." President Clinton signed the Kyoto Protocol in 1997 but the U.S. Senate refused to ratify it, citing potential damage to the U.S. economy.

2001 U.S. WITHDRAWS FROM TALKS ON KYOTO In March, George W. Bush ends U.S. negotiations on the Kyoto Protocol claiming the deal is not in America's economic interest.

2005 KYOTO ENTERS INTO EFFECT, notably without the U.S., the largest carbon emitter. It does cover an estimated 55% of global emissions.

2007 TALKS ON KYOTO 2.0 take place in Bali, Indonesia (COP13). An IPCC report claims that global warming is "most likely" caused by human activity.

2009 COPENHAGEN DISAPPOINTMENT in the Danish capital (COP15), where the parties only agree to a non-binding document. This Copenhagen Accord agrees that global temperatures should not increase by 2 degrees Celsius above pre-industrial levels.

2010 CANCUN (COP16) SETS TEMPERATURE TARGET at no more warming than 2 degrees Celsius, and establishes a $100 billion climate fund to assist developing countries to mitigate and adapt to climate change. As of 2019, countries have only submitted $3 billion to the fund.

2011 DURBAN, SOUTH AFRICA (COP17) Parties agree to draft a binding agreement by 2015 that will apply to both developed and developing countries.

2012 NO DEAL AT DOHA (COP18) to extend the Kyoto Protocol to 2020. The U.S. never signed on, Canada withdraws, and Japan and Russia decide to accept no new commitments. Those who remain account for only 15% of global emissions.

2015 PARIS (COP 21) CLIMATE AGREEMENT REACHED which requires all countries—developed and developing—to set emissions reductions goals. On April 1, 2016, the U.S. and China issue a joint statement that they would sign the Paris Agreement, doing so on April 22. The agreement goes into force on November 4, 2016, four days before the American election.

2017 On June 1, 2017, President Trump announces the U.S. withdrawal from the agreement citing its negative effects on the economy.

2018 RULES FOR PARIS AGREEMENT DECIDED in Katowice, Poland (COP24). A new IPCC report warns of devastating consequences including sea rise, stronger storms, and heatwaves by 2030. The meeting turns into a free-for-all with coal, oil, and gas-producing countries negating any progress.

2019 UN SECRETARY-GENERAL CALLS CLIMATE ACTION SUMMIT in New York in September. Antonio Guterres urges leaders to cut emissions by 40% by 2030 and reach carbon neutrality by 2050. On September 24, President Trump addresses the UN and asserts "The future does not belong to globalists, it belongs to patriots."

1992 and the Paris Climate Agreement of 2015.

Albert Gore, Jr., a former student of Roger Revelle, went on to serve in the U.S. House of Representatives (1977–85), the U.S. Senate (1985–93), and as the 45th vice president of the United States (1993–2001). In 1992 he wrote his first environmental book, *Earth in the Balance: Ecology and the Human Spirit*. Then, in 2006, Gore wrote the book, *An Inconvenient Truth*, with an accompanying documentary that addressed the emerging human challenge of global warming and climate change. The documentary received an Academy Award, and in 2007, Gore along with the UN's IPCC received a Nobel Peace Prize for his efforts to raise awareness about global warming.

On October 8, 2018, the IPCC released a Special Report on Global Warming of 1.5 degrees Celsius. This report, commissioned by the UNFCCC in 2015, lies at the heart of the current international debate over climate change. Countries in favor of more drastic action support its conclusions; nations who see it as too alarmist, politically motivated and dangerous to their national economic growth, downplay its significance—as became obvious at the December 2018 meeting in Katowice, Poland.

Key findings of the report include:
■ By 2100, If warming is kept to 1.5 degrees Celsius, coral reefs will still decline by 70–90% but if temperatures rise 2 degrees Celsius virtually all the world's reefs would be lost;
■ Global sea-level rise would be 10cm lower with global warming of 1.5 degrees Celsius compared to 2 degrees Celsius;
■ Extreme heatwaves will be experienced by 14% of the world's population at least once every five years at 1.5 degrees Celsius. But that figure rises to more than a third of the planet if temperatures rise 2 degrees Celsius; and
■ Arctic sea ice would remain during most summers if warming is kept to 1.5 degrees Celsius. But at 2 degrees Celsius, ice-free summers are ten times more likely leading to greater habitat losses for polar bears, whales, seals, and sea birds.

Making Coal, Oil and Gas Great Again

On November 8, 2016, the election of Donald J. Trump brought with it a domestic political promise to cancel the Paris Climate Agreement in favor of reinvigorating the coal, oil, and gas sectors to create more jobs, U.S. energy independence, and American-based wealth.

Coal: The top five coal-producing states are Wyoming (40.2%), West Virginia (12.6%), Pennsylvania (6.6%), Illinois (6.6%), and Kentucky (5.2%). Secretary Clinton only won Illinois out of these five states. In her book about the campaign, *What Happened*, Clinton wrote that her biggest regret involved saying she would "put coal miners out of business."

Oil: In 2018, about 68% of crude oil production came from five states: Texas (40.5%), North Dakota (11.5%), New Mexico (6.3%), Oklahoma (5%), and Alaska (4.5%). Of these five states, Mrs. Clinton only won New Mexico.

Gas: The top five state producers of natural gas are: Texas (23.7%), Pennsylvania (19%), Oklahoma (8.7%), Louisiana (7.4%), Ohio (6.2%) and Colorado (5.9%). Mrs. Clinton only won the state of Colorado on this list. According to the American Petroleum Institute (API), "The natural gas and oil industry is a critical part of the U.S. economy. In 2015, these energy resources supported 10.3 million jobs and contributed more than $1.3 trillion to the U.S. economy." A July 2017 API Factsheet argued "Research shows that for every oil and gas job, an additional 2.7 jobs are supported elsewhere in the economy. These jobs make up 5.6% of the nation's total employment."

Fracking, also known as hydraulic fracturing, has been used as a technique to drill for oil for some 65 years. Today, the combination of hydraulic fracturing and new horizontal drilling technology is responsible for the surge in U.S. oil and natural gas production. Once an oil well is drilled, small perforations are made in the horizontal portion of the well pipe, though which a mix of 90% water, 9.5% sand and .5% additives is pumped at high pressure to create micro-fractures in the rock. Fracking permits the U.S. to tap vast oil and gas reserves previously locked away in shale and other rock formations. 95% of natural gas wells drilled in the next decade will require hydraulic fracturing.

In 2016, out of the top 12 state producers of coal, oil, and natural gas, Donald Trump won 75% of them. Since energy policy plays to his strong suit domestically, we can expect the 2020 campaign—no matter the Democratic candidate—to embrace keeping coal, oil, and natural gas production great. Knowing the stakes, leading coal, oil, and gas CEOs have contributed millions of dollars to Donald Trump's 2020 reelection campaign.

The automobile industry will also play a role in November 2020. As of 2017, the American people drove 272.48 million vehicles. These include cars, motorcycles, trucks, buses and other vehicles. About 92% of American transportation fuel for vehicles now comes from fossil fuels. The automobile industry creates 9.9 million jobs coast-to-coast, or about 5.1% of American employment. According to the Auto Alliance, half of the companies on the Dow Jones industrial average depend on autos for revenue. Any disruption of the current automobile and parts industries, such as would happen under a Green New Deal, would have immediate effects on employment, manufacturing, and the American stock market. As of August 2019, stocks have gained 29% during the Trump presidency.

President Trump's appointment of Exxon-Mobil CEO Rex Tillerson as Secretary of State (February 21, 2017, to March 31, 2018) clarified the new administration's energy policy. Out of the gate, Tillerson received criticism for his leading a fossil fuels corporation that funded climate change skeptic groups, and for his ties with Russia's state-owned Rosneft corporation that facilitates oil and gas drilling in the Arctic Ocean and Black Sea. While acknowledging "the risks of climate change are real and require serious action," Tillerson also had stated that the potential solutions amount to "an engineering problem."

"LOOKS LIKE AN INSIDE JOB."

Secretary of State Tillerson's replacement, Mike Pompeo, has picked up the pro-U.S. energy development baton to promote U.S. interests abroad. On March 12, 2019, in a speech to the U.S. oil industry in Houston, Secretary Pompeo asserted that America's newfound shale oil and natural gas abundance "strengthens our hand in foreign policy." In calling upon oil producers to support Trump's foreign policy against certain bad actors that produce oil, Pompeo noted the use of sanctions against Venezuela with the intent to hasten the demise of Nicolas Maduro, Iran for conducting state-sponsored terrorism in the Middle East, and Russia for its annexation of the Crimea and support of Russian separatists in Eastern Ukraine.

On September 10, 2019, the president refilled the UN ambassador slot with Kelly Craft. Ambassador Craft hails from Kentucky, and is married to Joe Craft, a billionaire coal-mining executive for Alliance Research Partners, the third largest coal producer in the Eastern U.S. The Crafts donated to the 2016 Trump campaign. Ambassador Craft will need to preside over the UN's increasing concern over climate change, criticism of the U.S. government's commitment to a fossil fuel economy, and, if President Trump gets re-elected, the U.S. withdrawal from the Paris Climate Agreement.

U.S. "energy dominance" backed by sanctions abroad and strong economic growth at home has become the operating Trump Doctrine for U.S. foreign relations. As such, any discussion of climate change that negates or reduces fossil fuel production logically undermines that strategy. Under this approach, the thawing of the Arctic just provides another opportunity to bolster U.S. energy independence and supremacy.

The Global Order: How Global, How Orderly?

Throughout history, world orders have come and gone with economic, political, and military change. Most global orders emerged from past catastrophic wars—not the possibility of catastrophic climate change that might occur 12–30 years in the future. Some milestones:

The Treaty of Westphalia (1648): A series of treaties that ends The Thirty Years War, a religious conflict fought between Catholics and Protestants in Central Europe's Holy Roman Empire between 1618-48. Most political scientists say this treaty lays the foundations for the modern-day sovereign nation-state. Exhausted by war, pestilence, and economic destruction, the warring parties agreed to fix boundaries, and after that, inhabitants of a given country become subject to the laws of their respective *state* authority. Today in the world we have 195 nation-state authorities—also known as countries.

The Concert of Europe (1815): A system of conflict resolution that helps restore the monarchies Napoleon Bonaparte tried to overthrow in The Napoleonic Wars (1803-1815). Created at the Congress of Vienna, the Concert saw the great powers of Europe—Britain, France, Prussia, Russia, and Austria—transition from political chaos to a balanced peace that lasted for almost a hundred years. The five states maintain their power, opposed revolutionary movements, and restrained nationalism with what they called "the European balance of power."

Bismarck's European Alliance System (1871–1914) Germany became a modern, unified country under Otto von Bismarck (1815–98) who secretly created complex alliances built on the balance of power. As Germany's first Chancellor, he manipulated European rivalries to make Germany a world power, setting the stage for two world wars.

The League of Nations (1920–46) The brainchild of President Woodrow Wilson, the father of liberal internationalism. Wilson's Fourteen Points, a statement of principles for peace he uses in the talks to end World War I, reflects an approach favoring self-determination, the spread of democracy, the spread of capitalism and support for collective security. The League becomes the first worldwide organization with a principle mission to maintain world peace. The U.S. Senate refuses to join the League largely because it resembles an "entangling alliance". Wilson fails to impose his world view on the Senate and the allied powers, so the League fails to keep the peace, leading to World War II.

The United Nations (1945-now) President Franklin D. Roosevelt (FDR), former Assistant Secretary of the Navy under Wilson, revives the idea of global collective security with the United Nations (UN). Fifty nations signed the UN Charter which went into effect on October 24, 1945. The UN Security Council has five permanent members, the P-5, that hold veto power to prevent the adoption of any substantive resolution. The P-5 members: China (formerly the Republic of China), France, Russia (formerly the Soviet Union), the UK and the U.S. All five have use their veto power to protect and promote their national interests.

The Superpower Condominium (1945–91) The cold war sees two superpowers with opposing economic and political systems compete for power and influence, one communist, the USSR, and the other capitalist, the U.S. They fight in proxy wars (Korea 1950–53, Vietnam 1955–75, and Afghanistan 1979–89). They build alliances, the Warsaw Pact and the North Atlantic Treaty Organization, and nuclear arsenals. Nuclear deterrence almost fails during the Cuban Missile Crisis (October 16–28, 1962) when nuclear war became palpable. The two sides compromise, the USSR withdraws its missiles, leading to the limited test ban treaty and the nuclear nonproliferation treaty.

The New World Order (1990–2001) The fall of the Berlin Wall (November 9, 1989) marks the end of the cold war. Not long after, Iraqi dictator Saddam Hussein invades Kuwait on August 2, 1990. On September 11, 1990, President George H.W. Bush announces to Congress that the U.S., its allies and the UN will go to war to evict Iraqi troops from Kuwait and create "A New World Order." "The Crisis in the Persian Gulf, as grave as it is, also offers a rare opportunity to move forward toward a historic period of co-operation."

The Global War on Terrorism (2001–now) Exactly 11 years later, on September 11, 2001, President George W. Bush faces **the terrorist attacks of 9/11**. With economic globalization and the blurring of state boundaries, non-state actors like Al-Qaeda present a threat to the global order of nation-states. Cooperation on counterterrorism increases. The UN authorizes Operation Enduring Freedom (October 7, 2001) against Afghanistan for harboring terrorist training sites. The American-led Operation Iraqi Freedom (March 20, 2003), however, does not receive UN approval as France and Russia threaten to use their veto.

The modern evolution of the global order has a mixed track record at achieving global consensus on matters of international security. Therefore, we should not feign surprise that larger nation states continue to view issues of climate change through the prism of their respective national interests. Looking through those lenses, international responses to past conflict have proven difficult so any attempt to prevent the future effects of global climate change requires new thinking. Compromises will need to occur between the extreme views of climate doomsday and environmental ignorance.

Can We Compromise on Climate?

Many approaches have emerged to tackle reducing the effects of climate change. No one proposal by itself will likely reduce emissions fast enough for those worried about climate catastrophe nor convince those who believe fossil fuels remain crucial to national greatness to reduce demand. Some current approaches include:

The Bottom Up Approach — In his book, *The Thinking Person's Guide to Climate Change*, Robert Henson argues we must adopt first political and then technological solutions to tackle the possible negative consequences of climate change. Politically, the voluntary emissions goals set for nation-states by the Paris Agreement will be difficult to achieve. Yet other stakeholders— individuals, cities, and states—have heard the UN message and become proactive at reducing emissions.

"Smart cities" technology can help manage our environmental future. Smart cities are urban areas that use a variety of electronics, including the Internet of Things (IoT) sensors, to collect data and then manage assets, resources and services more efficiently. With 60% of the world population expected to live in cities by 2050, managing urban hubs will become key to managing emissions. In 2016, global smart city technology spending ran at $80 billion, and is expected to grow to $135 billion by 2021. A Smart Cities Council website has begun to share ideas for smart technology and data from 200 smart city projects.

Solar panels stand at the Ivanpah Solar Electric Generating System in the Mojave Desert near Primm, Nevada, U.S., on Monday, March 10, 2014. The 392-megawatt California Ivanpah plant developed by Google, NRG and Bright Source, which began operating in February, brings utility-scale solar to more than 5.5 gigawatts, up 1,089% since 2010. (JACOB KEPLER/BLOOMBERG/GETTY IMAGES)

Half of the 50 largest cities in the U.S. have adopted climate action plans. Twenty-three states plus the District of Columbia have adopted specific greenhouse gas reduction targets. The National Climate Assessment tracked these developments and acknowledged while adaptations and mitigations have expanded, however, "they do not yet approach the scale considered necessary to avoid substantial damages to the economy, environment, and human health over the coming decades."

The U.S. only represents 4.29% of the world population and emits 15% of global greenhouse gases. China and India remain the largest countries in the world, each with over a billion people, with 37% of the global population. According to *Forbes*, China alone emits more carbon dioxide than the U.S. and Europe combined. For the bottom-up approach to work globally, it will require global adoption.

The Corporate Accountability Approach — One UK-based organization, the Carbon Disclosure Project (CDP), takes what it considers "a fresh angle to

Environmental activists display a banner calling for action on climate change as they arrive on St. Peter's square prior to Pope Francis's Sunday Angelus prayer on June 28, 2015 at the Vatican. The activists included Christians, Muslims, Jews, Hindus and those of other denominations to urge adoption of an ambitious legally binding global agreement on climate change at the forthcoming UN conference in Paris, December 2015. (GABRIEL BOUYS/AFP/GETTY IMAGES)

an old debate." CDP keeps and publishes a Carbon Majors Database, essential measuring the largest corporate-level carbon dioxide and methane emissions worldwide. The data suggests that "since 1988, more than half of global industrial greenhouse gases can be traced to just 25 corporate and state producers." CDP reports aim to inform companies and

Andree Muntingh, Steenkampskraal (SKK) mine geologist, points to where the monazite reef (darker rock) containing the rare-earth minerals is, underground at the SKK rare-earth mine on July 29, 2019, about 80Km from the Western Cape town of Vanrhynsdorp. - SKK has been confirmed as one of the highest grade deposits of rare-earth minerals in the world. (RODGER BOSCH/AFP/GETTY IMAGES)

investors of the climate implications of their fossil fuel holdings.

As Pedro Faria, Technical Director of CDP, asserts, "Climate Action is no longer defined to the direction given by policy makers—it is now a social movement commanded by both economic and ethical imperatives and supported by growing amounts of data." This approach looks at working with—not just damning—the largest international corporate and state emitters to innovate ways to reduce the effects of climate change.

Some corporations have taken it to heart. According to the World Economic Forum, Apple's operations now run on 100% renewables and they have committed to 100% recyclable materials along its entire supply-chain. Google has become the largest corporate buyer of renewable energy in the world.

Market-Based Approach — As Michael Bloomberg and Carl Pope argue in their book, *Climate of Hope*, "Enlightened beneficence is not going to solve the problem of climate change. Only when self-interest acts are also climate-friendly acts, will success be possible. In other words, reducing carbon must offer profit opportunities for us to win the battle against climate change." They believe investors and consumers have begun looking at data more carefully for the environmental consequences before they invest and buy.

The Center for Climate and Energy

Solutions believes a carbon tax strategy provides another market-based solution. "Market-based strategies help fight climate change by putting an explicit price on carbon emissions and spurring businesses to find cost-effective ways to reduce those emissions. The cost of climate impacts—such as higher sea levels, and more frequent and severe heat waves, droughts, wildfires, and downpours—are not reflected in the goods and services that emit greenhouse gases." State and federal governments can and have also created tax incentives to install solar panels, and buy hybrid and electric cars.

Market-based approaches can work in democratic societies with liberal economic systems that welcome them and encourage innovation. Climate skeptics see a carbon tax as a regressive tax that will disadvantage the poor, stunt growth, and advantage illiberal countries that will not restrain their own coal, oil, and gas industries. Acceptance of market-based fixes may work in some countries, but on a global scale proves problematic.

The Technological Approach – The emergence of green technology looks to develop markets and create economies of scale for products that eliminate or reduce emissions. Green tech can include biomass, hydroelectric, geothermal, wind and solar (renewables), or cleaner coal and methane power generation with carbon dioxide capture and storage.

Nuclear power plants do not emit greenhouse gases. The United States, France, China, Russia, and South Korea have produced third generation nuclear reactors. While they have become safer, disastrous nuclear accidents with earlier generation plants at Chernobyl, Ukraine (1986) and Fukushima, Japan (2011) have doomed the chances of nuclear energy in many nations politically. France and China have no such concerns. Nuclear power is the main source of energy in France, and China hopes to produce 6% of its electricity via nuclear power by 2020.

The Nonproliferation Treaty (NPT) raises concerns about nuclear fuel from reactors getting diverted and reprocessed for nuclear weapons. Terrapower, a fourth-generation reactor company co-founded by Bill Gates, aims to fix both safety and proliferation worries. This "travelling wave reactor" breeds plutonium from uranium and then uses the plutonium as fuel, all contained with the reactor. The same fuel operates and generates electricity for decades. Earlier breeders required taking the plutonium off-site for reprocessing. China will build and operate the first of the Terrapower reactors by 2025.

Thorium reactors, another fourth-generation idea, would use thorium and uranium as the main fuel. Inside the reactor, the thorium converts to uranium-233 which fissions. The fuel lasts eight years, cannot melt down, cannot produce nuclear weapons, and is "walkaway safe" according to one of the U.S companies, Thorcon, developing the technology. India has indicated it hopes to use thorium as its main nuclear fuel in the coming decades.

The Top-Down Approach – On September 22, 2019, The United Nations adopted a 10-year Climate Action Plan aimed at a 45% reduction in greenhouse gases and sourcing 80% of electricity from renewable energy sources by 2030. The plan incorporates nine independent tracks and workplans: mitigation, social and political drivers, industry transition, infrastructures, cities and local action, nature-based solutions, resilience and adaptation, and climate finance and carbon pricing. Now comes the hard part-inducing nation-states to cooperate to achieve these ambitious goals.

The global challenge of rising seas: politics at the water's edge

Many environmentalists at home and abroad pin their hopes on the election of a new American President in 2020. This desire may fall fallow in light of the strong U.S. economy fueled in part with many new jobs, low unemployment, and a strong stock market. Moreover, the United States, while still a key player, does not represent the entire global order, nor even one fifth of global greenhouse emissions. Nonetheless many American citizens and leaders at local and state levels have started hedging against climate change by adjusting their lifestyles to lighten their carbon footprints.

For most of modern history, protecting peace and security has dominated the global order's agenda. Environmental issues requiring gradual lifestyle changes have been overshadowed by more immediate life and death imperatives. Deciding on who owns the Arctic, on how to adjust to rising seas, and developing new approaches and technologies to cope with climate change will require compromises both at home and abroad. Are we up to it?

Have we in fact become that caged canary destined to perish in our own coal mine, or can we unlock the cage by using creative innovation to continue promoting and prolonging human existence on this planet? In the epilogue of his 2019 book, *The Ice at the End of the World*, John Gertner wonders if "we seem disinclined to think too far—or too selflessly—as a species." Overcoming this inherent human trait remains an international challenge.

In another time, May 1948, in the aftermath of World War II, U.S. Senator Arthur Vandenberg (R-MI), Chairman of the U.S. Senate Foreign Relations Committee, introduced a landmark resolution supporting the creation of collective security in Europe which led directly to the formation of NATO. Presidential elections also loomed in the background, and Vandenberg was a leading candidate for the GOP against Harry Truman. In asserting, "politics stop at the water's edge," Vandenberg worked with Truman to build bipartisan support on this key foreign policy issue in the Senate, and the resolution passed 82–13.

Now that the water's edge is rising due to a melting Arctic, can Americans, let alone the global order, have the courage to work together and compromise on a foreign policy issue that treats the environment as seriously as a collective security agreement? Only time, and rising tides, will tell.

Kutubdia, in the Bay of Bengal, has roughly halved in size over the last 20 years as the waves overwhelm houses and fertile farmland. The island is prone to extreme weather, including cyclones and storm surges, which have increased in frequency in recent years.. (ZAKIR HOSSAIN CHOWDHURY/BARCROFT MEDIA/GETTY IMAGES)

discussion questions

1. The author presents a history of treaties, alliances, and international organizations working to establish a stable global order. Then, he notes that most progress occurred as a response to catastrophic wars. Do you think that progress on climate change is doomed to follow the same scenario? What climate change events might be enough to bring about change?

2. What are the potential international impacts of climate change in the absence of corrective action? What impacts have we experienced already?

3. Who are the stakeholders in the United States who will suffer if action is not taken to reduce climate change? Who are stakeholders who have an interest in not reducing greenhouse gasses? What actions can be taken by government or non-governmental actions that might better align their interests? (Regulation, incentive for renewable energy, specifically adding greenhouse gasses to environmental impact statements, taxes on carbon, education, funding of research, etc.)

4. Does the participation of the U.S. in the Paris Agreement make any difference to overall progress on climate change? Does it diminish the status of the U.S. to avoid participating with groups looking for solutions?

5. As the U.S. focuses inward, should it concentrate on mitigation of damage from climate change (as Miami is doing), slowing climate change (restricting emissions from coal and other plants as Obama-era regulations attempted), or developing new techniques for handling carbon emissions. How can all stakeholders in U.S. be encouraged to participate? (Federal, state and local governments; private sector; NGOs; schools; regulated companies such as utilities; and fossil fuel producers.) Will improvement be quicker with a top down or bottom up approach?

6. Is there an opportunity for economic gain and leadership for U.S. producers by developing and selling new technology to deal with climate change? Should the U.S. government be funding development of these technologies?

suggested readings

Harvey, Hal, Orvis, Robbie and Rissman, Jeffrey. **Designing Climate Soultions: A Policy Guide for Low-Carbon Energy.** 376 pp. Washington, DC: Island Press, 2018. Written by Hal Harvey, CEO of the policy firm Energy Innovation, with Robbie Orvis and Jeffrey Rissman of Energy Innovation, Designing Climate Solutions is an accessible resource on lowering carbon emissions for policymakers, activists, philanthropists, and others in the climate and energy community.

Bloomberg, Michael and Pope, Carl. **Cimate of Hope: How Cities, Businesses, and Citizens Can Save the Planet**. 272 pp. New York, NY: St. Martin's Press, 2018. From Mayor Michael Bloomberg and former head of the Sierra Club Carl Pope comes a manifesto on how the benefits of taking action on climate change are concrete, immediate, and immense.

Goldstein, Joshua S. and Qvist, Staffen A. **A Bright Future: How Some Countries Have Solved Climate Change and the Rest Can Follow.** 288 pp. New York, NY: PublicAffairs, 2019. In this clear-sighted and compelling book, Joshua Goldstein and Staffan Qvist explain how clean energy quickly replaced fossil fuels in such places as Sweden, France, South Korea, and Ontario. Their people enjoyed prosperity and growing energy use in harmony with the natural environment.

Gore, Al. **An Inconvenient Sequel: Truth to Power: Your Action Handbook to Learn the Science, Find your Voice, and Help Solve the Climate Crises.** 320 pp. Emmaus, PA: Rodale Press, 2017. The follow up to the #1 New York Times bestselling An Inconvenient Truth and companion to Vice President Al Gore's new documentary, An Inconvenient Sequel: Truth to Power, this new book is a daring call to action. It exposes the reality of how humankind has aided in the destruction of our planet and delivers hope through groundbreaking information on what you can do now.

Gertner, Jon. **The Ice at the End of the World: An Epic Journey into Greenland's Buried Past and Our Perilous Future**. 448 pp. New York, NY: Random House, 2019. In *The Ice at the End of the World*, Jon Gertner explains how Greenland has evolved from one of earth's last frontiers to its largest scientific laboratory.

Vollman, William T. **No Good Alternative.** 688 pp. New York, NY: Penguin Books. Volume 2, 2019. As with its predecessor, *No Immediate Danger*, this volume seeks to understand and listen, not to lay blame--except in a few corporate and political cases where outrage is clearly due.

Don't forget: Ballots start on page 98!!!!

To access web links to these readings, as well as links to additional, shorter readings and suggested web sites, GO TO www.fpa.org/great_decisions and click on the topic under Resources, on the right-hand side of the page.

India and Pakistan
by Barbara Crossette

BIP party workers celebrate their victory in the Lok Sabha elections at BJP's main office on May 23, 2019, in Mumbai, India. (VIJAYANAND GUPTA/HINDUSTAN TIMES/GETTY IMAGES)

India's national elections in the spring of 2019 were historic by any measure. A record 67% of India's 900 million registered voters cast their ballots in about a million polling stations managed by 10 million election officials. In the contest for 542 available seats in the 545-member lower house of the Indian Parliament, the Lok Sabha, more than 30 political parties secured places, according to results from the Election Commission of India. Beyond the metrics and logistics, however, one other number has become troubling for many Indians: 303. When the final results were tallied, Prime Minister Narendra Modi and his Bharatiya Janata Party, the BJP, had swept the boards with a huge majority of 303 seats –augmented to 353 by including its allied, mostly regional, partners in a coalition called the National Democratic Alliance.

For the BJP, a hardline, right wing political organization promoting Hindu nationalism while proposing vast welfare programs that have strong populist appeal, it was a near total sweep of political power. Analysts have since been measuring the profound depths to which India's secular

BARBARA CROSSETTE *is a former* New York Times *bureau chief in Southeast Asia and South Asia and a Fulbright Fellow in India. She won the 1991 George Polk Award for coverage of the assassination of Rajiv Gandhi, a 2008 Fulbright Award for International Understanding and the 2010 Shorenstein Prize for writing on Asia. She is a member of the Council on Foreign Relations, and the Foreign Policy Association Editorial Advisory Committee, and a co-founder of PassBlue.com, an online news site focused on the United Nations.*

democratic traditions and global reputation as the world's most populous democracy may have been shaken. Will India become, in essence, a one party state, guided by the concept of Hindutva, an all-embracing Hindu culture that marginalizes and endangers minorities? What will this mean to majority-Muslim Pakistan?

Little than more than two months after that election victory, the BJP, enjoying its near absolute political power, played its ideological hand. In early August, in a stunning strike against Muslim-majority Kashmir, Modi and his team remade the map of northernmost India. Kashmiri Muslims were stripped of their limited political autonomy placed under military rule, confined to their homes with all communications to the outside world cut off for months. Pakistan's prime minister, Imran Khan, who had been in office barely a year after a political upset, was enraged. Independent human rights experts reported to the United Nations that Kashmiris were suffering under collective punishment that they had done nothing to provoke.

For the South Asian region no political development on this sweeping scale and intensity had taken place for years if not decades, and violence by restive, angry Kashmiris was widely expected to follow if and when the clampdown is lifted.

Modi and the BJP: 'all about himself'

Looking back to the 2019 Indian elections that enabled the BJP to carry out its strike on Kashmir, Indian analysts of most political persuasions seem to agree that the outcome of the voting was all about Narendra Modi. Polling during and after the election found that large numbers of people would not have chosen the BJP had he not been its leading candidate. Since Modi first became prime minister in 2014, there have been plenty of negative developments in India: high unemployment, a spate of farmer suicides and deadly assaults on Muslims and Dalits, the Hindu caste system's most disadvantaged people, some killed in documented lynchings. There had been a bungled attack on Pakistan and a catastrophic currency decision to recall large banknotes in an effort to curb corruption in a cash society. All had been called out in the media, think tanks and secular civil society organizations. But those factors under Modi's administration seem not to have given pause to his followers.

Soutik Biswas, the BBC's trenchant, Delhi-based commentator on Indian politics and society, analyzed how Modi, 70, had consolidated his personal power to make the 2019 campaign "all about himself." Five years ago, when Modi began his first term in office, Indian commentators wondered how the prime minister would balance his record as an economic modernizer while chief minister in Gujarat state with his long years of activity in the Rashtriya Swayamsevak Sangh, the RSS, a disciplined paramilitary volunteer force of Hindu zealots some of whose founders were inspired by European fascism. In the cancellation of Muslim Kashmiri autonomy, they got their answer.

Voters in 2019 apparently accepted his two-track reputation: one part an uncompromising Hindu ascetic dressed in traditional Indian garb, who fasted during his first official visit to the United States in 2016 amid meetings with President Barack Obama, business leaders and technology titans. The other part is his skill as a brilliant political strategist adept at the use of both old-fashioned oratory and contemporary social media. He communicates not in press conferences but on Twitter. Often forgotten, or hidden, was his failure to prevent or stop a pogrom against Muslims in Gujarat in 2002, which left an estimated thousand people dead. The United States subsequently revoked his U.S. visa until he became prime minister in 2014, after which it was restored as a diplomatic courtesy.

The BJP and Modi could ignore the critics. "The more liberals agitated against Modi, the stronger it made him," Barkha Dutt, an influential television journalist in New Delhi and author of *This Unquiet Land: Stories from India's Fault Lines*, wrote as 2019 election results were being released. Her conclusion was shared by many across India: "Narendra Modi's unprecedented victory in the 2019 elections is proof that India and her politics have been irrevocably altered," she wrote. Amartya Sen, India's Nobel prize-winning economist and philosopher at Harvard, remarked that like other uncompromising nationalists around the world, Modi has made political use of "hatred and loathing."

The prime minister's close aides have become ruthless enablers and enforcers, most notably 56-year-old Amit Shah, a former BJP party president, who was appointed minister of home affairs. His portfolio includes border controls, internal security and the activities of a central government police force, among other law-and-order responsibilities. He is tough on immigration, and has been quoted calling Muslim migrants from neighboring Bangladesh "termites." More than a million ethnic Bengali Muslims, not all of them immigrants, are facing possible deportation from the Indian Northeast.

Devesh Kapur is director of Asia programs and Starr Foundation Professor of South Asian studies at the Johns Hopkins University School of Advanced International Studies in Washington. Writing in *The Washington Post*, he stepped back to explain the

Before you read, download the companion **Glossary** that includes definitions, a guide to acronyms and abbreviations used in the article, and other material. Go to **www.fpa.org/great_decisions** and select a topic in the Resources section. (Top Right)

deep social forces in India behind the Modi phenomenon.

"The fact that India's weak economy, rising joblessness and pervasive agrarian crisis did not dampen support for the BJP says something about Modi's high leadership quotient and the fecklessness of the opposition.," Kapur wrote. "But it also reveals something about how Indian society has changed — in ways that have perhaps been misrepresented by the English-speaking interlocutors who interpret India for the West," he argued.

"The reality is that Indian society has become more aspirational, more assertive and less deferential, with more pathways to social mobility than ever before," Kapur said in his essay. "Rising social groups are resentful of the social and cultural capital that privileges the elite and are increasingly willing to express this resentment electorally," he wrote.

Those in that elite, in Indian terms, are English-speaking, well educated, more cosmopolitan and secular in outlook. Jawaharlal Nehru, India's first

Indian women, from the 'Dalit' or 'Untouchable' caste listen to a speaker during a Dalit Dignity Rally against Congress-led UPA government near Parliament House in New Delhi, 05 December 2007. (RAVEENDRAN/AFP/GETTY IMAGES)

prime minister after independence, symbolized these traits. "Now, that old Nehruvian India is giving way and is being replaced by Modi's India, one that is less embarrassed by its limited English and heavy accents," Kapur added. "Its nationalism is unapologetic about India's Hindu roots, and it is prepared to be more assertive in defense of what it regards as its national interests — even if it means redefining the idea of the 'nation.'"

Can India's Congress Party Recover?

Long before the voting began in India in 2019, many experienced political analysts were predicting a dismal showing for the Indian National Congress, the party that under Nehru, Mohandas Karamchand Gandhi – the Mahatma --and other luminaries had led the long, nonviolent campaign against British colonialism, and then dominated Indian politics, for better or worse, in the decades that followed. By 2014, plagued by increasingly weak leadership, however, Congress won only 44 seats in the lower house of Parliament. Adding the 16 seats captured by its coalition allies in the Congress-led United Progressive Alliance, brought the total to 60, compared with the BJP and its allies at 336.

In 2019, Congress did only slightly better in the general election, winning 52 seats, which rose to 92 counting partners in the center-left United Progressive Alliance. (The upper house of parliament, the Rajya Sabha, is composed of 233 members elected by states according to population, with 12 additional members nominated by the president of India; it does not figure in the selection of a prime minister.)

Rahul Gandhi, the son, grandson and great-grandson of Indian prime ministers, led the Congress party into its 2014 and 2019 debacles. He appeared to many voters as a half-hearted candidate, who in the end had lost even his safe Congress seat in Amethi in northern India, which his family had held for decades. He did win in another constituency, in Kerala, as allowed in Indian electoral law, and will still be a member of Parliament. Gandhi, 49, did not seek or savor a life in politics, nor did his father, Rajiv. Both bore the heavy baggage of dynastic duty and a sense of entitlement – high caste Brahmins, the elite of elites, in a rapidly evolving society.

Eager strivers for recognition and opportunities for advancement are emerging from the 200 million Dalits of India, formerly known as "untouchables," who have suffered and still feel crippling social discrimination as the formal Hindu caste system's literal "outcastes." The Congress Party once could count on Dalit "vote banks" to support it candidates in return for handouts and promises. Now young Dalits whose families were once consigned to a scavenger life, are acquiring university educations, technology training and professional careers. A growing number are also creating a new Dalit literature, both in India and in the global Indian diaspora. The increasing numbers of Dalit immigrants in the United States and their continuing social disadvantages have been the subject of groundbreaking articles by reporters for the American newspaper *India Abroad.*

Dalits are reviving interest in Bhim Rao Ambedkar, a greater hero to them than Mahatma Gandhi. Dalit-born,

The Enduring Tragedy of Kashmir

When Prime Minister Narendra Modi acted on Hindu nationalist demands that Muslims be stripped of their political autonomy and other protections in Kashmir, he defied the Constitution that had established independent India's democracy. The sudden siege on the night of August 4–5 was quickly approved by the BJP-dominated Parliament. The state of Jammu and Kashmir—which the United Nations and many countries around the world still recognize as territory in dispute with Pakistan and not legally Indian—was reconfigured as a "union territory" controlled by the central government in Delhi. Part of the region was also carved out as a separate territory for Ladakh and its dominant Buddhist population.

All communications were cut to the Kashmir Valley, the heart of Muslim Kashmiris' unique culture, and hundreds of local politicians, journalists, business people and any others perceived to be critics were arrested. Dozens disappeared. Independent human rights monitors reporting to the UN High Commissioner for Human Rights called this "collective punishment…without even a pretext of a precipitating offense." The effects of the remaking of Jammu and Kashmir and the loss of Kashmiris' constitutional rights—Article 370 on political autonomy and Article 35A on citizenship and property rights—are likely to be felt in the region for years.

Pamela Philipose, a senior fellow with the Indian Council

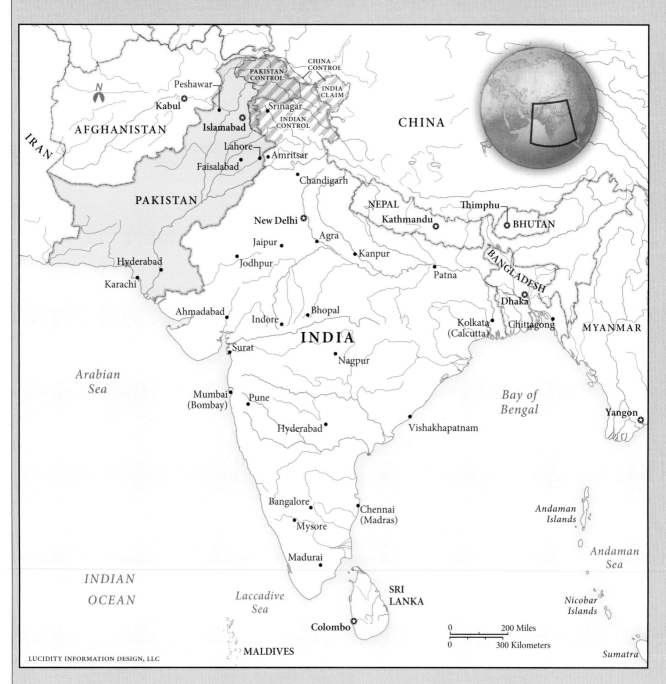

of Social Science Research, is a distinguished journalist and author with experience at *The Times of India* and *The Indian Express,* who later directed the Women's Feature Service in Delhi. She recently turned her attention to Kashmir in an essay on her fear of a nexus of two critical factors developing under the Modi regime: media controls and militarization.

Analyzing how the Hindu nationalist BJP strategized to end the safeguards for Muslim Kashmiris in Article 370, she wrote of the takeover: "Its lynchpin was the combination of military force and media manipulation, both conducted on an unprecedented scale. The muzzled media and the unmuzzled gun have always coexisted in the dystopic landscape of Kashmir. On 5 August, however, there was a media gag so impenetrable, so sudden, so cynical, so ruthless, that an entire population was blindsided…. The impact of this climate of fear and mass muting on ordinary lives can well be imagined."

In the days that followed the remaking of Jammu and Kashmir, two

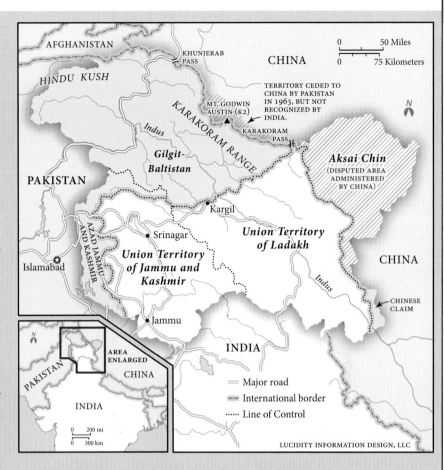

of India's neighbors, Pakistan and China, succeeded in bringing the fate of the Kashmiris to the United Nations Security Council for the first time in more than half a century. They argued that the Modi government was in violation of UN resolutions dating back to 1948, a year after British colonial India gained independence. One of the resolutions, number 38, barred India and Pakistan from altering status or borders without consulting residents or involving the Security Council. India has refused to abide by those demands. China's situation was not covered by Resolution 38, but China has an interest in this dispute. It claims and occupies an area in the eastern edge of Jammu and Kashmir.

All three countries, China, India and Pakistan, are nuclear armed, but of the three only China has signed and/or ratified international treaties banning the proliferation and testing of nuclear weapons. India tested its nuclear arsenal in 1974 and again in 1998. That second event prodded Pakistan to test a nuclear device for the first time, elevating an already tense situation in the region and stoking fears of an accidental war. Kashmir has long been considered a potential flashpoint.

India asserts that since Indian and Pakistani leaders agreed in a 1972 accord that they would settle the dispute together and that the UN has no further role to play. However, on August 8, 2019, Secretary-General António Guterres, expressed his concern at developments and noted that UN policy on the region is governed by the organization's charter and extant Security Council resolutions.

Since 1949 the UN has deployed a small international monitoring mission along the "line of control" that has served as a de facto border for more than 70 years. The future of the mission, the United Nations Military Observer Group in India and Pakistan, known by its acronym UNMOGIP, may now be uncertain. A Security Council military staff delegation was refused permission by India to visit the Indian-controlled side and report on the group's activities in 2018, though the fact-finding group was welcomed in Pakistan.

Indian paramilitary forces stand in Srinagar,Kashmir on May 25, 2019. Anti India clashes erupted in many area of Srinagar soon after Indian forces left curfew-hit areas. Police used tear gas canisters to disperse the angry protesters. (FAISAL KHAN/NURPHOTO/GETTY IMAGES)

Ambedkar, with a Columbia University graduate degree in economics and legal training at Grays Inn in London, led the commission that wrote independent India's constitution. His hopes for a more equitable society based on the constitution were denied, however, by persistent caste opposition. In October 1956, not long before his death, he converted from Hinduism to Buddhism with more than 300,000 of his supporters. Many other Dalits became Christians.

In a recent book, *Emergency Chronicles: Indira Gandhi and Democracy's Turning Point*, Gyan Prakash, a historian of modern India and the Dayton-Stockton Professor of History at Princeton University, raises questions about whether democracy in India was ever fully and broadly formed as Ambedkar and other writers of the constitution intended. "Indian politics showed scant concern for turning democracy into a philosophy of achieving social equality," Prakash wrote. "Instead it diminished the meaning of democracy into a competition between political parties and interests for state power. To be sure, adult franchise brought the backward castes out of the shadows of India's hierarchical society and placed them on the avenue to state power. But this was not the sum total of what Ambedkar had meant when he implored Indians to develop political democracy into social democracy.... he wanted social equality to become inseparable from political freedom."

Marshall Bouton, president emeritus of the Chicago Council on Global Affairs, among numerous other institutional positions, is a scholar and writer on India who has served as director of policy analysis for the Near East, Africa and South Asia in the U.S. Defense Department and as an assistant to the American ambassador in India. Over years of work on India, beginning with analyzing and writing on agricultural development, he has maintained close ties to numerous officials and influential people in Congress party circles. In a conversation at the Center for the Advanced Study of India at the University of Pennsylvania after the 2019 election results were published, he spoke

of many Indians concerned about the direction in which the BJP is taking India, and how Congress party leadership essentially allowed this to happen.

On his frequent recent visits to India, he said, he has heard comments about a stagnant Congress party "devoid of elders" or the kind of effective strategists who would not have missed the current profound changes in Indian society that Narendra Modi saw and tapped into. Moreover, there is a sense, Bouton said, that "dynasticism is going to be the death of the Congress party."

With Rahul Gandhi lacking in charisma at this critical time for the party, Congress seems to show that it has lost its political capital, Bouton said. Urban India is teeming with young people from rural areas aspiring to join the middle class, he noted. The Congress party did not seem to grasp how Modi's message was attracting young Indians, including the poor. "They didn't want a handout, they wanted a hand up." Bouton said.

Bouton said that India's political viability as a democracy requires a balance of power among party policies and ideas, and the task of Congress at this point is to establish a strong left-of-center approach and alternative to the BJP. "There has to be competition," Bouton said. Instead, critics have seen some

Congress politicians tailor their message to the Hindu right. The Congress party manifesto for the 2019 election was stripped of the word "secular" for the first time. Leading candidates, including Rahul Gandhi and his sister, Priyanka Vadra (who also lost a parliamentary seat in 2019), made well publicized visits to Hindu temples while campaigning.

Shashi Tharoor, a Congress party member of Parliament from Kerala, was outraged. In *The Week,* an Indian newsmagazine, Tharoor, a former under secretary-general for communications at the United Nations, wrote:

"Those who are suggesting that the answer to the party's woes in the Hindi heartland is to become more like the BJP in 'majority appeasement' are making a cardinal error. If the voter is presented with a choice between an original article and a pale imitation, he will choose the original every time. Rather than allowing ourselves to be intimidated by the BJP's success, it is far better for U.S. to stand up for what we have always believed in and urge the country to follow our principles," he wrote. "The loyalist will respect a party that demonstrates the courage of our convictions rather than offering some sort of 'Hindutva Lite.' Like Coke Lite and Pepsi Zero, 'Hindutva Lite' will end up with 'Congress Zero'."

In Pakistan, a new political party takes charge

In 2018, traditional politics and politicians in Pakistan were challenged by an upstart party with a youthful following, culminating in the first election victory of now-Prime Minister Imran Khan's Movement for Justice (Tehreek-e-Insaf). Prime Minister Khan, who was best known as an international celebrity cricket star before building a political career, spoke at a meeting at the United States Institute of Peace in Washington on July 23, 2019 about his plans.

He told his audience that he had inherited a bankrupt and politically corrupt country with the largest financial deficits in its history. He blamed what

he described as a collective "mafia" of traditional politicians that included the feudal, landed Pakistan Peoples Party of the Bhutto family in Sind Province and the Pakistan Muslim League faction under the Sharif clan of Punjabi industrialists.

"What happens," Khan said, "is the ruling elites, when they make money out of corruption, they have to take it out of the country because otherwise people ask questions – 'where did the money come from?' So, you suffer in two ways. Money which should go to human development ends up going into people's pockets. But the other aspect of corruption is that in order for the ruling elites to take money out, they have to destroy the state institutions. Because if the institutions are strong —for instance, if your anti-corruption body is strong, if your justice system is working, your taxation department —you cannot take money out. That's the biggest damage these corrupt, ruling elites do to the developing world."

Pakistan, created on the military western frontier of British India, was once a region where Hindus, Sikhs and Muslims had lived in relative harmony. When Britain's Indian empire was collapsing in 1947 and was divided into two nations, Pakistan was established as a country primarily for Muslims. Horrific, colliding stampedes ensued, leaving between a million to 2 million people dead – no one will ever really know exactly many – as Hindus fled to Hindu-majority India and Muslims raced toward their new country. Ever since, the days of carnage are known simply as Partition. It has been estimated that tens of thousands of women were raped as families on both sides were torn apart in the lethal mayhem.

Muhammad Ali Jinnah, the leader of the Muslim League, founded in 1906 to give Muslim's a political voice and later to campaign for an independent Muslim nation in South Asia, became Governor-General, of Pakistan and its first national leader, in 1947. He was considered by many to be a "secular" Muslim, born into a politically active family in Karachi, Pakistan's largest city. Jinnah, who had studied law in England, was in this early 70s and in failing health. He died the following year, and is remembered as Quaid-i-Azam, "Father of the Nation."

Pakistan has been politically unstable more or less ever since his death, with long periods of military rule several wars with India and the loss of part of its territory to what became Bangladesh in 1971 with assistance from the Indian army. Post-Jinnah history began with the assassination of his successor, Liaquat Ali Khan in 1951. Pakistan was officially declared an Islamic state. In 1973, Zulfikar Ali Bhutto, a political populist, became prime minister and was later arrested, tried in a controver-

Pakistani cricket star-turned-politician and head of the Pakistan Tehreek-e-Insaf (PTI) Imran Khan gestures as he delivers a speech during a political campaign rally, in Islamabad, on July 21, 2018. (WAKIL KOHSAR/AFP/GETTY IMAGES)

sial case and executed by the military in 1979. His daughter, Benazir Bhutto, a former prime minister twice deposed by the army, was killed nearly four decades later while campaigning to return to power in 2017. Her son, Bilawal Bhutto Zardari, is now leader of her Pakistan Peoples Party.

Imran Khan, born in Lahore to a rich ethnic Pashtun family, is an Oxford University graduate with a degree in politics, philosophy and economics, known as the PPE, a popular course of studies for or those students planning to enter public service and the media. His cricket career followed, during which he led Pakistan to its first cricket World Cup title by defeating England in 1992. In South Asia some say that as a cricketer, he is as popular in India as he is in Pakistan – at least until he became the face of the Pakistani government. After retiring from his sports career that year, he turned to philanthropy, building the first specialized cancer hospital in Pakistan in honor of his mother, who had died of the disease. He also became politically active, was elected a member of the Pakistan Parliament and a became an outspoken critic of Pervez Musharraf, a four-star army general who was president from 2001 until 2008.

By 2013, Khan was garnering a

strong showing for his party, the Pakistan Movement for Justice, buoyed by young people. The BBC, while covering the 2018 election, noted that "his campaign against corruption and dynastic politics in Pakistan, and a promise to raise a whole new class of 'clean' politicians -- that seems to have chimed with his supporters." Khan, "has sought to ride a wave of disillusionment at Pakistan's old political order, particularly among the urban middle class and young voters, who are tired of living in a country with an economy and currency on the slide, and water and power supplies in constant crisis," the BBC said.

When the Panama Papers emerged in 2015 from investigative reporters working in numerous countries tracking allegations of politicians' links to offshore companies used to channel funds to assets abroad, one of Khan's primary political targets toppled. Among those named in reports was Prime Minister Nawaz Sharif of the Pakistan Muslim League, whose family was implicated in the acquisition of foreign properties. Sharif was forced to resign in 2017. He was sentenced to 10 years in prison by an anti-corruption court. Another former prime minister and close Sharif associate, Shahid Khaqan Abbasi, was also arrested in July 2019 on corruption charges. Supporters of the Nawaz faction of the League say these are part of a political vendetta.

Khan, who met with President Trump in July 2019 the day before his U.S. Institute of Peace session, told his audience there that he had a package of development plans for Pakistan, including in agriculture, export industries and education. He spoke of various overtures he had made to India but received no response. In February 2019, India sent fighter planes over Pakistan to destroy a militant camp linked to a reported ISIS-backed suicide bombing in Kashmir earlier in the month that killed 40 Indian paramilitary troops. No serious damage was apparently done on the ground, but during the aerial attacks, Pakistan shot down an Indian plane, rescued the pilot and returned him to India. In July, Pakistan finally arrested the founder of a militant group blamed for terror attacks in Mumbai, India in 2008 that killed more than 160 people, including six Americans. In the same month, Khan's administration reopened a thousand-year old Hindu temple in Sialkot that had been closed for 72 years, with plans to turn it over to a Hindu organization.

Then came August 5 and the Indian seizure and political conversion of Muslim Kashmir into a territory to be administered from New Delhi by a Hindu nationalist government. Khan will now face the huge challenge of keeping Pakistani hotheads and the military under control, no matter what India may do to provoke them in Kashmir. Domestic programs may suffer. The leadership of Pakistan will be severely tested.

On September 27, in his address to the 74th United Nations General Assembly opening session, Prime Minister Khan spoke in blunt terms about what he saw as the potential dangers ahead in Kashmir. He said that the clampdown on the region, a tactic warped by "an ideology of hate," will lead eventually to widespread protests among the more than four million Muslims in the territory, and that will in turn prompt more repressive use of force by the Modi government. "There will be bloodshed," he said.

As economies grow, or slow, so do aspirations

As 2019 was drawing to a close, India and numerous other countries were becoming jittery about the global economy. Trade and tariff disputes, sanctions regimes, predictions of recessions ahead and concerns about mounting effects of climate change and its threat to agriculture and other economic sectors, were being analyzed almost daily. India, already stressed, is on the verge of becoming the world's most populous nation – if it hasn't already crossed that line; the next decennial national census takes place in 2021. This adds strain to already overburdened and often underperforming social service.

The Indian population at the end of 2019 was reliably estimated to be 1.36 billion and growing, with China steady or shrinking at 1.41 billion. Two leading United Nations demographers formerly from the organization's Population Division, Joseph Chamie and Barry Mirkin, have concluded that India will double China's growth rate and remain in first place for the rest of this century, possibly with a population of 1.9 billion by 2100.

For India, there are other important numbers. The median age of population is 27 (for China it is 38) and more than a quarter of Indians in the age range at which they will be looking for higher education, technology training—and jobs. (And wives, if the widening gap between female and male births continues because of sex-selective abortions.) In Pakistan, according to the UN Development Program, 64% of the nation of about 218 million people is younger than 30 and 29% are between 15 and 29. This growth among the young is forecast to continue to increase until at least 2050. On both sides of a tense border divide, there will be ample recruits for both protest movements and the military.

In July, Prime Minister Imran Khan told an audience in Washington that this makes education reform in Pakistan imperative, given that school enrollments expose social and ideological gaps. He said that students attending elite schools where teaching is in English number about 800,000, while 33 million children study in local languages in government schools and 2.5 million are in madrassas.

India had some disappointing economic news in 2019. From July 2016 to July 29, 2019 growth of India's Gross Domestic Product (GDP), which measures the value of most economic activity within a country, shrank from 8.7% to 5%, according to Trading Economics.com, a New York-based tracker for 196 countries using more than 300,000 economic indicators, including exchange rates, stock market indexes, government bond yields and commodity prices. In August 2019, a report from the World Bank showed that India had dropped two notches to Number 7 on global GDP rankings year-on-year between 2017 and 2018, behind, the U.S., China, Japan, Germany, Britain and France. It was the weakest showing since the first quarter of 2013, the World Bank said. India's all-time high GDP growth was 11.4% in the first quarter of 2010. Slowdowns in construction and manufacturing were singled out as problems. The crisis in Kashmir could cost significant losses in tourism nationally as well as in the popular Kashmir Valley.

In May 2019, after the recent Indian election, President Trump ended India's preferential tariff status given to developing countries, making Indian imports more expensive in the U.S., as the administration accused India of failing to provide "equitable and reasonable access" to its markets for American goods and services. On August 23, Moody's Investors Services cut its estimate of Indian GDP growth for 2019 to 6.2% from 6.8% and for 2020 to 6.7%. The Reserve Bank of India, the country's central bank had earlier lowered its growth estimate from 7% to 6.9%. Moody's noted weak hiring and "financial distress among rural households."

In July 2019, in a report refining his earlier estimates, a former Indian government chief financial adviser, Arvind Subramanian, now at Harvard University and the Peterson Institute for International Economics, questioned the veracity of official government GDP figures. Subramaniam and his team, working on a detailed, mathematical economic profile of Indian growth going back to the last years of a Congress party-led government, suggested that "Measurement changes likely caused India's GDP to be overestimated in the post-2011 period. Moreover, while it is not possible to say precisely what India's GDP would have been absent the measurement changes, the evidence suggests that the discrepancy in measured GDP growth post-2011 is likely to be significant." The debate continues.

Domestically, Narendra Modi has taken justifiable pride in his projects to improve living standards and reduce financial strains on rural households in his first term from 2014 to 2019. Now, however, prominent Indian commentators on economic and social issues are doubting reported results. Amartya Sen, who won the 1998 Nobel Prize in Economics for his work on poverty and famine, along with Mahbub ul Haq, a development economist from Pakistan, had led in the creation in 1990 of the United Nations Human Development Reports and the accompanying Human Development Index to measure the reality of peoples' lives in human terms.

In February 2019, speaking in Shantiniketan, where another Indian Nobelist, Rabindranath Tagore, established a haven for scholarship and the arts in 1901, Sen said that India could learn from China, where good basic education and primary health care have spurred the economy. India has one of the lowest government expenditures on healthcare in the world at about one percent of GDP.

A critical factor in improving the health of the poor and the conditions in which they live, especially in rural areas, is ending hunger and malnutrition. In June 2019, Marshall Bouton, the American expert on Indian agriculture quoted earlier in this chapter, wrote an illustrative paper for the India in Transition series of the Center for the Advanced Study of India at the University of Pennsylvania. Titled "The Paradox of India's Green Revolution," the study said that the story is complex, involving outdated government welfare policies, problems in the food distribution system, changes in diet and a failure to reform tax policies that ask too much of the agricultural sector, among other factors. "Today, agricultural households account for 50% of extreme poverty in India," Bouton wrote.

Paradoxically, India is self-reliant in the production of food grains. It is the world's second-largest producer of both wheat and rice and the largest exporter of rice, Bouton writes, but adds that " per capita availability of all food grains has increased only modestly as the population has more than tripled since the mid-1960s."

The International Food Policy Research Institute's 2018 Global Food Policy Report projects that 93 million Indians will be at risk of hunger by 2030. "India ranks 103rd out of 119 countries on the institute's Global Hunger Index and is home to the largest number of malnourished people in the world—about one quarter of the global total."

Pakistan's economy is very much smaller and less diverse than India's, and its starting point for future development is dire, as Prime Minister Khan has acknowledged. The Asian Development Bank, of which Pakistan was a founding member in 1966, is working with the Pakistanis on a 2019-2021 to expand the government's income through a combination of project loans from the bank to support reforms, and mobilizing financing for public-private partnerships. Urban development, water resources, energy and transportation rank high on the economists' list. Such plans, however, assume peace between India and Pakistan.

Pakistan's economic growth rate was a relatively healthy 5.5 to 5.8% in 2018 figures vary—but is forecast to drop to 3.3% for 2019 and 2.8% in 2020. By social measures, Pakistan it is more or less on a par with India: The percentage of people living below the national poverty line is 21.9 in India and 24.3 in Pakistan; Maternal mortality (deaths per 100,000 live births is 174 in India, 178 in Pakistan. Where Pakistan falls well behind India, however, is in deaths of children under 5 years of age and incidence of undernourishment, among other measures.

The World Bank had some good news for the Khan government, which pledged to bring back money stashed overseas and increase tax collection within the country. "Financial flows had a boost in FY19 due to a significant increase in central bank deposits and bilateral inflows from China, UAE and Saudi Arabia," the report said. In July, the International Monetary Fund extended a three-year, $6 billion loan package according to the Reuters news agency, but asked that the Khan government, which had initially wanted to avoid foreign borrowing, to agree to "tough conditions."

The U.S., Modi's India and Pakistan: works in progress

Despite the awkward image of Trump and Modi strolling into a political rally in Houston on September 22 holding hands, the administration's interests in South Asia have been at best episodic. The president's 2019 actions against India on trade and related economic issues have apparently unsettled some Indians focused on the country's strategic partnership with the United States and on an Indian Ocean Pacific regional security project created in response to Chinese expansion. That had seemed to be the top American priority—not a trade war.

One of China's biggest projects in the region is the rebuilding and upgrading of the deep water port at Gwadar, on Pakistan's west coast. Yet Prime Minister Imran Khan claimed in Washington in July 2019, that relations between his country and the U.S. are now very good. "So, why do I think that we will now have the very best of relationship with the U.S.?" he asked rhetorically in remarks at the United States Institute of Peace . "Because we're all on the same page." No mention of China.

"The period from 2003 or 2004 to 2015 was the worst in the relationship between Pakistan and the U.S. Pakistanis felt that they were fighting the U.S. war. No Pakistani was involved in 9/11," he said. "Taliban were in Afghanistan, Al Qaeda was in Afghanistan. But, Pakistan ended up involved in that war. We lost 70,000 people. We lost over 100 billion dollars to the economy. And yet, there was mistrust." Khan was in the political opposition during the bad years and critical of Pakistan's role. Now, he said, American officials finally understand that there can be no military solution in Afghanistan and Pakistan needs to turn inward to national development..

The Trump effect on American diplomacy is felt widely in Asia. "President Trump's belligerent nationalism and his use of trade as a political weapon are being emulated by key American allies, compounding the damage to U.S. strategic interests," a *Washington Post* editorial on September 6, 2019, said, pointing to heated disagreements between Japan and South Korea, "which have become caught up in an escalating feud about 20th-century grievances that animate nationalists in both countries."

Americans have not been very knowledgeable about South Asia, including India, the dominant regional power. Unlike the British, French or Portuguese with their long colonial histories in India, Americans do not have the same lingering political, economic, familial and even literary links to the Subcontinent. In the United States there were only moments of interaction with South Asians until they began to immigrate in larger numbers in the mid-20th century. Yet the first Sikhs who came to the U.S. from India in the late 19th century with their agricultural expertise soon emerged as the most successful farmers in California. In 1893, Swami Vivekananda, the best known Hindu religious leader and yoga master of his era to visit America, spoke at the first meeting of the Parliament of the World's Religions in Chicago, bringing messages of universal brotherhood and dedication of service to the poor. His erudite speeches captured the attention of American intellectuals – there are now numerous Vedanta centers following his philosophy in the U.S.

The recognition of Indian-Americans and their contributions to society, the media and politics has been magnified many times over since those early days. By the turn of the 21st century, exuberant accounts were appearing such as books such as Mira Kamdar's *Planet India: How the Fastest Growing Democracy Is Transforming America and the World*. (2007) American readers were also drawn to books built on Western experiences of more somber life in contemporary India. *Behind the Beautiful Forevers: Life, Death, and Hope in a Mumbai Undercity*, by Katherine Boo (2014) is one example.

The most scholarly, comprehensive study of Indian migration, the background to understanding the growing political influence of Indian-Americans, is the book *The Other One Percent*, by Sanjoy Chakravorty, Devesh Kapur and Nirvikar Singh, published in 2016. Pratap Bhanu Mehta, who until July 2019 was president of the Center for Policy Research in New Delhi and also taught at Harvard and New York University School of Law, called it a "riveting and textured portrait of the Indian diaspora, its formation, its political preferences, its social and economic base." Calling attention to its usefulness for policymakers, who are interacting frequently with Indian-American political activists, Mehta added "The book will unsettle many entrenched assumptions and open up a large research agenda."

From Indian independence in 1947 to the rise of radical Hindu nationalism under Prime Minister Narendra Modi and the BJP, the U.S.-India relationship has not always been smooth. Jawaharlal Nehru, India's first prime minister after independence, was closer to the 'civilized' British than to the more rough-cut Americans, his sister, Vijaya Lakshmi Pandit, told me in an interview a year before her death in 1990. She was India's ambassador to the United States from 1949 to 1951 and later the first female president of the United Nations General Assembly.

Nehru's daughter, Indira Gandhi, was close to the Soviet Union, with which she had concluded a Treaty of Peace, Friendship and Cooperation. She was perceived by influential Americans as hostile to the U.S. and too pro-Moscow during the Cold War. India-U.S. relations improved somewhat under her successors, her son Rajiv and later Manmohan Singh, an economist and economic reformer who was prime minster from 2004 to 2014, during the administrations of Bill Clinton, George W. Bush and Barack Obama.

India-U.S. relations during those years is the subject of an article by Robert D. Blackwill and Ashley J. Tellis in the September-October 2019 issue of Foreign Affairs, the journal of the Council on Foreign Relations. Both authors are strong defenders and promoters of India. Blackwill is the Henry A. Kissinger senior fellow for U.S. foreign policy at the Council on Foreign Relations, and Tellis holds the Tata Chair for Strategic Affairs at the Carnegie Endowment for International Peace in Washington. The title of their article acknowledges their point of view: "The India Dividend," subtitled "New Delhi Remains Washington's Best Hope in Asia." Not all policymakers would agree with that assertion, but Blackwill and Tellis were insiders during the years when American policy shifted significantly from treating India as a distant friend to a "strategic partner," and their account establishes the background to the current state of relations. Blackwill was the U.S. ambassador in India in 2003–04 and later deputy national security adviser to President Bush, and Tellis was senior adviser to the U.S. embassy in New Delhi from 2001 to 2003.

The authors argue that the idea among some Americans that "sooner or later, the two countries would become allies in all but name" is a misunderstanding. "If the United States' aim is to turn India into a close ally, formal or otherwise, it will come to grief," they write. "Instead

Washington and New Delhi should strive to forge a partnership oriented toward furthering common interests without expecting an alliance of any kind." Now under Trump, when the most pressing common interest the is expansion of Chinese influence, India's rogue nuclear weapons are ignored, though the country refuses to sign global nonproliferation or testing agreements. The U.S. has moved to support for civilian programs in India, such as nuclear safety, technology and missile defense.

The foundation of this U.S. policy is a 2005 agreement between President George W. Bush and Prime Minister Manmohan Singh that would allow American companies to build or invest in India's civilian nuclear power systems. Some U.S. companies were eager to seize the opportunity. But the plan did not turn out well because in 2010 the Indian Parliament passed a liability law that would make nuclear suppliers solely responsible in case of an accident, which stalled implementation of the deal as interested partners backed off.

On the nuclear weapons in South Asia, the fact remains that as long as India has them, Pakistan will keep or even enhance its arsenal. If Prime Minister Khan would even consider unilateral denuclearization it could invite military intervention and jeopardize his political career. Furthermore, all Asians see North Korea becoming an unofficial but increasingly openly recognized nuclear state, as the Trump administration has been stymied repeatedly by Kim Jong Un on demands for denuclearization.

What has fallen off the White House's ever-changing list of priorities appears to be India's worsening human rights record under the BJP. State Department experts, however, continue to catalogue Indian abuses and shortcomings in annual reports on human rights and religious tolerance. The department's 2019 report of the United States Commission on International Religious Freedom concluded that "In 2018 religious freedom conditions in India continued on a downward trend." Members of the Commission, which was created by an act of Congress, are

Indian Prime Minister Narendra Modi (L) and U.S. President Donald Trump attend the "Howdy, Modi!" rally in Houston, Texas, on Sept. 22, 2019. (STEVEN SONG/XINHUA/EYEVINE/ REDUX)

barred from visiting India. Their latest report was harsh, saying that violence against Muslims and other minorities, much of it perpetrated by Hindu extremists, was going unpunished. The Commission consequently placed India on its list of countries of "particular concern." Indian actions in Kashmir, a Muslim majority area where a stranglehold on communications has been imposed by the Modi government have been accompanied raids on homes and offices of civil rights lawyers and human rights advocates across India.

Some members of the U.S. Congress are beginning to protest, including Senator Bernie Sanders (D-VT), have joined a loosely organized movement called Stand with Kashmir. A Congressional Research Service report that was circulating on Capitol Hill in mid-August after Modi had stripped Kashmiris of their political rights, pointed to the dearth of expertise on foreign affairs under Trump and Pompeo, and its effects on policymaking. It said: "At present, the United States has no Assistant Secretary of State leading the Bureau of South and Central Asia, an Acting Ambassador to the United Nations, and no Ambassador in Pakistan,

leading some experts to worry that the Trump Administration's preparedness for India-Pakistan crises remains thin. Developments in August 2019 also have renewed concerns among analysts that the Trump Administration's 'hands-off" posture toward this and other international crises erodes American power and increases the risk of regional turbulence."

The UN position has since been filled. The new ambassador, Kelly Knight Craft, has no South Asian experience or other international policy expertise. Her first and only diplomatic job was as U.S. ambassador to Canada, a political appointment. Her husband, Joseph Craft, is a wealthy coal mining executive from Kentucky, Senator Mitch McConnell's home state. The Crafts were generous donors to Trump's political campaigns. As ambassador in Ottawa for 22 months, Knight Craft spent a third of her time out of Canada. The UN post is, or should be, a full time appointment. Every major global crisis sooner or later turns up there, as Kashmir did in August 2019 in the Security Council for the first time in half a century. Downgrading the American presence at the UN at this point is hard to explain.

discussion questions

1. Considering that each of these nations possess nuclear weapons, a miscalculation could lead to a major disaster. Despite previous failed efforts by other nations and the United Nations to attempt to reach a resolution with these two sovereign nations, why has this not been deemed a crisis priority by the world community that must be addressed now? If you were a mediating party to such a negotiation, what proposals would you consider placing on the agenda as a potential solution to this issue?

2. What should India do to meet the rising tide of population growth and demands by an increasing number of young aspirants for a "better life"?

3. What problems confront the United States in its relationship with Pakistan? What solutions might be proposed to bridge the gap between the two nations?

4. Can the United Nations play a more constructive role in bringing feuding parties to the negotiating table than it has in the past? What suggestions might you propose?

5. Is it in the best interest of the Untied States to keep strong relations with President Modi, despite the controversy surrounding his adminstrations recent actions? Should the U.S. take into special consideration the opinions of Indian-Americans?

6. Do you agree that some blame must be laid at the feet of the Trump administration for not having ambassadors for either India or Pakistan? How can the U.S. restore trust and a good working relationship with both nations?

suggested readings

Prakash, Gyan. **Emergency Chronicles: Indira Gandhi and Democracy's Turning Point.** 456 pp. Princeton, NJ:Preinceton University Press, 2019. *Emergency Chronicles* provides the first comprehensive account of this understudied episode in India's modern history. Gyan Prakash strips away the comfortable myth that the Emergency was an isolated event brought on solely by Gandhi's desire to cling to power, arguing that it was as much the product of Indian democracy's troubled relationship with popular politics.

Crabtree, James. **The Billionaire Raj: A Journey Through India's New Gilded Age.** 386 pp. Danvers, MA: Tim Duggan Books, 2018. India is the world's largest democracy, with more than one billion people and an economy expanding faster than China's. James Crabtree's *The Billionaire Raj* takes readers on a personal journey to meet these reclusive billionaires, fugitive tycoons, and shadowy political power brokers.

Guha, Ramachandra. **India After Gandhi: The History of the World's Largest Democracy.**. 944 pp. New York, NY: Ecco Press, 2008. Taking full advantage of the dramatic details of the protests and conflicts that helped shape the nation, politically, socially, and economically, Guha writes of the factors and processes that have kept the country together, and kept it democratic, defying the numerous prophets of doom.

Cohen, Stephen P. **The Idea of Pakistan.** 367 pp. Washington,DC: Brookings Institution Press, 2004. To probe beyond the headlines, Stephen Cohen, author of the prize-winning *India: Emerging Power,* offers a panoramic portrait of this complex country; from its origins as a homeland for Indian Muslims to a military-dominated state that has experienced uneven economic growth, political chaos, sectarian violence, and several nuclear crises with its much larger neighbor, India.

Lieven, Anatol. **Pakistan: A Hard Country**. 608 pp. New York, NY: PublicAffairs, 2012. Anatol Lieven's book is a magisterial investigation of this highly complex and often poorly understood country. Engagingly written, combining history and profound analysis with reportage from Lieven's extensive travels as a journalist and academic,

Snedden, Christopher. **Understanding Kashmir and Kashmiris.** 288 pp. London, England: Hurst, 2015. Snedden weaves a compelling narrative that frames the Kashmir dispute, explains why it continues, and assesses what it means politically and administratively for the divided peoples of J&K and their undecided futures.

Don't forget: Ballots start on page 98!!!!

To access web links to these readings, as well as links to additional, shorter readings and suggested web sites,
GO TO www.fpa.org/great_decisions
and click on the topic under Resources, on the right-hand side of the page.

Competition and cooperation in the Red Sea region
by David Shinn

U.S. Navy ships and partner force ships conduct a formation as a part of the International Maritime Exercise 2019. IMX19 is a multinational engagement involving partners and allies from around the world in sharing knowledge and experiences across the full spectrum of defensive maritime operations. The exercise serves to demonstrate the global resolve in maintaining regional security and stability, freedom of navigation and the free flow of commerce from the Suez Canal south to the Bab-el-Mandeb through the Strait of Hormuz to the Northern Arabian Gulf. (U.S. NAVY/ZUMAPRESS/NEWSCOM)

The Red Sea, a vital waterway accessed through the Suez Canal on the north and narrow Bab el-Mandeb (Gate of Tears) passage and Gulf of Aden on the south, both divides and links Africa and the Middle East. It is one large choke point that connects the Indian Ocean to the Mediterranean Sea. The Suez Canal accounts for more than 9% of international trade and additional shipping exits or enters the Red Sea through Bab el-Mandeb. By comparison, about 5% of global trade passes through the Panama Canal. The Red Sea is especially important to commercial shipping interests, both container vessels and oil tankers, of European countries and major trading powers in Asia such as China, Japan, and India. The United States is more concerned about free passage by U.S. Navy ships to support its security inter-

ests in the Mediterranean, Indian Ocean, Persian Gulf, and Gulf of Oman. The region has increasingly attracted great power attention and military engagement.

The Red Sea serves variously as a bridge and a barrier between Africa and the Middle East. Both sides have experienced conflict in recent years. African countries have been drawn into disputes in the Middle East, especially the Gulf States, while Middle Eastern countries have engaged, both

DAVID SHINN *served in the U.S. Foreign Service for 37 years, including assignments as ambassador to Ethiopia, deputy chief of mission in Sudan, State Department coordinator for Somalia during the international intervention, and director in the State Department for East Africa and the Horn. Since 2001, he has been teaching in the Elliott School of International Affairs at George Washington University.*

positively and negatively, in African issues. The net result has been to complicate political and security relationships on both sides of the Red Sea and between African and Middle Eastern countries. The current conflict in Yemen, which borders the shipping lanes of both the Red Sea and Gulf of Aden underscores this point.

Nine countries have shoreline on the Red Sea: Egypt, Israel, Jordan, Saudi Arabia, Yemen, Somalia/Somaliland, Djibouti, Eritrea, and Sudan. Other key regional players include landlocked Ethiopia on the African side and five other Gulf Cooperation Council (GCC) states: United Arab Emirates, Qatar, Kuwait, Oman, and Bahrain. Two important regional powers—Iran and Turkey—are also actors in the Red Sea region. The regional players constitute a volatile mix of political differences, religious beliefs, wealth, and poverty. The relationship between the two sides of the Red Sea is inherently asymmetrical; the African side is generally fragile and poor while the Gulf side, except for Yemen, is wealthy and stronger.

Egypt, Sudan, Eritrea, Yemen and Saudi Arabia have important ports on the Red Sea. Eritrea and Sudan are dependent on the Red Sea for all seaborne commerce. Saudi Arabia has the most developed Red Sea ports, which account for 70% of its seaborne cargo. Jeddah is the headquarters for the Saudi Western Fleet. Saudi Arabia's East-West pipeline carries crude from the eastern province near Bahrain to the port of Yanbu on the Red Sea. This increases the percentage of Saudi oil and gas that leaves Saudi Arabia through the Bab el-Mandeb. Jordan's only sea access and small navy is in the Gulf of Aqaba, which enters the Red Sea. Israel has a secondary port at Eilat in the Gulf of Aqaba. Djibouti, Somaliland, and Yemen have major ports in the Gulf of Aden. The economies of all of these countries rely heavily on the Red Sea and Gulf of Aden ports, except for Israel, which has two major ports on the Mediterranean.

Rich in natural resources, the U.S. Geological Survey estimates there are 5 billion barrels of undiscovered, technically recoverable oil and 112 trillion cubic feet of recoverable gas in the Red Sea Basin. The Red Sea also holds an estimated 3 million metric tons of zinc, 500,000 to 700,000 tons of copper, 6,500 tons of silver, and 46 tons of gold, potentially worth billions of dollars. Eventual exploitation of this undersea wealth could lead to either competition or cooperation among the Red Sea littoral states.

A combination of increased conflict on both sides of the Red Sea, al-Qaeda and Islamic State-affiliated terrorism in several states, Somali piracy, arms smuggling, people and narcotics trafficking, and the inherent strategic and commercial importance of the region have led to a sharp increase in great power and regional military engagement. A number of naval task forces were created to counter these threats in the Red Sea and wider region. The United States established Combined Task Force 150 after the 2001 terrorist attacks in an effort to disrupt terrorist organizations. The European Union Naval Force ATALANTA began in 2008, mostly to protect vessels delivering supplies to Somalia. NATO's Operation Ocean Shield also started in 2008 in response to Somali piracy but ended in 2016 as piracy decreased in importance. Combined Task Force 151 began in 2009 and continues to function as a counter-piracy force. Foreign military bases subsequently proliferated in Djibouti, Eritrea, Somalia, and Somaliland.

History of conflict in the region

The Red Sea was a backwater until the Suez Canal opened in 1869. The 1888 Constantinople Convention guaranteed, at least in theory, that the canal is open in peace and war to every commercial vessel or warship without distinction of flag. Great Britain, when it controlled the canal, honored this provision during the Spanish-American War, Russo-Japanese War of 1904–05, and the Italian-Ethiopian War of 1935–36. After Egypt took control of the canal, it denied in 1949 access to Israel and all ships trading with Israel.

Egypt and Israel signed a peace treaty in 1979 in which all ships, including Israeli, were permitted to transit the canal.

Today, warships from many nations, including Israel, regularly transit the canal and the Red Sea without incident. There was a hiatus from 1979 until 2011 in the passage of Iranian warships, although it was not clear if Egypt refused permission or Iran did not request access. Two Iranian naval vessels passed through the canal in 2011 in route to and returning from Syria and two more entered the Mediterranean Sea the following year.

Northeast Africa has been one of the most conflicted regions of the world since the end of World War II. Egypt was a key participant in the Arab-Israeli War of 1948. The Suez Canal crisis in 1956 pitted France, the United Kingdom, and Israel against Egypt, which closed the canal for six months. Israel's 1967 preemptive attack on Egypt, Jordan, and Syria led to the shutdown of the canal until 1975. Egypt and Syria attacked Israel in the Yom Kippur War of 1973 and briefly stopped Israeli shipping going through the Red Sea by blockading the Bab el-Mandeb. While this was the last of Egypt's wars with Israel, terrorist attacks by Islamic fundamentalist organizations have become common occurrences and the Islamic State affiliate, Wilayat Sinai, began operations in the Sinai and beyond. Egypt has a long history of tension over allocation of Nile water with Sudan and Ethiopia, the source of 82% of the water that reaches Egypt's Aswan Dam. Egypt's policy toward Ethiopia is driven by Nile water concerns.

Before you read, download the companion **Glossary** that includes definitions, a guide to acronyms and abbreviations used in the article, and other material. Go to **www.fpa.org/great_decisions** and select a topic in the Resources section. (Top Right)

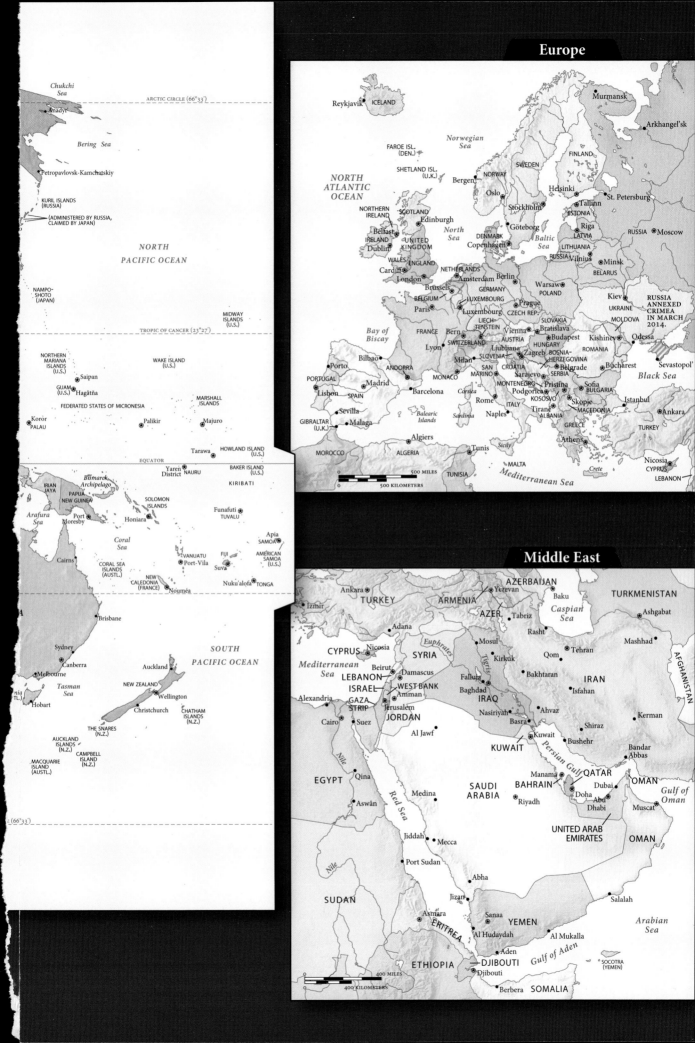

For over 100 years, the Foreign Policy Association has served as a catalyst for developing awareness, understanding and informed opinions on U.S. foreign policy and global issues. From mass media to grassroots organizations, the FPA promotes active civic participation in the U.S. foreign policy process, by engaging with the global public, heads of state and pre-eminent experts on foreign affairs. Founded in 1954, the FPA's flagship program Great Decisions is the largest nonpartisan public education program in the world, and provides the American public with the tools to become informed members of the global community.

ARCTIC OCEAN

Queen Elizabeth Islands

Ellesmere Island

GREENLAND (DENMARK)

Beaufort Sea

Baffin Bay

Baffin Island

Victoria Island

Davis Strait

ARCTIC CIRCLE (66°33')

ALASKA (U.S.)

Great Bear Lake

Denmark Strait

Reykjav

Anchorage

Gulf of Alaska

Great Slave Lake

Churchill

Hudson Bay

Labrador Sea

Juneau

NORTH AMERICA

CANADA

Lake Winnipeg

NORTH PACIFIC OCEAN

Vancouver
Seattle

NORTH AMERICA

Great Lakes

Montréal
Ottawa ⊛
Québec

NORTH ATLANTIC OCEAN

AZORES (PORTUGAL)

UNITED STATES

Toronto
New York

Chicago

Denver

St. Louis

Washington, D.C.

San Francisco

Atlanta

BERMUDA (U.K.)

CANARY ISLANDS (SPAIN)

Los Angeles

Dallas

WESTERN SAH ADMINISTE BY MORO

Monterrey

Gulf of Mexico

Miami

Nassau

TROPIC OF CANCER (23°27')

HAWAII (U.S.)

Honolulu

MEXICO

Havana

THE BAHAMAS

Nouakchott

Mexico City

Veracruz

CUBA
HAITI
Port-au-
Prince

DOMINICAN
REPUBLIC

VIRGIN ISLS. (U.S.)
BRITISH VIRGIN ISLS. (U.K.)
ANGUILLA (U.K.)
ST. KITTS AND NEVIS
ANTIGUA AND BARBUDA

CAPE VERDE
Praia

Dakar
Banjul

SE

ATOLL

GUATEMALA
Guatemala City
BELIZE
Belmopan
HONDURAS
Tegucigalpa
San Salvador
EL SALVADOR
Managua
NICARAGUA

JAMAICA
Kingston

Santo
Domingo

PUERTO RICO
(U.S.)

GUADELOUPE (FR.)
DOMINICA
MARTINIQUE (FR.)
ST. LUCIA
BARBADOS

THE GAMBIA
Bissau
GUINEA-BISSAU

Caribbean
Sea

MONTSERRAT (U.K.)
ST. VINCENT AND
THE GRENADINES

Conak
Freeto

GRENADA

SIERRA LEO

REEF

PALMYRA ATOLL (U.S.)

COSTA RICA

ARUBA (NETH.)

NETHERLANDS
ANTILLES (NETH.)

Port-of-Spain
TRINIDAD AND TOBAGO

M

San
José

Panama
PANAMA

Caracas

KIRITIMATI (CHRISTMAS ISLAND)

Medellín

VENEZUELA

Georgetown
Paramaribo

IS ISLAND
U.S.)

Bogotá

GUYANA
SURINAME

Cayenne
FRENCH GUIANA (FR.)

EQUATOR

Cali

COLOMBIA

Quito
ECUADOR

GALAPAGOS ISLANDS (ECUADOR)

Manaus

Belém

MARQUESAS ISLAND (FR. POLYNESIA)

Iquitos

BRAZIL

Recife

FRENCH POLYNESIA (FRANCE)

PERU

Lima

SOUTH AMERICA

Brasília

TUAMOTU
ARCHIPELAGO
(FR. POLYNESIA)

Cusco

La Paz
BOLIVIA

SOCIETY ISLANDS (FR. POLYNESIA)

NDS

Sucre

Rio de
Janeiro

TROPIC OF CAPRICORN (23°27')

PARAGUAY

São
Paulo

TUBUAI ISLANDS (FR. POLYNESIA)

PITCAIRN ISLANDS (U.K.)

EASTER
ISLAND
(CHILE)

ISLA SALA
Y GÓMEZ
(CHILE)

Antofagasta

Asunción

SOUTH
ATLANTIC OCEAN

CHILE

JUAN FERNÁNDEZ
ISLANDS
(CHILE)

Santiago

Buenos Aires
La Plata
ARGENTINA

URUGUAY
Montevideo

SOUTH
PACIFIC OCEAN

Bahía
Blanca

VENEZUELA   Independent state

GUADELOUPE (FRANCE)   Dependent territory

Ottawa ⊛ Capital

Bangalore ● Major city

Scale 1:35,000,000

Robinson Projection with standard parallels 38°N and 38°S
Source: CIA World Factbook

FALKLAND ISLANDS
(ADMINISTERED BY U.K.,
CLAIMED BY ARGENTINA)

SOUTH GEORGIA AND THE
SOUTH SANDWICH ISLANDS
(ADMINISTERED BY U.K.,
CLAIMED BY ARGENTINA)

Punta Arenas

Stanley

Scotia Sea

Drake
Passage

SOUTH ORKNEY, ISLANDS
(B.A.T.)

SOUTHERN

OCEAN

Bellingshausen Sea

Weddell Sea

Amundsen Sea

Ross Sea

Ronne
Ice Shelf

Ross
Ice Shelf

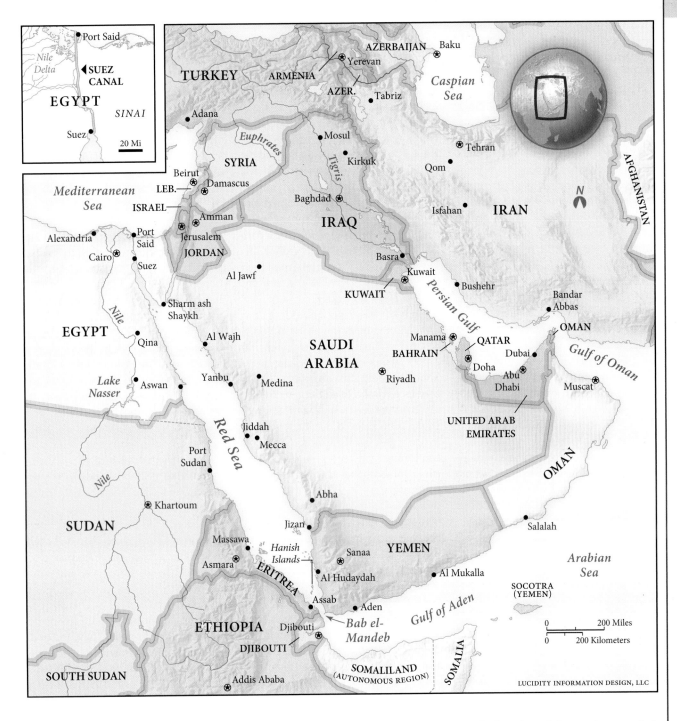

A border conflict between Egypt and Sudan dating back to 1958 over control of the Hala'ib Triangle, which borders the Red Sea, remains unresolved. Egypt periodically gets drawn into the conflict for control of neighboring Libya.

Sudan was embroiled in civil war between the northern and southern parts of the country from 1955 to 1972 and then again from 1983 until a peace agreement in 2005 led to a referendum and secession of South Sudan in 2011. The same year, the UN sent a peacekeeping mission to South Sudan. Several border disputes between Sudan and South Sudan remained unresolved, requiring a separate UN peacekeeping operation along the border. In 2013, civil war began in South Sudan, threatening instability in the wider region. Serious ethnic conflict broke out in Darfur in western Sudan in 2003, resulting eventually in a United Nations/African Union peacekeeping mission. While the situation in Darfur is quieter, it has not been settled. There have also been periodic conflicts in eastern Sudan. Until early in this century, Sudan supported al-Qaeda-affiliated groups and has been subject to terrorist attacks aimed primarily at foreign interests. Historically, Sudan also supported rebel groups in neighboring Chad, Libya, Uganda, Eritrea, and Ethiopia. Sudan meddled in Middle Eastern affairs by supporting Iraq in both the Iran-Iraq War of 1980-1988 and the

Gulf War of 1990-1991. It subsequently cooperated with the network that illicitly moved Iranian arms through the Red Sea to Sudan for ultimate delivery to Hamas in Gaza.

In 1941, following the end of brief Italian control and a legal/diplomatic contest for ownership of Eritrea, Ethiopia faced a succession of regional crises. Independence of Somalia in 1960 resulted in an immediate attempt to incorporate Ethiopia's Somali-inhabited territory into Somalia. This led in 1977–78 to full-fledged war and the Somali invasion of the Ogaden region of Ethiopia. Ethiopia also confronted an Eritrean independence movement that began in the mid-1960s and continued until the overthrow of the Ethiopian government in 1991 and Ethiopia's acceptance of de facto independence for Eritrea the same year. In 1998, a border war broke out between Ethiopia and Eritrea that continued until 2000 and resulted in as many as 100,000 deaths. This led in 2000 to creation of a UN peacekeeping mission along the Ethiopian-Eritrean border that ended in 2008 due to an inability to carry out its mandate. Ethiopia-Eritrea diplomatic relations remained broken until 2018. In the meantime, an al-Qaeda-affiliated group known as al-Shabaab gained strength in Somalia and threatened the security of Ethiopia and Kenya. Since 2006, Ethiopia has sent troops into Somalia either bilaterally in support of the Somali government or as part of the African Union peacekeeping mission to defeat Islamic fundamentalists and al-Shabaab. Beginning in 2018, a second terrorist group, the Islamic State in Somalia, began operations as a rival to al-Shabaab.

Legally independent since 1993, Eritrea was consumed by the war with Ethiopia from 1998 to 2000 and then suffered economically due to the broken diplomatic and trade relationship with its neighbor until 2018. During much of this period, Eritrea supported rebel groups operating against Ethiopia and groups in Somalia that opposed Ethiopia, which the latter reciprocated by supporting Eritrean dissident groups. In 1995, a dispute broke out between Eritrea and Yemen over control of the Hanish Islands in the southern Red Sea. Conflicting oil exploration claims contributed to the conflict. International arbitration awarded the largest and most important islands to Yemen and delimited the maritime boundary between Eritrea and Yemen. In 2008, Eritrea provoked an incident along the Djiboutian border that overlooks the Bab el-Mandeb; this resulted in limited fighting. Both countries accepted mediation by Qatar, which subsequently sent troops to monitor the border. In 2017, Qatar pulled out its troops following a dispute with Saudi Arabia and the United Arab Emirates and their implicit support for Eritrea.

Djibouti has experienced less conflict than the other countries in northeast Africa, but because its population is 60% Somali it was also a target of Somalia's irredentist ambitions to take over its territory. In addition to the unresolved border dispute with Eritrea, Djibouti once faced dissident activity by the Front for Restoration of Unity and Democracy, representing the Afar ethnic minority that now functions as a political party.

Following independence, Somalia was at the center of regional conflict because of its irredentist program to incorporate the Somali-inhabited territory of neighboring countries. The overthrow of the dictatorial Siad Barre government in 1991 ended with a failed state and the unilateral independence of Somaliland. The failure of government and rise of Somali warlords based on clan support resulted in a serious famine and U.S.-led international humanitarian intervention in 1993 followed by a UN peacekeeping mission. As Somali warlords ravaged the country, the UN mission pulled out and the Islamic fundamentalist group, al-Shabaab, eventually seized control of much of the state. The African Union peacekeeping mission created in 2007 and succession of Somali governments reestablished control over most of the country but al-Shabaab held on to rural areas and terrorist attacks became a common occurrence. Further undermining regional stability, pirates based in Somalia carried out many successful attacks in the Gulf of Aden, southern Red Sea, and western Indian Ocean from 2005 to 2012.

The eastern side of the Red Sea, except for the regional impact of the Arab-Israeli wars and frequent fighting in Yemen, has, by comparison, experienced less conflict than the African side. But it too contributed significantly to wider regional instability in past years. Iraq's invasion of Kuwait in 1990 united all the GCC states and Egypt with Kuwait. But Jordan, Yemen, and Sudan sided with Iraq. With the passage of time conflicts on each side of the Red Sea have increasingly attracted involvement from the other side.

Saudi Arabia had been a relative haven of political stability among the Gulf States. In 1998, it had a minor military clash with Yemen over control of Duwaima Island in the Red Sea. Yemen contests two other nearby, strategically located islands and the Saudi claim to land in the Empty Quarter in the southeastern part of the Arabian Peninsula. In 2009, Saudi forces attacked Zaidi Shia Houthi rebels inside Yemen. Saudi Arabia's most serious engagement has been its military intervention in Yemen since 2015 on behalf of the internationally recognized government. Saudi Arabia has important ties with the African countries on the other side of the Red Sea. Hundreds of thousands of Sudanese, Ethiopians, Eritreans, and Somalis come to Saudi Arabia for employment, while the annual Haj to Mecca attracts additional thousands. During the 1990s and early 2000s, Saudi Arabia encouraged the export of fundamentalist Wahhabism to countries such as Somalia and Ethiopia. In addition, funding from wealthy Saudi and other Gulf State individuals supported terrorist organizations in the region, especially Somalia.

Yemen has been ground zero for conflict in the Arabian Peninsula. The North Yemen civil war from 1962 to 1970 pitted royalist rebels against the republican Yemen Arab Republic. Jordan and Saudi Arabia supported the royalists while Egypt sided with the republicans. In 1979, there was a brief border war between Saudi-allied North Yemen and Soviet-allied South Yemen. In 1986, civil war between different factions of the Marxist government in South Yemen occurred. In 1994, there was a civil war between North Yemen and South Yemen. Southern leaders declared secession but it was not recognized by the international community. A rebellion by the Houthis in North Yemen broke out in 2004 and continues to the present. An estimated 100,000 people have died in the conflict.

Yemen has historically had considerable interaction with the Horn of Africa. Economic and political refugees move both directions in large numbers. Yemenis along the Gulf of Aden coast were complicit during the height of Somali piracy. Somali terrorist groups have collaborated with al-Qaeda in the Arabian Peninsula (AQAP), which has benefited from the war in Yemen. AQAP is now experiencing competition from an Islamic State affiliate in Yemen.

Current regional competition

In the political/security arena, states on both sides of the Red Sea, especially the Arabian side, have abetted competition on the other side more than they have facilitated cooperation. The priority of the GCC states, is political stability and the absence of extremism in northeast Africa and Yemen. There is not always agreement among them on achieving these goals and their actions are often not in the best interest of the other parties. Qatar, for example, believes support for Islamists aids regional stability; the UAE disagrees.

Perhaps the most important theme currently driving the policies of key Gulf States in both the Gulf and northeast Africa is the effort to rein in Iran's influence throughout the region. It is led by Saudi Arabia and the UAE and supported by Bahrain. It began with pressure and financial incentives by Saudi Arabia and the UAE on African states to break relations with Iran, which once had significant influence in the region, especially in Sudan. In 2016, Sudan, Somalia, and Djibouti complied but they resented being pressured into taking sides in the Saudi-Iran dispute. Oman, on the other hand, retains friendly relations with Iran while Kuwait just tries to stay out of the disagreement. In 2017, Saudi Arabia, the UAE, Bahrain, and Egypt broke relations with Qatar, which led to Qatar developing a stronger alliance with Turkey and a more nuanced relationship with Iran. A major reason for disagreement between Turkey/Qatar and Saudi Arabia/UAE is the latter's strong opposition to any country with ties to the Muslim Brotherhood; Turkey and Qatar have cordial relations with Muslim Brotherhood affiliates. Turkey relies on Qatar's financial support but does not want to be sucked into its disputes in northeast Africa with other GCC countries.

The cross currents within the GCC are most pronounced in the war in Yemen, which is consumed by fighting, internal divisions, and presence of terrorist groups. There are three major factions—the internationally recognized but weak government of President Abed Rabbo Mansour Hadi based in Aden, the northern Shia Houthi rebels based in Sanaa and supported by Iran, and the secessionist Southern Transitional Council based in Aden. Because of the war, Yemen is in no position to influence significantly events in northeast Africa, but has become a contentious issue within the GCC. Saudi Arabia and Bahrain support the Hadi government against the Houthis financially and with military forces. Although the UAE is part of the anti-Houthi coalition, its forces favor the Southern Transitional Council. Qatar was part of the anti-Houthi coalition until Saudi Arabia expelled it in 2017; it now balances relations between the Houthis and the Hadi-aligned Islah Party. Kuwait and Oman have stayed out of the war. Houthi drone attacks against Saudi Arabia have significantly increased the tension, although the most serious attack in September 2019 that damaged Saudi oil facilities apparently originated in Iran. The United States has provided air refueling and intelligence and sold arms to the coalition partners.

Egypt joined the Saudi-led intervention in Yemen principally to support

Abu Dhabi's Crown Prince Sheikh Mohamed bin Zayed Al Nahyan (C) receives Ethiopian Prime Minister Abiy Ahmed (L) and Eritrean President Isaias Afwerki (R) at the presidential palace in the UAE capital Abu Dhabi on July 24, 2018. (KARIM SAHIB/AFP/GETTY IMAGES)

the Hadi government, reign in Iran's regional ambitions, and prevent the Houthis in Yemen from obstructing or controlling Bab el-Mandeb, which could disrupt shipping through the Red Sea and Suez Canal. Since 2015, the Houthis have conducted a number of attacks against ships in the Red Sea. The attacks on shipping off Yemen are considered to be at least as serious as those in the Strait of Hormuz, although they receive less international media attention. While Egypt opposes the Houthis, however, it has not sent troops to Yemen. Egypt is also engaged in a long running competition with Saudi Arabia for influence in the Red Sea region.

The war in Yemen and Gulf State efforts to solicit support for the war from countries in northeast Africa have had mostly negative consequences for the region. Sudan contributes between 8,000 and 12,000 troops that have a light infantry capability to the Saudi/UAE coalition in Yemen. These troops, who are paid for by the UAE, come from the highly controversial Rapid Support Forces (RSF), a quasi-private militia that has not yet been integrated into Sudan's national army. As of 2018, the UAE transferred almost $8 billion to Sudan's central bank before it decided to abandon President Omar al-Bashir, contributing to his overthrow. Sudan also received significant financial support from Qatar and agreed in 2018 to a $4 billion project to develop with the help of Turkey the Red Sea port of Suakin off Sudan's coast. Turkey has a military base in Qatar; Saudi Arabia and Egypt feared Turkey intended to revive the Ottoman dream and build a military facility on Suakin. Early in 2019, probably to help ensure Sudan's continued supply of troops in Yemen and to undercut Qatar, Saudi Arabia and the UAE pledged $3 billion in aid to Sudan's new military leaders. The civilian opposition movement in Sudan, which opposes military rule, interpreted this pledge as taking sides on behalf of the national army and the RSF. The overthrow of al-Bashir, the Saudi/UAE rupture with Qatar, and, most recently, creation of a combina-

tion military/civilian government in Sudan raise questions about the future of Sudanese troops in Yemen and whether the Qatar/Turkey project at Suakin will go forward.

In 2015, the UAE signed a 30-year lease with Eritrea for a major air base and small naval facility at the port of Assab immediately after UAE and Saudi troops had been evicted from Djibouti following a diplomatic incident in Djibouti involving the UAE. The sole purpose of this base is to support the war in Yemen, which the UAE, contrary to Saudi wishes, began to withdraw from during the second half of 2019. The UAE is also constructing a military base at Berbera in Somaliland and Saudi Arabia received permission to establish a base in Djibouti, but has not yet begun construction. As the UAE exits the war in Yemen, it raises questions as to the need for military bases in Assab and Berbera. While these bases earn foreign exchange for the African countries, they also drag them into Gulf disputes that they may one day regret. Ethiopia has retained diplomatic relations with Iran and refrained from choosing sides in Gulf State disputes but still managed to receive a pledge in 2018 from the UAE of $3 billion in aid and investments. Ethiopia may be sufficiently strong to avoid a UAE *quid pro quo*.

Some of the Gulf States' most disruptive policies have occurred in Somalia, a fragile state threatened by the al-Shabaab terrorist organization and one struggling to maintain the loyalty of its federal components. The Gulf States continue to use these divisions for their own purposes. Turkey was the first to develop a strong relationship with the Somali central government in Mogadishu. By aligning with Qatar, which provided Mogadishu with more than $1 billion in aid, however, it has indirectly become involved in Gulf State intrigue in Somalia. Turkey has become Mogadishu's most important foreign backer and invested $50 million in the establishment in 2017 of a military base staffed by 200 Turkish soldiers whose goal is to train more than 10,000 Somali soldiers. A Turk-

ish company also operates the port of Mogadishu.

The Somali central government, although it broke relations with Iran and supports the war against the Houthis, balked at Saudi and UAE pressure to sever relations with Qatar. This refusal especially irritated Saudi Arabia, Somalia's largest trading partner and a source of significant financial aid. Mogadishu's decision to maintain relations with Qatar is also linked to its unhappiness over UAE assistance to two of its autonomous federal components, Puntland and Jubaland, and to breakaway Somaliland. The UAE funds and trains the Puntland Maritime Police Force and supports its air wing in the port of Bosasso. This situation has not only worsened relations between Mogadishu and its federated states but led to disagreement within the central government concerning the wisdom of maintaining relations with Qatar. In the meantime, Somalia is trying to balance its relations between Qatar and the UAE.

Iran is a wild card in the Red Sea region. It is currently preoccupied with events in the Persian Gulf and Gulf of Oman and has no diplomatic relations with Red Sea littoral countries, thus limiting its actions. But its support for the Houthis still gives it leverage and, since 2008, Iranian warships have participated independently in the Gulf of Aden anti-piracy operation. This gave them periodic access to the Red Sea, which they used to smuggle weapons to Syria and Hamas in Gaza. At the end of 2018, Saudi Arabia was instrumental in establishing the Arab and African Coastal States of the Red Sea and the Gulf of Aden for the propose of enhancing security, trade, and investment in the region. All of the Red Sea/Gulf of Aden littoral states except Eritrea and uninvited Israel are part of this new organization, which has a secondary goal of thwarting Iranian expansionism in the region. Saudi Arabia then hosted a joint drill with the seven countries for promoting naval security in the Red Sea region. Saudi-Egyptian competition for leadership in the region may, however, limit its effectiveness.

Current global competition

The inherent strategic importance of the Red Sea for commercial shipping and passage of warships has increased global attention to the region, especially in the aftermath of Somali piracy, the war in Yemen, growing tension between Arab states and Iran, persistent terrorist activity, and significant political change in countries such as Sudan and Ethiopia. While threats to shipping, drone and missile attacks on Saudi oil facilities, and rising tension between the Gulf States and Iran have recently focused international attention on the Persian Gulf, Strait of Hormuz, and Gulf of Oman, it would be a mistake to neglect what is happening in the Red Sea region, which is an equally fraught neighborhood.

Great Power (and not so great) competition has become a feature of the Red Sea region. This has become most evident with the proliferation of military bases in Djibouti. France has had a military presence in Djibouti dating back to the early days of colonial rule. The number of personnel assigned there has declined from 4,300 in 1978 to 1,450 today. The United States established a naval expeditionary base at Djibouti in 2001, primarily to combat terrorism in the region. Two years later it became a permanent military base and now hosts about 4,000 military and civilian personnel. Some 50 German military personnel have operated out of the French base in Djibouti since 2001 as a counterterrorism force and subsequently to protect shipping in the region. In 2008, Spain assigned about 50 military personnel to the French base to assist with protection of commercial shipping. In 2011, Japan established a base in Djibouti with about 200 personnel to support its anti-piracy contribution. India is reportedly in discussion with Japan concerning access to the base. Both Japan and India envisage Djibouti as a location from which to monitor Chinese military activity in the region. In 2013, Italy opened a military base, which averages 80 personnel at any given time, to support Italian naval activity in the region.

A picture shows containers and a general view of the port of Djibouti, on March 27, 2016.. (SIMON MAINA/AFP/GETTY IMAGES)

The most important new arrival in Djibouti is China, which in 2017 opened its first ever foreign military base. China's stated reasons for the base are to support the Somali anti-piracy operation in which Chinese naval vessels have participated since 2008, the emergency evacuation of Chinese nationals from the region, countering terrorism, and support for Chinese troops assigned to UN peacekeeping operations. China constructed a pier that can accommodate large warships. An estimated 2,000 Chinese military personnel are assigned to Djibouti, but it may be able to accommodate up to 10,000 personnel. China reportedly allows Russia to use the facility; Russia requested permission to open a base at Djibouti, but was turned down by the Djiboutian government. U.S. officials have expressed concern about the purpose of the Chinese base and believe it portends additional Chinese military facilities in the Indian Ocean and Mediterranean region and the global expansion of China's economic and political influence.

Competition in the region is not confined to the establishment of numerous military installations at Djibouti. Among non-littoral Red Sea states, the United States can bring the most naval and air power to the Red Sea on short notice. In addition to the base at Djibouti, Bahrain is the location of two airbases, the Naval Forces Central Command, and the headquar-

ters of the Fifth Fleet. Kuwait hosts an estimated 15,000 U.S. personnel while Qatar has another 10,000 at the Al Udeid Air Base. Some 3,000 personnel are assigned to the Al Dhafra Air Base in the UAE and the number can surge to 6,000. The United States has a major naval support facility and airfield on the island of Diego Garcia in the middle of the Indian Ocean and a much smaller presence in Kenya, Somalia, Seychelles, and Ethiopia. U.S. and Egyptian naval ships periodically conduct exercises in the Red Sea to enhance interoperability and war-fighting readiness. After a long hiatus, the United States and Egypt resumed Operation Bright Star, which brings to Egypt land, naval and air forces from a number of countries to train on counterterrorism and non-traditional warfare. The United States is an important source of arms for Egypt, Israel, and several of the Gulf States.

The Trump administration's national security policy regards China and Russia globally as strategic competitors. This has the effect of treating both countries' actions in the Red Sea with deep concern and enormous suspicion. China's military base in Djibouti and Russian attempts to establish a base there, as well as apparent successful efforts to negotiate some kind of military arrangement with Sudan and Eritrea compound this concern. In 2015, Chinese and Russian naval vessels held a joint exercise in the Mediterranean and in 2019 both countries joined Egypt for an exercise in the Mediterranean. China and Russia are major arms suppliers to the region, especially the African side of the Red Sea. China's popular nationalistic movie, "Operation Red Sea," which is a highly fictional account of the People's Liberation Army Navy's (PLAN) evacuation in 2015 of some 800 Chinese and foreign nationals from Aden, only fuels this concern. The PLAN helped the Hong Kong studio film the movie. It is, however, the more assertive global foreign policy of Xi Jinping and Vladimir Putin that has put the United States on edge. The stability and security of this region has become a central part of Xi Jinping's principal foreign policy, the Belt and Road Initiative.

European members of NATO, especially those with military facilities at Djibouti, generally support U.S. interests in the Red Sea region. France, in particular, wants to maintain freedom of navigation through the Suez Canal and

Red Sea to resupply its Indian Ocean overseas departments of Réunion and Mayotte, where it has a modest military presence. These and other small islands in the southern Indian Ocean give France control over 2.5 million square kilometers of exclusive economic zone. While the United Kingdom has pulled back significantly from the Red Sea region, it has about 400 British military personnel based in Kenya, opened a naval base in Bahrain, and a military training facility in Oman. In 2018, the UK deployed 20 troops from the Special Boat Service to protect its vessels after Houthi rebels in Yemen attacked an oil tanker in the Red Sea.

India and Japan are potential American allies in the Red Sea region. India is more important because it is closer but Japan has the stronger navy. India is seeking additional military bases in the Indian Ocean region, mainly to counter China's rising military presence. It has reached an agreement with Oman for logistical support and is constructing military facilities on the Mauritian archipelago of Agalega that will enable

India to sustain naval operations in the south-western Indian Ocean. The Red Sea and Gulf of Aden are among the sea lanes that are considered crucial to Japan's maritime transport. Japan is expanding the role of its base at Djibouti to include emergency evacuation of Japanese nationals from the region. The base is also clearly an effort to counter China's influence in the Red Sea region.

Iran, although currently an adversary of the United States, is preoccupied with developments closer to home. It has been pushed out of the Red Sea region by the Gulf States, but will at some point renew efforts to develop allies in the region and return as a major force. It continues periodically to send naval vessels to the Gulf of Aden and could theoretically mount a blockade of the Bab el-Mandeb. It is highly unlikely, however, that Iranian vessels would be capable of maintaining a blockade for an extended period of time or would even risk doing so as they would be highly vulnerable to attack from the air.

Regional and global cooperation

There is a positive side to regional interaction and global engagement in the Red Sea region. The GCC states are an important source of investment in northeast Africa and non-regional states in Europe, Asia, and North America are important investors on both sides of the Red Sea. This investment creates jobs and aids economic growth. GCC investment in northeast Africa is arguably the most constructive aspect of the relationship. It can also result in profits for companies in GCC countries and, in the case of agricultural investment, improve food security in the Gulf States.

Aid to the region's poorest countries is another positive contribution. The GCC countries and Turkey are aid donors to countries in northeast Africa and could help develop Yemen when the war ends. International development partners, including China, provide significant assistance to coun-

tries in northeast Africa. It is important that loans, especially those offered by China, not contribute excessively to debt. In an extreme case, for example, China holds an estimated 68 to 82% of Djibouti's total external debt. At the same time, China's loans financed a $590 million multipurpose port at Djibouti and an electrified railway from Djibouti to Addis Ababa.

Trade has both positive and negative effects but has not yet become an important part of the northeast Africa-Gulf State relationship. The Gulf States are, however, an important market for livestock from Somalia/Somaliland, Ethiopia, and Djibouti and charcoal from Somalia, which has serious negative environmental implications for Somalia. China is the largest trade partner with most countries in the Red Sea region. It runs a large trade surplus with the poorer countries such as Ethiopia, Egypt, and Djibouti but a sizeable

trade deficit with energy suppliers such as Saudi Arabia, Oman, and Kuwait. Trade has the potential for becoming a more important positive factor if the countries of northeast Africa can substantially increase agricultural production and exports to the Gulf States, which import 80 to 90% of their food. The Gulf States also employ hundreds of thousands of workers from northeast Africa, thus reducing the unemployment problem.

There have been numerous occasions when non-regional countries have helped end or mitigate conflicts in the region. In 1991, the United States helped bring together the Ethiopian government and rebel forces as their war was coming to an end. In 1995, France was instrumental in bringing Eritrea and Yemen to the negotiating table to settle the dispute over the Hanish Islands. China played a key role in convincing Sudan to accept a hybrid UN/African

Union peacekeeping force in Darfur. The United States, United Kingdom, and Norway helped to end the north-south conflict in Sudan and to convince the government to accept a referendum on the independence of South Sudan.

In recent years, there has been less enthusiasm by non-regional countries to engage in mediation efforts; some of the slack has been picked up by the Gulf States. Beginning in 2010, Qatar provided 400 observers to monitor a ceasefire on the Red Sea island of Doumeira, claimed by both Eritrea and Djibouti, until disagreements with Saudi Arabia and the UAE forced the Qatari troops to leave in 2017. In 2018, the UAE and Saudi Arabia helped convince Eritrea to accept a peace offer from Ethiopia that ended their twenty year-long conflict, demonstrating that GCC states can play an important peace-making role. The UAE also provided $3 billion in aid and investment to Ethiopia and, together with Saudi Arabia, helped lift the UN sanctions regime against Eritrea.

States on both sides of the Red Sea have also demonstrated that they can resolve problems themselves. In 2016, Egypt and Saudi Arabia signed a maritime border demarcation agreement that ceded to Saudi Arabia sovereignty over the islands of Tiran and Sanafir in the Red Sea in the Strait of Tiran leading to the Gulf of Aqaba. The agreement, which was not popular among the Egyptian public, allowed Egypt to drill for gas and oil in deep territorial waters and averted a conflict with Saudi Arabia.

Moving forward

The complexity of issues in the Red Sea region is enormous and from the point of view of U.S. foreign policy further complicated by the fact that responsibility for them crosses bureaucratic lines in both the Department of State and Department of Defense. The State Department divides responsibility between the bureau in charge of Sub-Saharan African affairs and the one in charge of the Middle East and North Africa. The Department of Defense has a similar division of responsibility.

The military commands of the Defense Department place responsibility for Africa with the Africa Command based in Stuttgart, Germany and for the Middle East, including Egypt, with the Central Command in Tampa, Florida. The Indo-Pacific Command also has an interest in the Red Sea region. Communication among these units is not always as good as it should be. The problem is further exacerbated because states in the region see the United States as largely absent from a policy perspective, although it does have a strong military presence. Increasingly, China is being looked to as the region's long-term partner.

In order to emphasize the importance that the United States attaches to the region and obtain a better understanding of the issues on both sides of the Red Sea, the United States could send a team from both regional bureaus of the State and Defense Departments at the deputy assistant secretary level or higher to key capitals in the Gulf States and northeast Africa. The team could include appropriate representatives from the Africa Command, Central Command, and Indo-Pacific Command. An additional option is to appoint a special envoy for Red Sea regional issues who would have responsibility for engaging countries on both sides of the Red Sea and for making policy recommendations.

Looking beyond increased U.S. engagement in the region, a strong argument can be made for creating an organization that brings together all nine of the Red Sea littoral states with some kind of participation by important contiguous countries such as Ethiopia and the other members of the GCC. No current organization, except for the United Nations and its sub-agency the International Maritime Organization (IMO), brings all of these countries together. Existing groups such as the African Union and Arab League have not been particularly effective in bridging the Red Sea divide. Bringing together all of these countries, including Israel, some of whom are not currently speaking to each other, would be a challenge. But if the mandate begins as a free-standing discussion forum or one managed by the UN or IMO, it might be feasible. One of the issues, at least for the littoral states, is the future development of undersea resources.

An Egyptian national flag flies on a boat as a container ship sails down at the new section of the Suez Canal in the Egyptian port city of Ismailia, northeast of Cairo, on October 14, 2019. (KHALED DESOUKI/AFP/GETTY IMAGES)

discussion questions

1.The United States during both the Obama and Trump administrations aligned with Saudi Arabia and the UAE in their war against the Houthis in Yemen, selling arms and providing air refueling. Has the time come to end that support?

2. For the most part, the Trump administration has not shown much interest in the conflicts of the Red Sea region. Should it be more engaged, for example, in efforts to encourage democratization in Ethiopia, transition to a civilian government in Sudan, and resolve differences between Saudi Arabia/UAE and Qatar/Turkey?

3. In view of its close security relationships with Israel, Egypt, Saudi Arabia, the UAE, Qatar, Bahrain, and Turkey; how does the United States manage this horribly complex situation?

4. What is the threat to the future of the only permanent U.S. military base in Africa at Djibouti? How can the United States minimize any potential threat?

5. The foreign policy focus of the Trump administration is strategic competition with China and Russia. Is this the best policy for the Red Sea region? Are there areas where cooperation makes more sense, especially in the case of China?

6. How will China's Belt and Road Initiative impact development in the Red Sea region? Is China's role in the region seen as positive by the regional countries? By non-regional countries?

Don't forget: Ballots start on page 98!!!!

suggested readings

Ehteshami, Anoushiravan and Emma C. Murphy. **The International Politics of the Red Sea**. 236 pp. London: Routledge, 2012. The authors analyze security, militarization, arms flow, land boundaries, maritime borders, and territorial issues. They also cover the economics of the Red Sea, migration, capital flows and transport.

International Crisis Group. **Intra-Gulf Competition in Africa's Horn: Lessening the Impact.** 44 pp. Brussels: International Crisis Group, 2019. The International Crisis Group provides a detailed analysis of the current conflicts in the Red Sea region with a particular focus on Saudi Arabia, the UAE, Qatar, Turkey, and Iran and how these conflicts impact northeast Africa.

Melvin, Neil. **The Foreign Military Presence in the Horn of Africa Region.** 31 pp. Solna, Sweden: Stockholm International Peace Research Institute, April 2019. Neil Melvin describes the military forces of China, Egypt, France, Germany India, Iran, Israel, Italy, Japan, South Korea, Russia, Saudi Arabia, Spain, Turkey, UAE, UK, and US on both sides of the Red Sea.

Miran, Jonathan. "The Red Sea" in **Oceanic Histories** edited by David Armitage, Alison Bashford, and Sujit Sivasundaram. 25 pp. Cambridge, UK: Cambridge University Press, 2018. Jonathan Miran focuses on how the Red Sea is viewed historically and why as a historical space and place it has attracted so little scholarly attention.

Shay, Shaul. **The Red Sea Region between War and Reconciliation**. 224 pp. Sussex Academic Press, 2019. Shaul Shay, former deputy head of the Israeli National Security Council, takes an alarming view of the future of the region. He argues that superpower confrontation is inevitable and a stable future for the region cannot be assumed.

Lackner, Helen. **Yemen in Crisis: Road to War.** 352 pp. Brookyln, NY: Verso Books, 2019. The democratic promise of the 2011 Arab Spring has unraveled in Yemen, triggering a disastrous crisis of civil war, famine, militarization, and governmental collapse with serious implications for the future of the region. Yet as expert political researcher Helen Lackner argues, the catastrophe does not have to continue, and we can hope for, and help build, a different future in Yemen.

To access web links to these readings, as well as links to additional, shorter readings and suggested web sites, GO TO www.fpa.org/great_decisions and click on the topic under Resources, on the right-hand side of the page.

Modern slavery
and human trafficking
by Ronald Weitzer

Children fetch water from the bottom of a 25-foot well. At the surface, they use the water to pan for gold. (LARRY C. PRICE/PULITZER CENTER ON CRISIS REPORTING)

Human trafficking and modern slavery have become major public issues over the past two decades. Almost every nation has enacted laws criminalizing human trafficking, and international organizations, governments, and NGOs sponsor a large variety of projects to curb trafficking and slavery. Billions of dollars have been allocated to these efforts. Between fiscal years 2001 and 2010, for example, the U.S. government spent more than $1.45 billion on domestic and international antitrafficking programs, and the funds allocated for FY2019–FY2021 total $430 million. Expenditures by other governments and by international organizations have been substantial as well.

Definitions

Definitional problems plague discussions of trafficking and modern slavery. Among the issues are whether a person's consent is relevant; whether slavery is distinct from or overlaps with human trafficking; the meaning of "exploitation";

RONALD WEITZER *is a professor of sociology at George Washington University. He has researched domestic policies regarding sex trafficking in the United States and in 2014 co-edited a special issue on human trafficking for* The Annals of the American Academy of Political and Social Science.

and whether bonded labor and coerced marriage qualify as slavery.

One of the biggest problems is the lack of clarity and consensus on the very definition of human trafficking, as well as the troubling conflation of trafficking and slavery. The U.S. Congress and government agencies and leading international organizations increasingly use the terms "trafficking" and "slavery" interchangeably. And a few governments equate trafficking with unauthorized, assisted migration regardless of whether the individual consented or sought out such assistance. Some governments mix human smuggling and trafficking in their official figures or in law. In Brazil, for example, sex trafficking is legally defined as "promoting, intermediating, or facilitating the entry of women who practice prostitution into national territory or the exit of women who practice prostitution abroad." As the U.S. State Department points out, "These statutes encompass activity that does not constitute trafficking . . . such as consensual smuggling or movement for the purpose of prostitution."

Most governments distinguish between human *smuggling* (where a facilitator helps a person illegally cross a national border and where the two parties have relatively brief contact) and *trafficking* (where at least some deception or coercion is involved in recruitment or transit and where the victim may have protracted ties to the trafficker). The two types may overlap, such as when a person first enters into a voluntary agreement with a smuggler but later experiences abuse from that handler or a third party – thus qualifying as trafficking.

In the United States the 2000 Trafficking Victims Protection Act (TVPA) criminalizes the "recruitment, harboring, transportation, provision, or ob-

taining" of (1) an adult for purposes of labor or sexual commerce through means of "force, fraud, or coercion," (2) a person under age 18 for labor via "force, fraud, or coercion," and (3) a minor for commercial sex acts irrespective of whether coercion or deception are involved. In other words, to qualify as trafficking some kind of *abuse* is central for adults and for minors involved in non-sexual labor, but is not a requirement for minors involved in the sex trade. Adults who willingly engage in commercial sex are not trafficking victims under TVPA.

The premier international trafficking convention, the U.N.'s *Palermo Protocol* (2000), likewise centers on coercion and deception but is broader than TVPA in prohibiting "the abuse of power or of a position of vulnerability or of the giving or receiving of payments or benefits to achieve the consent of a person having control over another person, for the purpose of exploitation." Remarkably, core indicators— "exploitation," "abuse of power," "benefits," "control," and "vulnerability"—are left undefined. Vulnerability may include risk factors such as being poor, unemployed, indebted, drug dependent, a minor, or an illegal immigrant, but it is imperative that such key terms be precisely defined in a legal instrument of such international importance. The Palermo Protocol is the model for some nations' domestic trafficking laws, but states have found it harder to implement than the more precise TVPA.

Although the term "trafficking" suggests movement from one place to another, relocation is not required by law. Both the Palermo Protocol and TVPA include in the definition *recruitment, receipt, or harboring* of persons, any one of which qualifies as trafficking provided that other conditions (coercion, deception, exploitation) are met, regardless of whether geographical movement occurred. Many victims are recruited and put to work locally, and "harboring" consists of maintaining or housing a person in compelled work. Human trafficking does not require travel.

Modern slavery is not defined in U.S. or international law, and the lack of a universal standard means that the term is used inconsistently. The League of Nations' 1926 Slavery Convention defined slavery as "the status or condition of a person over whom any or all of the power attaching to the right of ownership are exercised." Today, owning another person is not included in definitions of slavery, because legal ownership is now outlawed throughout the world. Instead, *slavery* is now considered a regime of maximum economic exploitation, social isolation, and total coercive control over the workers. Some analysts use the term *slavery-like conditions* to describe circumstances that are less onerous and comprehensive than outright slavery. These conditions include confiscation of legal documents, restrictions on one's freedom, harsh working conditions, meager pay, and debt that mushrooms over time.

Although TVPA contains language portraying trafficking as a "manifestation of slavery," U.S. government reports and official pronouncements in the 2000s focused on trafficking per se or distinguished it from slavery. By 2012, however, the State Department had begun equating trafficking with slavery, forced labor, and bonded labor – resulting in a huge spike in the alleged number of trafficking victims (27 million in 2012). The growing conflation of distinct problems has been driven by activists' interest in drawing greater attention to the problem.

To simplify matters, it seems prudent to treat human trafficking as acts of coercion or deception occurring at the recruitment or transit stage, and slavery as forced labor and comprehensive control of a person inside and outside of the work setting. As other experts have noted, trafficking is a *process* of recruitment into a labor arena and slavery is a potential *outcome* of trafficking. Bonded labor – when a person incurs a debt with a middleman or employer in return for a job opportunity – is included under slave-like conditions only if it involves at least some coercion, deception, economic exploitation, or other abuse.

Before you read, download the companion **Glossary** that includes definitions, a guide to acronyms and abbreviations used in the article, and other material. Go to **www.fpa.org/great_decisions** and select a topic in the Resources section. (Top Right)

How many victims?

Estimates of the number of victims worldwide vary widely and have changed radically over time. In 2000, TVPA declared that "at least 700,000" persons were trafficked into slavery annually worldwide. For several years thereafter, the State Department's *Trafficking in Persons Reports* put the total at 600,000–800,000. In 2012, however, the figure skyrocketed to 27 million, comparable to the Global Slavery Index's (GSI) figure of 29.8 million in 2013. GSI's total ballooned to 45.8 million in 2016, but two years later was cut to 40.3 million. GSI explains both the 2013-2016 increase and the 2016-2018 decrease as a result of changes in the methodology it uses to arrive at estimates. Regarding the overall increase from 2013 to 2018, GSI cautions that "we are not asserting that modern slavery has increased in the intervening period."

Part of the overall increase is due to the inclusion of "forced marriage" in GSI's total – an alleged 15.4 million people in its 2018 report. It is questionable whether the notion of a culturally ordained but not fully consensual marriage is tantamount to slavery. Instead of assuming that all forced marriages qualify as slavery, it is important, as the State Department points out, to examine specific cases and "look particularly at the terms of the marriage and the possible conditions of exploitation encountered afterward."

The shifting worldwide numbers mentioned above are troubling in their own right, raising questions about attempts to quantify globally a problem that is largely hidden from view. While the State Department asserted in 2010 that 0.18% of the world's population had been trafficked, the agency no longer provides national or global prevalence figures in its annual reports, now using the default term "millions" instead. Some leading analysts argue that we should dispense entirely with expensive big-data projects (like GSI's) and focus instead on the ground: specific cities or small regions of a country with the goal of identifying and rescuing victims in those places. The IOM, for example, restricts its figures to individuals that it directly assists. These individuals are interviewed at IOM field offices before they are deemed credible trafficking victims and provided with services. IOM's interviews with about 100,000 such individuals over the past 20 years can be used by authorities to target the main "hot spots" where they are recruited and enslaved.

There are international figures on *certified victims*: i.e., those officially confirmed as victims by government authorities. However, as the table on the next page shows, the two leading sources differ substantially: the number of confirmed victims in one source is *double or triple* that of the other source! It is not known which is more reliable, but both show that the number of officially-identified victims is but a tiny fraction of the alleged millions of undetected victims worldwide. Either the latter claim is grossly exaggerated or detection efforts have been immensely unsuccessful, or both.

Victim experiences

There is no such thing as a "typical" victim. Victims' experiences range along a broad spectrum and depend on the amount and duration of economic exploitation, working and living conditions, the victim's age and gender, and the extent and kind of control exercised

Global Slavery Index

There are serious problems with the Global Slavery Index:
■ It is based on miscellaneous, unstandardized sources across countries: estimates come from NGOs, the media, government reports, or population surveys.
■ One of the main sources, a poll of households, is deficient because so many countries are left out. Only 48 countries were polled in the 2018 GSI, and only one Southeast Asian and two Arab nations. Countries experiencing armed conflict are not surveyed, although slavery may be prevalent there.
■ Poll respondents are asked whether they or any family member has experienced forced labor, forced marriage, deception about work, and some other questions. Surveys on such sensitive issues risk immense under-reporting by victims, and respondents may know nothing about their family members' experiences.

GSI uses a bizarre "imputation" procedure. For countries where there is no information whatsoever, GSI applies a "regional average" estimate to that country. This procedure obviously assumes that the regional estimates are themselves reliable (a dubious assumption), but also creates potential error in extrapolating from a region to a single nation.

For these and other reasons, some analysts and NGOs like Anti-Slavery International consider GSI's *prevalence* estimates totally unreliable. This does not necessarily mean that GSI's overall *categorization* of countries is erroneous, however. It should come as no surprise that countries where slavery is most pervasive are in the Third World, with the second highest prevalence in developing nations and the best record in the developed world.

TRAFFICKING VICTIMS WORLDWIDE

Year	Victims Identified (STATE DEPT.[1])	Victims Detected (UNODC[2])
2008	30,961	N/A
2009	49,105	N/A
2010	33,113	12,500
2011	42,291	14,000
2012	46,570	15,500
2013	44,758	17,000
2014	44,462	20,500
2015	77,823	24,000
2016	68,453	24,500
2017	96.960	N/A
2018	85,613	N/A

[1] U.S. Department of State, Trafficking in Persons Report 2019 (p.38) and prior years. Figures based on data provided "by foreign governments and other sources and reviewed by the Department of State." The "victims identified" category is not further defined in the report but apparently refers to victims who have been officially certified as such by state officials, not alleged victims.

[2] U.N. Office on Drugs and Crime, Global Report on Trafficking in Persons 2018 (p.21). Regarding the term "victims detected": "UNODC surveys governments on trafficking victims identified in their respective countries using a common questionnaire with a standard set of indicators, and then aggregates the results." The figures presented here are rounded, based on a UNODC bar chart.

by traffickers and bosses. At one pole are those who have been kidnapped and forced into work, lack all freedom of movement, receive little or no pay, suffer physical or sexual assault, or labor under extremely unhealthy or dangerous conditions. Others face none of these. Between these two extremes are those who have shifting experiences over time or are subjected to milder forms of mistreatment. The following examples illustrate these types.

Moderate Mistreatment/ Mixed Experiences.

An unknown number of victims (1) endure moderate levels of abuse or (2) have mixed or shifting experiences over time. Examples of "moderate" victimization include being informed about the kind of work awaiting them but not the actual working conditions; receiving somewhat less pay or working longer hours than what was agreed to; having a passport confiscated but enjoying some freedom outside working hours;

or being occasionally subjected to verbal abuse, demeaning tasks, or arbitrary fines, but not physical or sexual assault.

Some migrants do not fully appreciate the terms of their agreement with a facilitator, are not informed about working conditions or risks of arrest in a new locale, or how difficult it can be to pay off a debt to a broker or boss. For those who performed the same kind of work at home, working and living conditions at the new worksite may be quite different than what they are accustomed to. And other laborers agree to perform a certain type of job reluctantly – a diluted form of consent – out of an obligation to support their families or because of pressure from relatives.

Filipinas working in Japanese hostess clubs enter into a standard debt-based arrangement with a middleman who facilitates their travel and employment in Japan. Many of the brokers and bar managers exploit the hostesses by inflating the debt owed; holding passports until the woman returns home; retaining earnings they are not entitled to; and overcharging for food and housing. Yet despite these arrangements, many of the women consider this bar work preferable to living in poverty back home.

A questionnaire administered to 476 Bangladeshi labor migrants who worked abroad found that 81% qualified as trafficking victims:

■ Two thirds of the victims discovered during transit that their travel documents were fraudulent

■ Four fifths had their passport confiscated by their employer

■ Three quarters were forced to work excessive hours and/or were poorly paid.

Compared to what many other migrants and workers experience, these violations may be considered "moderate," but one pattern was especially disturbing: 96% of the female respondents experienced sexual harassment and/or sexual assault by a broker or employer.

One's experiences can change dramatically over time. A positive experience during recruitment or transit may be inverted after one arrives at a work-

place. An initial employer who treats someone properly and fully abides by a prior agreement may be followed by one who subjects the worker to at least some wage exploitation or other mistreatment. And some victims switch roles, becoming traffickers or slave managers themselves.

Moreover, a worker's assessment of and feelings about a job can flip over time. For example, women who are recruited to work as waitresses in bars along the Lao-Thai border have been pressured to engage in prostitution. They initially found sexual commerce distasteful and refused to engage in it, but once they discover that it is far more lucrative than waitressing and interact with women who like the work, many begin to normalize it and end up preferring it over low-paying jobs. This illustrates how a situation that is initially perceived as undesirable may be gradually redefined and embraced. Not only the working conditions but also the worker's attitude toward those conditions may shift radically over time.

Extreme or Polymorphous Victimization.

A victim can be subject to any or all imaginable types of serious abuse, including beatings, humiliation, denial of health care, and total confinement. Determining which kinds of mistreatment are most prevalent in any given setting is tricky, given the lack of representative victim samples, but a rough sense of the experiential dimension can be obtained from interviews with confirmed victims and calls to hotlines. For example, the five main kinds of abuse recorded in 10,615 calls to a hotline staffed by the Polaris Project in the U.S. in 2017 were isolation or confinement, emotional abuse, economic abuse, threats, and physical abuse.

Victims can be recruited and enslaved in bizarre ways. Nigeria is a case in point. Women and girls began to be trafficked into prostitution in Europe in the late 1980s, and the number has skyrocketed in recent years. The number of Nigerian females arriving in Italy grew from about 1,500 in 2014 to 11,000 in 2016. Most are recruited in one region

Sex Trafficking

Multiple victimization is revealed in a survey of 4,559 woman subjected to sexual exploitation, who were interviewed at IOM field missions in Europe and Central Asia:

■ 96% were denied the freedom to choose clients and 88% were not allowed to determine the kinds of sexual services they would provide

■ 40% were regularly prevented from using condoms and 9% were never allowed to use them

■ 9% experienced psychological abuse, 17% sexual assault, and 31% physical assault

■ 60% were denied all freedom of movement, while 36% were allowed some mobility but only if accompanied by a handler

■ Medical care was denied to 58%

■ They worked seven days a week and served an average of five clients per day

■ On average, they were allowed to keep just one sixth of their earnings

These findings – which qualify as slavery-like conditions if not outright slavery – demonstrate both intense and polymorphous mistreatment. It should be noted, however, that the data were drawn from individuals who managed to access IOM field missions, not a representative sample of victims. People who contact service providers may over-represent those who have had the worst experiences.

of Nigeria (Edo State) and most were trafficked into European sex markets.

Some of the women fly to Europe, but most travel overland through Libya and then cross the Mediterranean into Italy. After arriving in Europe, the women quickly discover that they must sell sex in order to pay off their enormous debt, up to 10 times the initial agreement. It typically costs a trafficker about $2,000 to buy a fake passport and transport someone to Europe, and they make colossal profits off these investments, to the tune of $40,000 to $80,000 per victim. A woman working in a Paris park, for example, was shocked to learn that her debt was €50,000. She was forced to work 12 hours a day; had to earn a minimum of €100 a day; and her handler took all of her income.

Some of the victims later return home and graduate to became traffickers themselves (madams), recruiting other women. Madams convince poor and vulnerable young women that a better life awaits them in Europe, where they will be working in a conventional job, such as waitressing or domestic work. Upon arrival they are forced into the sex industry. What makes this process distinctive is the ritualized use of the supernatural. Before they leave for Europe, a madam and village priest perform a voodoo ceremony whose purpose to secure spiritual leverage over the victim. The voodoo priest is paid by the madam for

conducting these ceremonies – as much as $1,000 – a strong incentive for doing so often. The following techniques have been used:

■ a woman is presented with photos of other girls who live the good life in Europe; naïve women believe these fake representations are genuine

■ the girl is told that her relocation debt is small, or told nothing about it at all

■ the ceremony involves the use of a woman's personal effects and an oath

to seal a "contract." A woman's hair or fingernails may be mixed with powdered animal bone and then rolled into a bundle bearing the woman's name. The scroll is retained by the madam or at a shrine, tangible evidence of the contractual agreement. Alternatives include eating a kola nut and chicken heart, drinking a brew of blood and gin, or symbolic cutting of the woman's skin. During the ritual the priest casts a spell on the woman.

To ensure compliance, the women

Sex workers of Sonagachi Kolkata, West Bengal, India, the Largest red light area of South East Asia, took part in a torch rally April 30, 2019, demanding dignity, labor rights and social protection on the eve of International Labor Day. (AVISHEK DAS/SOPA IMAGES/LIGHTROCKET/ GETTY IMAGES)

are instructed that if they tell anyone about the oath and debt a "juju curse" will be activated, resulting in insanity, death, or harm to a family member. The latter is not a mere threat; family members have been assaulted when a victim puts up resistance or is a poor earner.

Concern for family members, coupled with an abiding belief in the power of the oath and the victim's traumatic experiences abroad, present huge obstacles for law enforcement. In 2018, for instance, Nigeria's Agency for the Prohibition of Trafficking in Persons reviewed 662 cases but prosecuted only 43 suspects and convicted 26.

In a recent, rare trial, 16 Nigerian traffickers (11 women and 5 men) were prosecuted in Paris for enslaving 49 women. Some of the victims testified that they were beaten, raped, denied medical care, or forced to have an abortion. The court convicted 15 of the defendants, imposed heavy fines on them, and meted out sentences ranging from 2 to 11 years in prison.

Perhaps some good news comes from Edo State. On March 9, 2018, its revered traditional king, Oba Ewuare II, convened a meeting with about 500 juju priests in an attempt to curb the practice. The king declared that he had nullified all pacts used in human trafficking and had also placed a royal curse on any priest, madam, or parent involved in these rituals. He also proclaimed

that victims were now freed of their oaths. It remains to be seen if this recent intervention will make a dent in the lucrative business of sex slavery in Nigeria, but it does illustrate one way in which religious leaders can play a constructive role in places where trafficking is grounded in mysticism elsewhere in the world.

Child victims

Under international legal instruments, the employment of minors in the sex industry differs from employment in other sectors. As noted above, *any* involvement of minors in commercial sex is criminalized in U.S. and international law. They are deemed victims irrespective of whether they seek out or consent to work in this sector.

For other types of labor, however, age and working conditions determine whether a minor is deemed abused or exploited. The ILO considers laborers under 15 years of age victims by definition: their labor is considered both harmful and unethical. For the 15-17 age group, a 1999 ILO convention permits them to work provided that they do not engage in the "worst forms of child labor" – e.g., forced labor, debt bondage, prostitution, armed conflict, drug trafficking or other illicit activities, or hazardous work. *Hazardous work* endangers a person's health and safety and includes:
■ long hours or night work

■ work underground, under water, in confined spaces, or at risky altitudes
■ use of dangerous machinery/equipment or carrying heavy loads
■ exposure to hazardous materials, high noise levels, or temperatures that jeopardize health.

ILO estimates that currently 152 million minors worldwide are involved in forbidden forms of child labor, half of whom (73 million) work under hazardous conditions.

With so much of their populations living below the poverty line, it is not surprising that African nations have the highest concentrations of child labor, half the worldwide total. Most of the victims work in agriculture, fishing, and forestry.

The mining industry in West Africa illustrates the challenge of ending underage labor victimization. The arduous and risky nature of this work clearly fit the ILO's "worst forms of child labor" category (long hours, heavy loads, hot temperatures, use of mercury to amalgamate gold, work in underground mine shafts). The problem is that most of these youths are encouraged to migrate by their parents, normalize the working conditions, and view their labor as an opportunity: it is one of the few options to earn money to support their families – given the lack of work in their home villages – and also provides the boys with prestige and social capital that helps in attracting marriage partners.

Commercial fishing

Commercial fishing is a known slavery site. Ships that spend long periods of time at sea can literally imprison workers, with no option to leave even when they become sick or injured. Reports of extreme fraud in recruitment and horrendous working conditions are commonplace. In Russian and Turkish waters, commercial fishermen were forced to work 18–22 hours 7 days a week, and were beaten, often denied water, not paid, and injured by the traps they used. Similar crimes against commercial shrimpers in Southeast Asia were documented in an *Associated Press* exposé in 2015. Thai men and boys were forced to work 20-24 hours a day 7 days a week, were beaten and whipped if they complained or tried to

rest, and were paid little or nothing. Some had been kidnapped by brokers and sold to captains of fishing boats or the companies that own the boats, and some were later abandoned and died on an island far from home. Once the boats return home, a parallel cycle of abuse takes place in the shrimp-processing industry, victimizing the women and children who peel shrimp for a living. They were slapped and cursed, denied part of their wages, given short lunch breaks, and accumulated debts while working. A 16-year old girl who labored under these conditions from 3am until 7pm every day showed the reporters arms that "were a patchwork of scars from infections and allergies caused by the shrimp."

These push and pull factors are mirrored elsewhere in the Third World, where minors suffer under slave-like conditions but do not perceive themselves as victims. Their decision to migrate for work stems from economic desperation and either filial obligation or outright pressure from family members.

It is clear that combatting such "consensual victimization" faces tremendous obstacles for both national governments and the international community. The good news is that the number of youths working in slave-like or hazardous conditions has decreased somewhat in recent years. According to the ILO, the number of minors involved in hazardous work fell from 170 million in 2000 to 73 million in 2016, with a comparable decline (245 million to 152 million) involved in impermissible but non-hazardous child labor.

Industry sectors

Victims are trafficked into many different industries: mining, agriculture, manufacturing, domestic work, fishing, construction, and the sex industry. Regarding the latter, it is important to stress that voluntary involvement in sexual commerce does not constitute trafficking. As the State Department points out, "Prostitution by willing adults is not human trafficking regardless of whether it is legalized, decriminalized, or criminalized."

Yet, sex trafficking has received the lion's share of attention over the past two decades. Indeed, it is typically the *only* focus in news reporting, feature films, television documentaries, and many anti-trafficking projects run by international organizations, NGOs, and governments. Moreover, most of the victims who have been rescued and most of the perpetrators arrested worldwide were involved in sex trafficking. Over the past three years (FY 2016–18), for example, the Justice Department prosecuted 753 cases of human trafficking, 94% of which involved sex trafficking.

Why? Sex trafficking is uniquely disturbing for many people, pulling at the heartstrings; it is easily sensation-

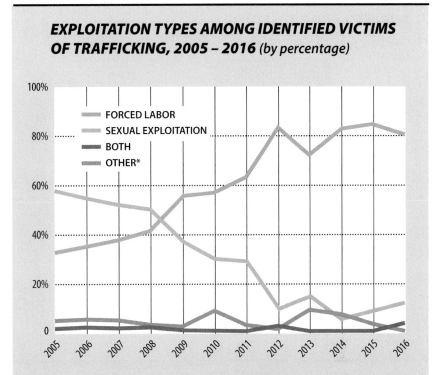

EXPLOITATION TYPES AMONG IDENTIFIED VICTIMS OF TRAFFICKING, 2005 – 2016 (by percentage)

*NOTE: "OTHER" INCLUDES: FORCED MARRIAGE, MILITARY SERVICE, LOW LEVEL CRIMINAL ACTIVITY, AND TRAFFICKING FOR BLOOD, ORGANS OR OTHER BODY PARTS.
SOURCE: IOM HUMAN TRAFFICKING GLOBAL DATABASE, 2017

alized; and it is gendered: women and girls are the vast majority of victims, which seems to generate more sympathy than for male victims. Many people view labor trafficking, by contrast, as "boring" or see it as a subset of disreputable illegal immigration, contributing to muted empathy for those involved. What is missing here is recognition that victimization in labor trafficking and forced work can be just as severe and life-altering as what sex trafficking victims may experience. This may explain why some activists now prefer the term slavery over labor trafficking; slavery is much more stigmatized and thus more likely to generate publicity and activism.

Whereas sex trafficking remains the main focus and some nations have only recently criminalized labor trafficking, today the latter is receiving slightly more attention from governments and international organizations. One of the most important facts is that the global market for exploited non-sexual labor *far exceeds* the market for sexual services. In other words, the commercial

sex market pales in comparison to the size of all other labor arenas, such as agriculture, manufacturing, domestic work, etc. In 2010, the State Department proclaimed that "the majority of human trafficking in the world takes the form of forced labor," a conclusion echoed by international and non-governmental organizations such as Anti-Slavery International. The International Labour Organization has consistently estimated that about four-fifths of all persons involved in forced or exploitative work worldwide were engaged in non-sexual commerce: 78% in 2012 and 81% in 2017. Another indicator of this pattern is that the number of labor-trafficking victims seeking assistance at IOM field offices now eclipses the number of assisted sex-trafficking victims, the latter comprising about 13% in 2016 (see graph above). Labor trafficking is therefore much more pervasive than sex trafficking.

Another important fact is that sex workers – more than many other laborers –have routine contact with customers and typically work and live near

FORCED LABOR BY SECTOR

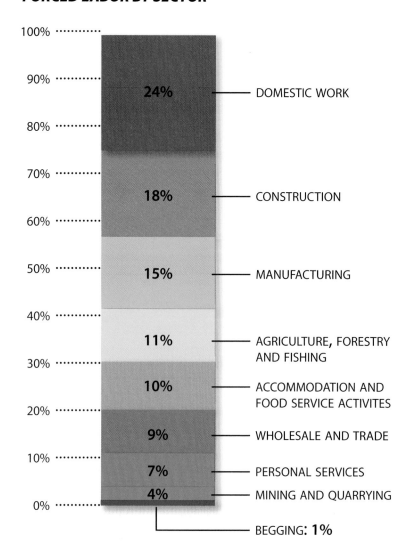

Source: International Labour Organization, Global Estimates of Modern Slavery, 2017, p. 32

NOTE: DUE TO ROUNDING, PERCENTAGES DO NOT ADD UP TO 100%   LUCIDITY INFORMATION DESIGN, LLC

neighbors. This increases the odds that they will be discovered – that some client or neighbor will inform the authorities of someone who appears to be abused or a minor. It can be argued that (1) reporting by a client or neighbor may help to explain, at least to some extent, why the authorities become aware of sex trafficking more often than labor trafficking and (2) the presence of clients and neighbors may serve as a partial deterrent to mistreatment in the sex sector in the first place, insofar as bosses are aware that unfree or abused sex workers may alert others. Sexual commerce is more visible because clients need to know its venues, whereas other industries can be much more isolated from public view. There are few if any visitors to mines, fishing ships, agricultural sites, and construction sites.

The consensus is that labor trafficking and slavery are *most prevalent in domestic work, agriculture, construction, and manufacturing.* (This is the global picture; the leading industries naturally vary by country, depending on their local presence and the government's anti-trafficking record.) Trafficking and forced labor appear to be somewhat less prevalent globally in the mining and fishing industries; but, again, this conclusion may be a function of the fact that mining and commercial fishing can be even more isolated than the top four sectors.

Law enforcement

Traffickers do not fit a standard profile. Some operate in organized-crime networks, others work in very small groups, and yet others are solo entrepreneurs. The proportion in each category is unknown, but data on traffickers caught by the authorities suggests that the majority are small-scale operators. And many victims are recruited by acquaintances, friends, or family members. Because of their strong social ties, it is particularly difficult for the authorities to build cases against a victim's relatives or close friends.

The conventional image of a trafficker is a middle-aged male. Yet, more than a third of those arrested, prosecuted, and convicted of trafficking offenses internationally are females: 37% of those convicted in 2014 and 38% in 2016. In some parts of the world, the *majority* of those convicted of trafficking are female: Eastern Europe, Central Asia, the Caribbean, and Central America. *Women are therefore much more involved in human trafficking than in almost all other types of crime*, where they represent a small fraction

of the offender population. Women are most active as brokers at the recruitment stage (trafficking) while men predominate at the exploitation stage (forced labor, slavery). And women are more prevalent in sex trafficking than labor trafficking enterprises. Remarkably, a sizeable number of female traffickers were former victims, as a 2016 UNODC report points out:

"particularly in the field of trafficking for sexual exploitation, many former victims are at some point offered the opportunity of recruiting new vic-

Cambodian Trafficking

Accounts from traffickers themselves are scarce and usually anecdotal. An exception is a unique study based on interviews with 91 individuals incarcerated for trafficking offenses in Cambodia. By comparing the interview transcripts with other sources, the researchers determined that 25% of the respondents had indeed been involved in trafficking as defined by Cambodian law. However, 16% had been involved simply in procuring for prostitution (not trafficking) and the remaining 59% had been "doubtfully convicted" of trafficking – meaning that their accounts did not fit the legal definition of trafficking. The narratives were cross-checked with other sources in some cases, but the researchers could not determine how many of the "doubtfully convicted" may have been wrongly convicted.

tims or serving as a "madam." Victims' motivation to switch to such roles may be to reduce their debt to traffickers or others, or to end their own exploitation. . . . Moreover, once victims are engaged in the enterprise, they become accomplices to the trafficking operation and are then less likely to cooperate with law enforcement."

Prosecutions and convictions of traffickers have steadily increased worldwide, doubling between 2007 and 2018 (see Table 2). However, law enforcement efforts are not evenly distributed throughout the world, with some countries much more active than others. In the United States, the Justice Department secured convictions against 439 traffickers in FY 2016, 499 in FY 2017, and 526 in FY 2018. At the other end of the spectrum, UNODC found that 9%

Worldwide prosecutions and convictions for human trafficking

Year	Prosecutions	Convictions
2007	5,682	3,427
2008	5,212	2,983
2009	5,606	4,116
2010	6,017	3,619
2011	7,909	3,969
2012	7,705	4,746
2013	9,460	5,776
2014	10,051	4,443
2015	19,127	6,615
2016	14,939	9,072
2017	17,471	7,135
2018	11,096	7,481

Source: U.S. Department of State, Trafficking in Persons Report 2019 (p.38) and prior years

of 181 countries reported no trafficking convictions and 27% reported only 1–10 convictions from 2014 to 2017.

It is not known whether "low" prosecution and conviction rates are due to low incidence of trafficking in a country or to meager enforcement efforts. What is clear is that prosecutions are inherently difficult everywhere, since they typically depend on the testimony of victims who may distrust the authorities, dread recounting traumatic experiences at trial, or fear retaliation from traffickers. When the perpetrators are police, military, or other state agents, the prospects for prosecution are much lower than for civilian traffickers.

There are no international data on the punishments meted out for persons convicted of trafficking, but we do know that sentences can be as severe as life imprisonment. In the United States, the federal penalty for someone convicted of trafficking is a fine and/or imprisonment for 10 years to life. The punishment for a slavery-like condition (i.e., holding a person in debt peonage or involuntary servitude) ranges from a fine to incarceration for 20 years. Each of the 50 states has its own trafficking law, and sanctions vary from state to state.

Of the U.S. federal trafficking cases that resulted in verdicts in 2015, 98% of those convicted received a prison term and the average length of sentence was 183 months, or 15.3 years. These figures combine forced labor, slavery, sex trafficking, and peonage. In FY 2018, trafficking sentences ranged from 3 months to life in prison, and more than 70% exceeded 5 years.

While the global pattern is clearly under-enforcement, there have also been instances when individuals were prosecuted and convicted for acts that do not legally qualify as trafficking offenses, as the Cambodian study shows. In the United States, a clear trend is to prosecute individuals engaged in pimping (i.e., supervising or living off the proceeds of a prostitute) under more severe trafficking statutes, and those convicted typically receive much longer sentences than they likely would have in the past. And in a notorious Seattle case, clients of Korean massage parlors who discussed their experiences on a client-centered website were charged with operating a "human trafficking ring." One of the accused later committed suicide. The prosecution was criticized for engaging in a gross misapplication of trafficking law to individuals who had simply purchased sexual services and discussed this online.

In both the U.S. and elsewhere in the world, relatively little is known about the crucial law enforcement dimension. We need much more research on the ways in which criminal justice systems, throughout the world, investigate and adjudicate cases of accused traffickers and slaveholders, as well as the reasons why some nations have such a poor record in this domain.

U.S. foreign policy

Since the passage of TVPA in 2000, the U.S. Government has taken the lead internationally in efforts to combat human trafficking. It does so through its embassies, collaborative initiatives with other governments, funding foreign NGOs, and in detailed annual reports on international trends and country compliance with a set of best practices.

Migrant workers from Cambodia at work on a fishing boat in Mahachai, on the outskirts of Bangkok, Thailand, February 25, 2010. (NICOLAS ASFOURI/AFP/GETTY IMAGES)

Since 2002 the Labor Department has issued its *Worst Forms of Child Labor Report*, which identifies countries that have made progress in fighting child labor, making them eligible for trade-preference programs. The second and more comprehensive international assessment is the State Department's annual *Trafficking in Persons Report*. The objective is to hold countries accountable for trafficking and to encourage them to adopt a set of best practices for detecting and combatting it. Since 2001, each country receives a detailed narrative evaluation of its record and is assigned a tier ranking, subject to revision if conditions change during the following year:

Tier 1: the government fully meets TVPA's minimum standards for the elimination of trafficking; 33 countries were listed under this tier in 2019, including most of Western Europe

Tier 2: the government does not fully meet TVPA's minimum standards, but is making significant efforts to comply with them; 93 countries in 2019

Tier 2 Watch List: the government does not fully meet TVPA's minimum standards and is making significant efforts to do so, but (a) the number of victims is substantial or significantly increasing and/or (b) the regime has failed to provide evidence of enhanced efforts to combat trafficking in the past year; 38 countries in 2019

Tier 3: the government does not fully meet TVPA's minimum standards and is not making significant efforts to do so; 22 countries in 2019, including Burma, China, Cuba, Iran, North Korea, Russia, Saudi Arabia, Syria, and Venezuela.

Minimum standards include the existence of an anti-trafficking law, ongoing "serious and sustained efforts" to eliminate severe forms of human trafficking, cooperation with other governments' anti-trafficking efforts, policies for meaningful protection of and assistance to victims, and "stringent" punishment of perpetrators. The State Department recommends prosecuting traffickers under trafficking laws, not as a civil offense or labor violation. Trafficking laws typically stipulate harsher punishments, and convictions under them send a stronger deterrent message to would-be criminals.

Tier 3 countries are subject to economic sanctions. The TVPA gives the U.S. government the power to deny foreign assistance to a regime in this category, although it has rarely done so, preferring soft pressure instead. Sanctions are usually waived for Tier 3 nations unless that country is already under U.S. sanctions for other reasons. From 2005 to 2016, sanctions were imposed on Burma, Iran, North Korea, Russia, and Syria, but only Iran and North Korea in recent years. The very fact that Tier 3 and Tier 2 Watch List nations are officially branded as such is intended to "name and shame" and thus encourage greater compliance. Over the past two decades, the threat of foreign aid restrictions has indeed catalyzed reforms in several nations, after which they were rewarded with a higher tier ranking. But many countries have remained stuck in a low tier.

The State Department did not rank the United States itself in its first nine annual reports; it was first included in 2010, in Tier 1 and retains that ranking today.

With its tier-ranking system it is clear that the U.S. is attempting to convert its own standards into global norms. International organizations – such as UNODC, IOM, and ILO – do not routinely reveal which governments are compliant with the Palermo Protocol and do not rank countries. It has thus fallen to the U.S. to take the lead in the worldwide anti-trafficking campaign, gradually building consensus on key norms and best practices.

The U.S. government also works directly with other governments, funding and staffing bilateral prevention initiatives, victim-assistance programs, and enforcement efforts. Regarding enforcement, in the past four years (FY 2015-2018) the State Department opened 780 human trafficking cases outside the U.S. Other international investigations and prosecutions are initiated by the Departments of Defense and Homeland Security. A major example is ongoing collaboration between Mexican and American authorities working to dismantle trafficking rings operating along the U.S.-Mexico border. This joint effort has resulted in successful prosecutions in both countries, including U.S. federal prosecutions of over 170 defendants, and the dismantling of some cross-border trafficking networks.

A policy that overlaps the domestic and foreign realms is the special visa available in the United States to immigrants who are certified as trafficking victims: a T-visa allows the immigrant to remain in the country. TVPA caps the number of T-visas at 5,000 per year, but the number applied for and granted has fallen well short of that. Under the Obama administration from 2009-2016, between one-sixth and one-third of such applications by victims were denied, depending on the year; during the first year of the Trump administration, one-fifth were denied.

The growing international attention to labor trafficking, mentioned earlier in the article, has prompted increased concern with working conditions throughout entire supply chains. Because a product passes through a lengthy chain of producers, distributors, and retailers, determining whether any given product is slavery-free is extremely difficult. Is the cocoa in the chocolate bar you are eating or the gold in the ring you are wearing a result of slave labor? Major corporations are beginning to take measures to decrease the risk of forced labor occurring at each stage in their supply chain, but governments can push corporations further. Australia and the UK recently passed legislation that requires major corporations to report annually on the risks of slavery in their operations and supply chains and to make efforts to reduce those risks. The laws are limited to disclosure; they do nothing to combat slave-like conditions other than the required statement of risks and remedies. No similar law exists in the United States, although some bills have been proposed recently in Congress. State intervention in the corporate world is not a conventional foreign policy issue, but the application of new legal norms to multinational corporations is clearly an attempt to increase accountability among entities that operate both domestically and internationally.

Public shaming is another way to compel corporate compliance. An example is the Department of Labor's annual *List of Goods Produced by Child Labor or Forced Labor*; the 2018 list identified 148 goods and 76 countries where they are produced. The Departments of State and Homeland Security publish similar lists, blacklisting foreign products that are suspected of being produced with forced labor, child labor, or convict labor. Listed products can be subject to an importation ban.

Businesses that appear to be implicated in trafficking and slavery, including a lack of supply-chain transparency, are vulnerable to grass-roots campaigns and consumer boycotts. One recent opinion poll found that a majority of consumers would stop buying a product if they discovered it was produced with forced labor.

Conclusion

It is often said that cross-border human trafficking is human smuggling gone awry. For those who cross national borders, social, economic, and political "push factors" in one's home country (lack of job opportunities, intense poverty, political persecution, pervasive violent crime, widespread disease, domestic abuse) are the flipside of a set of "pull factors" in other countries (job or educational opportunities, political asylum, enhanced health care, physical security). When people decide to move across a border, they usually need the assistance of smugglers, some of whom are traffickers who engage in deception or coercion. The more restrictive the barriers to cross-border migration, the greater the odds that the migrant will be victimized by middlemen.

The circumstances are somewhat different for those who are seeking opportunities in their native country, not crossing a national border. Nevertheless, these domestic cases share the core characteristic of *vulnerability* to economic exploitation and other mistreatment at the hands of recruiters and nefarious employers. What ties domestic and cross-border types together is abuse during the recruitment stage and exploitative or coercive conditions at the worksite.

At the same time, we must remember that migration, trafficking, and labor conditions vary from one location and social network to another and that participants' lived experiences vary contextually as well. Relations between workers, middlemen, and employers range from extreme physical and psychological abuse, severe economic exploitation, and terrible working conditions to less extreme and less oppressive working and living conditions.

We have questioned the preoccupation with "guestimating" the number of victims nationally and worldwide. Some analysts consider this an inherently flawed exercise, given the clandestine nature of much trafficking and slavery. Recall that the U.S. State Department has now abandoned numerical estimates and instead simply notes that there are "millions" of victims worldwide. It can be argued that resources should be shifted downward: away from costly big-data quantification of trafficking and slavery at the macro level toward sponsoring micro-level research in specific cities and with distinct victim populations, as IOM does. Such research on the ground has important policy and enforcement implications: When findings pinpoint specific "hot spots" of victimization, they can help the authorities locate perpetrators and disrupt trafficking rings and slave-based enterprises.

Activists take part in a 'Walk for Freedom' to protest against human trafficking in Berlin, Germany, October 20, 2018. (FABRIZIO BENSCH/REUTERS)

discussion questions

1.What are the main differences between human trafficking and human smuggling?

2. The author argues that estimates of human trafficking and slavery are inherently flawed, especially at the national and international level. What is the basis for this argument, and what does the author recommend as an alternative focus.

3. Sex trafficking receives most of the attention from activists, the media, governments, and international organizations. If labor trafficking is far more prevalent throughout the world, why is so much of the focus on sex trafficking, and what can we do to rebalance official discourse and policy priorities?

4.What is the difference between slavery and slave-like conditions?

5. Every year the U.S. government ranks nations into one of four tiers and uses the threat of economic sanctions to pressure countries into conformity with a set of minimum standards for combatting trafficking. Many countries have remained stuck in one tier, while others have improved their ranking. Is this an effective foreign policy method? Are there alternative ways of convincing other nations to crack down on trafficking in their countries?

6. Should minors who willingly engage in hazardous work be considered victims?

Don't forget: Ballots start on page 98!!!!

suggested readings

Gozdziak, Elbieta, and Micah Bump. **Data and Research on Human Trafficking.** 56 pp. Washington, DC: Institute for the Study of International Migration, 2008. A review of 1,500 publications on human trafficking. The authors found that the vast majority were overviews or commentaries; only one-third reported empirical research findings; and most of the empirical writings either did not identify their research methods or used convenience samples instead of random samples. The analysis can serve as a litmus test for writings produced since this study was published.

International Labour Organization. **Global Estimates of Child Labor: Results and Trends 2012-2016**. 65 pp. Geneva: ILO, 2017. The definitive analysis of labor among minors.

Siskin, Alison, and Liana Sun Wyler. **Trafficking in Persons: U.S. Policy and Issues for Congress.** 70 pp. Washington, DC: Congressional Research Service, 2013. Overview of trafficking in the United States and the U.S. government's foreign policies toward trafficking.

Aronowitz, Alexis. **Human Trafficking: A Reference Handbook.** 406 pp. Santa Barbara, CA: ABC-CLIO, 2017. Covers all major dimensions of human trafficking including official documents, legislation, resources, and major organizations involved in anti-trafficking work. Also features several short essays by experts.

U.S. Department of State. **Trafficking in Persons Report 2019**. 538 pp. Washington, DC: Department of State, 2019. Comprehensive examination of worldwide patterns and trends and detailed narratives on conditions in virtually every country.

Weitzer, Ronald, and Sheldon Zhang (eds.). **Human Trafficking: Recent Empirical Research.** Annals of the American Academy of Political and Social Science. 265 pp. Volume 653, May 2014. A special issue of the prestigious journal devoted to various dimensions of human trafficking, including youth involvement, pimping practices, law enforcement, celebrity involvement in anti-trafficking campaigns, and sex and labor trafficking in selected countries.

To access web links to these readings, as well as links to additional, shorter readings and suggested web sites,
GO TO www.fpa.org/great_decisions
and click on the topic under Resources, on the right-hand side of the page.

Panic at the border: U.S. relations with the Northern Triangle

by Michael Shifter and Bruno Binetti

Anti-narcotics and military police officers incinerate more than 200 kilos of cocaine seized in southern Honduras near the border with Nicaragua, on the outskirts of Tegucigalpa on August 5, 2016. (ORLANDO SIERRA/AFP/GETTY IMAGES)

The United States has had a dominant presence in Central America for more than a century, but the region received little media and public attention here except during the region's civil wars in the 1980s. Today, Central America is once again at the center of political debates in the U.S. as a result of rising undocumented immigration from El Salvador, Guatemala and Honduras, also known as the Northern Triangle of Central America (NTCA). While citizens of NTCA countries have been migrating to the U.S. for decades, a combination of factors including widespread violence and criminality, economic inequality and rural poverty, and the desire to reunite with family members who already live in the U.S. has led to a vast increase in their numbers.

Since the Great Recession, undocumented immigration from Mexico—the traditional source of immigration to the U.S.—has been steadily declining, while that from NTCA

MICHAEL SHIFTER *is president of the Inter-American Dialogue and an adjunct professor of Latin American Studies at Georgetown University. He speaks and writes widely on U.S.-Latin American relations and hemispheric affairs. Shifter is a member of the Council on Foreign Relations and a contributing editor of* Current History.

BRUNO BINETTI *is a non-resident fellow at the Inter-American Dialogue. He is a doctoral student at the London School of Economics. He holds an MA from the Elliot School of International Affairs at George Washington University.*

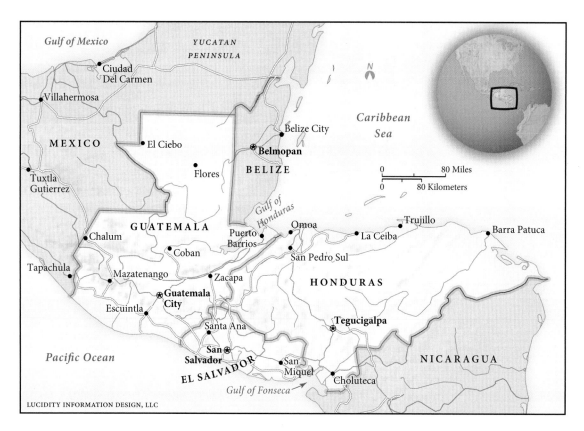

LUCIDITY INFORMATION DESIGN, LLC

countries continues to rise. Further, a significant share of entries from NTCA countries are families and unaccompanied minors, who request asylum in the U.S. This situation has overrun the U.S. immigration system, which is inefficient and in desperate need of reforms due to decades of political blockage.

Under the Trump administration, combating illegal immigration has become a priority of the United States. President Donald Trump has proclaimed a "zero tolerance" policy on the issue, including curtailing the right to asylum, separating children from their families to expedite deportation processes, and increasing the number of raids and arrests of undocumented immigrants, some of whom have been in the U.S. for decades. These policies have deeply divided U.S. society and caused great human suffering, while doing little to stem the number

Before you read, download the companion **Glossary** that includes definitions, a guide to acronyms and abbreviations used in the article, and other material. Go to **www. fpa.org/great_decisions** and select a topic in the Resources section. (Top Right)

of NTCA citizens attempting to enter illegally through the U.S. southern border.

This essay will analyze the relationship between the United States and Northern Triangle countries, in order to explain the structural causes behind the recent increase in undocumented immigration from the area. To do so, it will explain the long history of U.S. influence over the NTCA, which Washington saw as a critical Cold War battleground in the 1980s and has become a strategic zone for drug-trafficking into the United States since then. This analysis will also address the particularities of recent emigration from NTCA countries, and how it differs from Mexico's. In addition, it will evaluate U.S. policy responses to this surge in undocumented emigration from El Salvador, Guatemala and Honduras under the Obama and Trump administrations. Finally, it will propose ways in which the U.S. can tackle this problem by focusing on the reasons that make people emigrate in the first place.

Historical background

The U.S. consolidated its influence over Central America in the early 20th century. The opening of the Panama Canal in 1914

under President Theodore Roosevelt was a testimony to U.S. hegemonic position in the area. Under Roosevelt and his successors, Washington intervened several times in the region in order to protect U.S. economic and political interests. In doing so, it undermined or deposed governments deemed hostile to U.S. goals and propped-up friendly regimes regardless of their respect for democratic norms or basic human rights. Meanwhile, Central American elites became entrenched, concentrating all political and economic power while most of the population remained desperately poor, especially in the countryside. As a result, rural revolts by peasants and indigenous populations became common, and were harshly repressed by the U.S.-backed security forces.

This trend became even more acute after the start of the Cold War in the mid-20th century. For Washington, authoritarian regimes in Central America were critical allies against left-wing forces supported by Moscow, and deserved assistance despite their corruption and violence. In

1954, the CIA supported a coup against Guatemalan president Jacobo Arbenz, a democratically elected leader falsely accused of sympathizing with communism for his attempts to implement an ambitious program of land reform. The destruction of Guatemalan democracy generated instability and led to a vicious civil war between the military regime and left-wing guerrillas, which lasted from the 1960s to the 1990s. A similar situation ensued in El Salvador in 1980, when several guerrillas united to form the Farabundo Martí National Liberation Front (FMLN) and—with Soviet support—launched an outright offensive against the state, even managing to take some neighborhoods of the capital, San Salvador.

The importance of Central America as a battleground of the Cold War became paramount during the Ronald Reagan administration. During the 1980s Washington spent billions of dollars in economic and military aid for the Salvadorian and Guatemalan regimes in their fight against left-wing guerrillas. In both countries the security forces and paramilitary groups supported by the state unleashed vicious violence against rural villages, which tended to support the guerrillas. More than 200,000 people were murdered in the Guatemalan Civil war, and 75,000 people were killed in El Salvador, most in the hands of government-backed death squads. Entire villages were razed, peasants murdered and buried in mass graves spread throughout these countries. One of the most infamous episodes was the *El Mozote* massacre, in which more than 1,200 people were slaughtered by the Salvadorian military in December 1981. Even after this operation became known, the Reagan administration resisted calls from Congress and civil society groups to cut ties with murderous Central American governments.

While Honduras did not experience a civil conflict, it was affected by the instability and violence of its neighbors. A strong U.S. ally, the Honduran government welcomed the deployment of U.S. troops in its territory and assisted the right-wing regimes in Guatemala and El Salvador.

The Memorial at El Mozote in 1993. It was built for families massacred in the village of Mozote, El Salvador, by the U.S.-trained Atlacatyl Batallion in the early years of the war. The plaque reads, "They did not die, they are with us, with you and with all humanity." (LARRY TOWELL/MAGNUM PHOTOS)

In addition, Honduras agreed to host a paramilitary force of right-wing Nicaraguans, who were being trained by the Reagan administration to fight against the leftist Sandinista regime that had taken power in Nicaragua. However, the U.S. Congress opposed further involvement in Central America following the revelations of massacres in Guatemala and El Salvador, and banned the government from funding the Contras. Instead of relenting, the White House decided to use the proceeds of a secret arms sale to Iran (a declared enemy of the United States) to keep supporting the Contras. In 1985, the scheme was revealed by the press, and the Reagan administration was crippled for months amid intense outrage in Congress and among the public.

As the Cold War came to an end in the late 1980s, all Central American governments came together to find a way out of the region's intertwined and violent civil conflicts. This led to the Esquipulas Agreements, which laid the groundwork for democratic elections in Nicaragua (1990) and national peace accords in El Salvador (1992) and Guatemala (1996). Through these deals, governments, militaries and guerrillas committed themselves to restore democratic rule, rebuild state institutions,

demobilize paramilitary forces, reform the security forces, and end human rights violations. As promising as these deals were, they were extremely hard to put into practice. Decades of conflict took a heavy toll on the NTCA: Infrastructure was in ruins, public services almost nonexistent, poverty was rampant, inequality was appalling, and state institutions were extremely weak, corrupt and inefficient. The democratically elected governments who took over in the 1990s managed to prevent a return to open armed strife, but the structural conditions caused by and that had contributed to the armed conflicts remained almost unchanged.

By that time, the region had ceased to be a priority for the United States, which offered little or no assistance for post-conflict reconstruction. Incapable of building strong democratic institutions, El Salvador, Honduras and Guatemala became fertile ground for the expansion of criminal groups and armed gangs in the 1980s and 1990s. Some of these criminal organizations became more powerful and sophisticated as they became involved in drug-trafficking: The NTCA is strategically located between cocaine production areas in South America and drug trafficking routes that go through Mexico and into the U.S., the largest consumer of illicit drugs in the world. The weakness of state structures gave way to widespread corruption and inefficiency among the security forces, judiciary systems and the political class. Moreover, former members of paramilitary forces and intelligence services who had acted with impunity during the civil conflicts recycled themselves as members of criminal organizations.

Even as the U.S. withdrew from the NTCA, its policies still had large repercussions in the region. In the 1970s the U.S. government had launched a war on drugs based on a hardline stance against drug consumption and traffic. However, the expansion of interdiction efforts in the Caribbean increased the importance of Central America as a drug-trafficking route. In addition, in the 1990s the U.S. government deported thousands of gang members from NTCA countries living in Los Angeles (mostly Salvadorians) to their countries of origin. These groups used their criminal skills to build powerful and violent branches of U.S.-based gangs such as MS-13 (also known as Mara Salvatrucha) and Barrio 18, among many others. The U.S. policy of deporting dangerous criminals back to NTCA countries remains in effect today, with tragic consequences.

By the early 2000s, gangs had taken over entire neighborhoods in El Salvador, Guatemala and Honduras, and were fighting each other and weak security forces over territory and drug routes. As a result, murder rates shot up in NTCA countries, becoming some of the highest in the world. The other Central American nations (Nicaragua, Panama and Costa Rica) also face significant criminal activity and are part of hemispheric drug-trafficking routes, but have been more able to cope with this threat due to their relatively more stable politics and stronger institutions. Meanwhile, Mexico launched a war on drugs of its own in 2006 under president Felipe Calderón, which led Mexican criminal groups to increase their presence in NTCA countries, building alliances with some local groups while violently fighting others.

Eventually, the dramatic rise in drug-trafficking activities and widespread violence got the attention of the U.S. government. In 2007 the George W Bush administration launched the Merida Initiative, a multi-billion-dollar assistance package designed to boost Mexican efforts to combat drug-trafficking organizations that included some funds for NTCA countries. While the Initiative was announced as a multi-dimensional effort, in reality most U.S. assistance was destined to provide training and equipment for widely distrusted security forces, neglecting much-needed reforms to state institutions and all but guaranteeing impunity for police abuses and political corruption.

Recent migration to the United States

Undocumented immigration from NTCA countries in the United States is not new, even if it only recently entered the public debate. In 1998, president Bill Clinton granted Temporary Protected Status (TPS) –an immigration category that protects undocumented immigrants from being deported— to more than 50,000 Honduran nationals who had moved to the U.S. after the country was hit by Hurricane Mitch. Three years later, president George W Bush approved TPS for approximately 200,000 Salvadorians, most of whom had fled a catastrophic earthquake. TPS for both groups had been periodically extended many times since then.

The number of undocumented immigrants entering the U.S. rose significantly during the 1990s and early 2000s; a great majority of them were Mexican citizens. In the year 2000, over 1.6 million people were detained while trying to cross the U.S.-Mexico border illegally, a historic high. According to Pew Research, in 2007 the overall population of undocumented immigrants in the U.S. reached its peak at 12.2 million: 6.9 million were Mexican citizens and 1.5 million came from NTCA countries. However, after the 2008 crisis undocumented immigration from Mexico began to decline, as the U.S. economy had less demand for undocumented workers in agriculture, construction and other sectors. In 2010, the number of people detained while attempting to illegally cross the southern border into the United States had dropped to less than 500,000.

However, since 2013 declining undocumented immigration from Mexico has been partially offset by a rise in im-

UNITED STATES

Mexicali
Tijuana
Nogales
Ciudad Juarez
Chihuahua
Nuevo Laredo
Monclova
Matamoros
La Paz
Mazatlán
MEXICO
Mexico City
Vera Cruz
Chetumal
BELIZE
HONDURAS
San Pedro Sul
GUATEMALA
Tegucigalpa
EL SALVADOR
NICARAGUA
COSTA RICA
PANAMA
COLOMBIA

Gulf of Mexico
CUBA
JAMAICA
HAITI
BAHAMAS
ATLANTIC OCEAN
PACIFIC OCEAN
Caribbean Sea

Major migration route

0   400 Miles
0   400 Kilometers

LUCIDITY INFORMATION DESIGN, LLC

migration from NTCA countries. Between 2007 and 2017, the number of unauthorized immigrants from Mexico living in the U.S. declined by about 1.5 million, while those from NTCA countries rose by 400,000 and have continued to increase since then. Moreover, most undocumented immigrants from Mexico are young males looking for employment, meaning that they cross the border in secret and seek to elude U.S. border authorities. In contrast, a large share of NTCA immigrants are families and unaccompanied minors who request asylum in the U.S., a novel situation that quickly turned into a crisis for the U.S. government.

Although it is impossible to pinpoint a single reason, there are several intertwined factors that can explain the rise in immigration from El Salvador, Guatemala and Honduras.

The first is the lack of economic opportunities in NTCA countries, which are among the poorest in Latin America: 53.2% of Hondurans, 50.5% of Guatemalans and 32.1% of Salvadorians are poor, according to the United Nations Economic Commission on Latin America (ECLAC). Despite relatively high GDP growth rates or over 2% annually, wealth in the NTCA is highly concentrated, unemployment is high, and most people subsist in the informal sector. Further, poverty is even higher in rural areas, where a significant part of emigrants to the U.S. come from. Rural infrastructure is very precarious and peasants lack access to credit. This makes peasants particularly vulnerable to natural disasters such as earthquakes, and to the effects of climate change including hurricanes, massive storms and droughts, which have been rising in recent decades.

Structural poverty and inequality have combined with the entry of more people into the workforce: more than half of the population in NTCA countries is under the age of 25. This age group is more likely to decide to emigrate in search for better living conditions than older people. Moreover, since immigration from the NTCA to the United States began to increase in the 1980s, the remittances sent by those working in the U.S. has become a critical source of income for families in these countries. In 2016 remittances represented at least 20% of GDP in Honduras, 17% of GDP in El Salvador, and 10% in Guatemala. Those who seek to emigrate, therefore, not only look for personal improvement, but to take care of those left behind.

A second factor that explains the surge in undocumented migration from NTCA countries is the desire of people to reunite with their family members. ECLAC estimates that 82% of recent migrants from NTCA countries already have relatives living in the United States. This type of immigration tends to be self-perpetuating: With 1.2 million Salvadorians, 880,000 Guatemalans and more than 500,000 Hondurans already living in the U.S. (nearly half of them undocumented), family reunification efforts are likely to continue.

A third factor that has been mentioned above is widespread violence and criminality in NTCA countries. According to the latest data available from the United Nations Office on Drugs and Crime, in 2017 El Salvador had a murder rate of 62 per 100,000 inhabitants, Guatemala of 26 per 100,000, and Honduras of 42 per 100,000. The global average is 5 murders per 100,000 inhabitants. In addition to murder, armed gangs engage in kidnapping and extorsion, and forcefully recruit young men, attacking those who refuse and their families. According to a 2010 study, people in NTCA countries are 30% more likely to consider migrating if they have been the victim of a crime in the previous year. Part of this violence is related to common criminality, but a significant share is connected to drug-trafficking: more than 80% of all cocaine entering the U.S. passes through the Northern Triangle.

Murder rates in NTCA countries are among the highest in the world, but have been slowly declining since their peak in 2012. At least part of this improvement is due to new government initiatives, including taking back prisons that were being run by criminal gangs. El Salvador, Honduras and Guatemala have also implemented hardline policies based on the use of massive force by the security forces to combat criminality. This can be a deterrent in the short term, but eventually leads to human right violations, police abuses, and lack of trust for the police among the people they are intended to protect. Further, lower murder rates in some areas are a consequence of the consolidation of criminal organizations: armed groups have become so powerful that they now face less resistance

Mara Salvatrucha gang members are seen behind the bars of cells at a detention center on February 20, 2013, in San Salvador, El Salvador. (JAN SOCHOR/LATINCONTENT/GETTY IMAGES)

from rival groups and from the security forces. In fact, in 2012 murder rates in El Salvador dropped precipitously after the government brokered a truce between MS-13 and Barrio 18, the country's two main gangs. The cease-fire collapsed in 2014, after the authorities faced growing criticism for ceding to gang leaders' demands.

A final reason for rising emigration from NTCA countries, and perhaps the most important one, is the weakness of democratic institutions. State structures in El Salvador, Guatemala and Honduras are incapable of providing basic public services to many of their citizens, such as healthcare and education, and have no presence in large parts of their territories. A legacy of the civil conflicts, security forces are corrupt, violent and underpaid, which makes them easy to permeate by criminal organizations. Judicial systems lack independence from both the political system and criminal groups. This creates an environment in which corruption flourishes and impunity is the norm.

Further, governments lack proper funding to do their jobs. In NTCA counties, tax avoidance is the norm: tax rates on the wealthy are still very low and most refuse to pay even that. As a result, Honduras only collects 19% of its GDP in taxes, El Salvador 16% and Guatemala about 10%. In comparison, the average for member states of the Organization for Economic Cooperation and Development (OECD), a club of high-income countries, stands at 34% of GDP.

Democratic governance: breakthroughs and setbacks

To be sure, the overall situation in NTCA countries has improved since the peace agreements of the 1990s. Civil society organizations work to defend the environment from predatory practices and to promote the rights of poor peasants and indigenous communities, despite suffering threats and violence from criminal groups. Similarly, brave journalists expose corruption from high-level officials and the brutality of the security forces throughout the region, and some public officials struggle to hold power accountable against all odds. Because of the efforts of activists, the media, and independent judges and prosecutors, some corrupt officials have been held accountable, and mobilized citizens are protesting against abuses in record numbers. Throughout the NTCA, however, there have been worrying signs of a further deterioration of democratic governance and the rule of law.

In 2007, under pressure from civil society groups, the Guatemalan government welcomed a United Nations-backed institution—the International Commission against Impunity in Guatemala, CICIG—to support the local judiciary in combatting human rights abuses by the security forces. With time, however, CICIG went beyond its original mandate and began working with judges and prosecutors in high-level corruption cases. With the international support and visibility brought by CICIG, these officials were able to make historic breakthroughs: in 2015, the president and vice-president of Guatemala were forced to resign after being charged with corruption, amid massive citizen demonstrations. Both are in custody awaiting trial. One year later, Guatemalans elected outsider and former comedian Jimmy Morales as president on an anti-corruption campaign. Soon, however, Morales clashed with CICIG and its chief prosecutor, especially after the body began investigating the president's family and advisors for alleged corruption and illegal campaign financing. Despite intense civil society protests, judicial rulings and citizen demonstrations, in September 2019 CICIG was forced to shut down after the Guatemalan government withdrew the authorization it needed to function.

Despite this significant setback, the example of CICIG inspired civil society groups, journalists and independent officials in other NTCA countries. It proved that local institutions could hold high-level politicians accountable provided they had the proper funding and outside support. In 2016, the Honduran government reached a deal with the Organization of American States to install a CICIG-inspired institution to

People hold national flags and a sign reading "I love CICIG (International Commission against Impunity in Guatemala)". (JOHAN ORDONEZ/AFP/GETTY IMAGES)

support the local judiciary: the Support Mission against Impunity in Honduras (MACCIH). Although this new body lacks the independence and strength of its Guatemalan counterpart, its creation shows that the anti-corruption agenda is alive and well in the NTCA.

At the same time, Honduran democracy has deteriorated severely in recent times. In 2009 president Manuel Zelaya was removed from office by the military, with support from the country's political class in Congress, when he attempted to change the constitution to allow re-election. The OAS and most countries in the region deemed this a coup and isolated Honduras until democratic rule was restored. In 2016, environmental activist Berta Caceres—who led a grass-roots campaign against the construction of a dam on indigenous territory—was brutally murdered: the case brought international condemnation but no convictions. Two years later, president Juan Orlando Hernández—who had strongly backed the ouster of Zelaya—managed to change the constitution himself, and won reelection amid serious allegations of fraud.

The situation in El Salvador is also defined by widespread impunity and corruption, dotted with glimmers of hope. In 2009 the former leftwing guerrilla group FMLN—which had turned into a political party after the end of the civil war—won power for the first time through democratic elections. This achievement was quickly overshadowed by rising violence and corruption. As in Guatemala and Honduras, some members of the Salvadorian judiciary dared nonetheless to investigate high-level officials: a former right-wing president is in prison, accused of embezzling nearly 250 million dollars, and the first president from the FMLN fled to Nicaragua to escape prosecution. Tired of traditional, political elites, in 2019 Salvadorians overwhelmingly elected Nayib Bukele, who ran as an anti-establishment candidate. It remains to be seen if Bukele will be willing or able to fulfill his promises of uprooting corruption, and if a MACCIH-inspired commission created in 2019 will be effective.

Salvadoran Armed Forces soldiers line up in the historic center of San Salvador on June 20, 2019. (MARVIN RECINOS/AFP/GETTY IMAGES)

Policy responses in the U.S.

In sum, the recent rise in undocumented immigration from NTCA countries—which began around 2013—responds to a combination of factors, including widespread violence and criminality, rampant poverty and unemployment amid a demographic boom, a desire to join family members already in the U.S., and the corruption and weakness of state institutions in El Salvador, Guatemala and Honduras.

Migrants face huge challenges after they decide to leave, since they have to travel for more than 2000 miles across some of the most violent areas in the world until they reach the United States. Throughout the journey, migrants are subjected to all sorts of violence including kidnapping, extortion, forced prostitution, sexual assault, and forced recruitment into criminal groups. Parts of the trip are made by foot, especially in highly-policed border areas. Some people travel through Mexico by bus, others ride "la Bestia" (the Beast), a freight train that crosses Mexico from South to North every few days. Thousands of men, women and children stay in the train for more than two weeks until they reach the U.S. border, crammed up on top of the train's cargo. Hundreds

die or are severely injured every year in the moving train.

Those who can afford it pay human smugglers between 3,000 and 10,000 dollars per person to provide protection during the journey, and then pay several thousands more to *coyotes* who help them cross the U.S.-Mexico border. Frequently smugglers themselves subject migrants to violence. For low-income migrants, the alternative is to join efforts with other people from their area who also want to reach the U.S., forming so-called "caravans" of several thousand people. These groups are created out of necessity, to try to protect each other and pull their resources on the long and perilous journey.

Nevertheless, even if they manage to reach U.S. territory and apply for asylum there, migrants from NTCA countries still face long odds. In fact, the relatively large presence of children among migrants—a new phenomenon—is partially due to the fact that they have special protections under U.S. law, which makes them more likely to stay in the country. For instance, unaccompanied minors can only be detained for a few days by border officials, after which they must be handed

A migrant caravan of Central Americans walked into the interior of Mexico after crossing the Guatemalan border on October 21, 2018. (JOHN MOORE/GETTY IMAGES)

to foster homes or to relatives living in the U.S. Family groups are similarly protected, and must be released and allowed to stay in the U.S. after 20 days while their case is processed by backlogged immigration courts. With more than 800,000 asylum requests pending by 2018, in practice many migrants from El Salvador, Guatemala and Honduras get to stay in the U.S. indefinitely after requesting asylum.

The growing number of asylum applications from NTCA citizens overflowed the U.S. immigration system, which had been designed to cope with only a few thousand requests a year. Between 2010 and 2017, for instance, asylum requests increased from 28,000 to 143,000, with most of the increase coming from citizens of El Salvador, Guatemala and Honduras. Many thousands more applied for "defensive" asylum in an attempt to halt their deportation procedures from the U.S.

As the Northern Triangle surpassed Mexico as the origin of undocumented migration to the U.S., the region received increased attention from U.S. officials. In response to what he called an "urgent humanitarian situation" at the border, created by the arrival of more than 50,000 unaccompanied minors from NTCA countries in a matter

of months, in 2014 president Obama asked Congress for almost 4 billion dollars in additional funding to build new detention facilities, increase surveillance and border patrols, and hire more immigration officials and judges in order to cope with the larger number of asylum applicants. The Republican-controlled Congress, however, resisted, amid serious clashes with the White House on immigration policy. Meanwhile, the Obama administration moved to protect undocumented immigrants who had been brought to the U.S. as children from deportation, while boosting deportations of undocumented immigrants with criminal records and recent arrivals.

To address the deep causes behind emigration from NTCA countries, the Obama administration launched the U.S. Strategy for Engagement in Central America, focusing on El Salvador, Honduras and Guatemala. This policy worked simultaneously on three fronts: economic development, democratic governance and security. Under this strategy, Congress channeled more than 1.2 billion dollars through the State Department and the United States Agency for International Development (USAID) to various programs on areas such as education, civil ser-

vice and judicial reform, energy infrastructure, social development, crime prevention, and others. These initiatives were complemented by the Alliance for Prosperity, a multi-billion plan with similar goals launched by the governments of the three NTCA countries with U.S. support. The objectives of the Alliance are to boost the productive sector, develop human capital, strengthen the rule of law and improve citizen security in El Salvador, Guatemala and Honduras. Then-vice-president Joe Biden became the visible face of the administration's efforts to engage Northern Triangle countries in a constructive way and dispel old notions of U.S. hegemony in the region.

At the same time, under president Obama the U.S. increased pressure on Mexico to stop migrants from NTCA countries from crossing its territory, to reduce the number of people arriving at the U.S.-Mexico border. Therefore, in July 2014 Mexican president Enrique Peña Nieto launched the Southern Border Program, deploying more troops and police officials along its 577-mile border with Guatemala. The greater security presence resulted in an increase of over 70% in deportations of NTCA citizens from Mexico between 2014 and 2015. It also led to more human rights violations, abuses and violence against migrants by the Mexican security forces, and provided new opportunities for human smugglers who controlled alternative routes into Mexico.

Despite these efforts, by the time Obama left office in January of 2017 the idea that there was an unprecedented and dangerous crisis at the border had taken hold in Washington and throughout the United States. A key factor behind this growing sense of alarm was the man elected in November 2016 to be Obama's successor.

Enters Donald Trump

Anti-immigration sentiments were one of the key drivers of Donald Trump's successful presidential campaign, together with opposition to free trade. As a candidate and later on as president, Trump has used harsh and racist language against migrants, falsely accusing them of being responsible for joblessness, drug-trafficking and allegedly rising crime in U.S. border areas.

Initially, President Trump focused on immigration from Mexican nationals, despite their declining numbers. His most infamous promise was to build a border wall to stop migrants and drugs from entering the U.S., even though by the time Trump took office about 650 of the 1954 miles of binational border were already covered by a fence. In addition to being highly insulting for Mexico, a key U.S. ally and important trade partner, this wall would be highly impracticable: it would dramatically uproot the lives of binational communities that move across the border sometimes daily, and would cost billions of dollars but do little to stop people from applying for asylum at U.S. ports of entry. Moreover, most of the drugs that enter the U.S. do it in small boats, or are smuggled in through legal border crossings. Facing growing resistance from Congress—including among his fellow Republicans—in early 2019 Trump declared a national emergency at the border to relocate funds toward the construction of the wall without Congressional approval. So far, however, no new sections have been built outside of already existing barriers.

At the same time, the Trump administration launched a "zero tolerance" policy toward undocumented immigration, targeted toward entries from NTCA countries. The government instructed the Immigration and Customs Enforcement (ICE)—the agency in charge of implementing immigration policy—to expand the number of raids, arrests and deportations of all illegal immigrants, regardless of their criminal records or how long they had lived in the United States, a sharp departure from previous policy.

In addition, the White House has gradually implemented a complete overhaul of U.S. immigration regulations, in order to restrict the right to asylum and worsen the living conditions of undocumented immigrants in detention. The proclaimed goal of these policies is to end "catch and release"

(the practice of releasing undocumented immigrants in the U.S. while their asylum case is decided on) and deter new immigrants from attempting to enter the U.S. For example, new rules impose a mandatory fee on asylum claimants, prohibit them from seeking employment in the U.S. while their case is heard, and state that families who have applied for asylum can be detained indefinitely. Further, the Trump administration has taken measures to immediately reject asylum requests from people who have entered the U.S. through another country: that would immediately ban immigrants from El Salvador, Honduras and Guatemala from seeking protection in the U.S. These changes have led to more people being detained in increasingly cramped detention facilities, with very limited access to legal counseling and healthcare. At least 8 children have died in these centers, most of them of dehydration and the common flu. Most of these measures have been challenged in court by civil society groups and some U.S. states, but the administration's relentless anti-immigration push continues.

President Trump's crackdown on immigration is not limited to newcomers. Breaking a decades-old precedent,

the president has also sought to end TPS status for citizens of El Salvador and Honduras, among other countries. This would allow ICE to deport over 300,000 people that have been in the U.S. since the 1990s. So far, the decision has been halted pending several judicial proceedings. The administration was also forced to partially reverse its decision to forcefully separate children from their parents in detention facilities, which was aimed at facilitating deportation procedures for adults.

In addition to making it harder for migrants from NTCA countries to enter and stay in the United States, president Trump has also increased pressure on Mexico, El Salvador, Guatemala and Honduras to stop migrants from reaching the U.S. border in the first place. Mexico's situation is probably the direst: So far, more than 60,000 people have been forced to wait in Mexican border cities for their asylum request to be heard in the U.S. Since the U.S. immigration system has a backlog of hundreds of thousands of cases, they are likely to stay in that geographical and legal limbo for years. In the meantime, migrants live in precarious encampments maintained by Mexican authorities and some NGOs. Others wait in the streets and are vulnerable

Hundreds of activists and immigration advocates took to the streets in New York City on October 11, 2019. (ERIK MCGREGOR/LIGHTROCKET/GETTY IMAGES)

to sexual exploitation and violence.

Despite Mexico's efforts to accommodate people who had been expelled from the U.S. and to boost security over its southern border, in May 2019 Trump threatened to impose massive tariffs on Mexican exports if the government of Andrés Manuel López Obrador did not do more to stem the "flow" of people coming to the United States. Facing an economic disaster (which would have gravely affected the U.S. economy as well), the Mexican government quickly accepted to take in even more Central American migrants while their asylum application in the U.S. is being processed, and to send over 8,000 additional troops to its border with Guatemala in order to stop migrants from NTCA countries from entering Mexico on their way to the United States. As a result, Trump "indefinitely suspended" his tariff threat.

Central American governments have also felt the anti-immigrant wrath of the White House. In March 2019, Trump ordered over 500 million in aid toward El Salvador, Guatemala and Honduras to be halted as punishment for their failure to stop their people from migrating to the United States. This is a dramatic reversal in U.S. policy toward these countries: instead of seeing assistance to the NTCA as a way to change the structural conditions that make people emigrate, Washington is now chastising them, which is likely to weaken these countries even further and increase emigration. Democrat and Republican members of Congress have opposed this move, but the government has discretion to withhold the funds if it chooses to.

So far, the governments of Mexico, El Salvador, Honduras and Guatemala have sought to accommodate the U.S. president as much as possible and avoid confrontation. In 2018, for example, Guatemalan president Morales followed the U.S. in recoating his country's embassy in Israel from Tel Aviv to Jerusalem, in an (unsuccessful) attempt to gain the favor of the U.S. president. In July 2019, after Trump threatened to impose sanctions, Morales agreed to sign an agreement declaring Guate-

mala a "safe third country" for asylum seekers. If enacted, under this deal the U.S. would be able to deport thousands of Salvadorian and Honduran migrants to Guatemala, which would be responsible for their well-being.

Regardless of the text of the deal, Guatemala is far from being safe for its own citizens, much less for asylum seekers from other NTCA countries. Human rights organizations and others have criticized the deal as being completely unworkable, and as an attempt of the U.S. to forcefully return thousands of migrants to the situation of poverty and violence that made them flee in the first place. Confirming these claims, Guatemala's Supreme Court halted the implementation of the agreement, and Morales' elected successor (who will take office in January 2020) questioned its efficacy and announced that he would seek to renegotiate it. Nonetheless, the Trump administration has defended the deal, and vowed to continue pushing for similar agreements with other NTCA countries.

The anti-immigrant rhetoric of the president and other high-level officials is at least as consequential as the policy changes they are implementing. In countless speeches, tweets and statements the president has normalized language that until then was confined to the most extreme right-wing fringes of the political spectrum. He has accused Mexican immigrants of being "rapists and killers", he has talked about Central American immigrants "invading" the United States, and falsely accused migrant caravans of being full of drug-traffickers and gang members. Further, he has directly tied undocumented immigration with crime and murder, promoting false and dangerous stereotypes that can lead to more xenophobia and even violent acts against migrants.

What lies ahead

Evidence suggests that punitive approaches do not work to deter desperate people from migrating. A long-term U.S. policy to gradually reduce the number of undocumented immigrants arriving at its border would need to focus on the structural factors fueling

this vast displacement of people from NTCA countries, both "push" and "pull."

In order to address the "push" factors that make people leave their countries, the U.S. will need to engage the region in a constructive way, with properly funded programs that work with local governments while holding them accountable. The approach used by the George W. Bush administration was based on free trade, and led to the signing of the Dominican Republic Central American Free Trade Agreement (DR-CAFTA). This deal generated new economic opportunities in NTCA countries, but the benefits have not reached most citizens. Under President Obama, U.S. assistance shifted toward more targeted, community-based projects, but did not have enough funding nor time to be implemented before recent changes under President Trump.

Existing assistance programs that focus on education, infrastructure development and health in the NTCA could be expanded instead of cancelled or used as bargaining chips. U.S. efforts could also focus on strengthening accountability and democratic institutions in El Salvador, Guatemala and Honduras. In that sense, the silence of the Trump White House while Guatemalan president Jimmy Morales expelled CICIG and Honduran President Hernández secured reelection by dubious means directly contradict the administration's efforts to reduce undocumented immigration from these countries. Every time the U.S. has tried to rely on authoritarian or corrupt leaders to pursue its strategic goals in Central America, it has backfired spectacularly. This is a lesson Washington should have learned by now.

In addition, there is much the U.S. can do to reduce violence and criminality in NTCA countries, which are decisive factors behind emigration. For instance, U.S. lax gun regulations make it easy to smuggle weapons toward armed gangs and criminal organizations in Mexico and the NTCA. According to a recent study, more than 70% of the arms Mexican authorities decommission from criminals are U.S. made. Further, U.S. assistance packages could focus more on accountability and human rights observance in the security forces: iron-fist policies based on brute force against organized crime overwhelmingly affect innocent citizens.

Ultimately, the massive demand for drugs in the United States creates overwhelming incentives and profits for Central American criminal groups. It is about time to accept that the U.S. decades-old war on drugs, focused on disrupting international supply routes and punishing all types of drug possession domestically, has failed miserably. Cocaine consumption in the U.S. has increased sharply in recent years, and shows no signs of abating. New drug policies—already being implemented in some U.S. states—should avoid punishing consumers and emphasize prevention and healthcare over repression. In addition, U.S. authorities could do more to prevent criminal organizations with presence in NTCA countries from using American financial institutions to hide and launder their assets.

But U.S. authorities must also accept that there are "pull" factors that attract immigrants. In particular, the U.S. economy continues to demand thousands of undocumented workers in sectors in which American-born people are less likely to participate, such as construction, restaurants, agriculture, and child and elderly care. Undocumented immigrants make about up 5% of the workforce force in the United States, or about 8 million people. The numbers are even higher in states such as California and Texas, where they constitute more than 10% of the total workforce. It is very difficult to attempt to repress a movement of people that is at least partially generated by the demand of U.S. citizens and businesses.

More broadly, it is impossible to separate the present crisis from the state of the U.S. immigration system, which is in desperate need of reforms. Unfortunately, political blockage in Washington—which predates Trump—has made it impossible to find an acceptable compromise. Reaching such common ground, however, is indispensable to finding a durable and humane

solution to the rise in undocumented immigration from NTCA countries. A bipartisan immigration reform—similar to those that were common until the 1990s—would include measures that would be unpleasant for both sides of the aisle: it must include the regularization of the nearly 9 million undocumented immigrants living in the U.S., some of whom have been here for many years. It would also include drastic changes to the asylum system, which was designed to process a few requests a year and is based on an outdated distinction between "forced" migration and "voluntary" migration. As we have seen, the exact reasons for emigration from NTCA countries are hard to pinpoint, and elements from both categories tend to overlap. A possible compromise might be to restrict the right to asylum while granting more temporary visas for humanitarian reasons and for workers in areas that demand them.

Perhaps most importantly, U.S. policy regarding immigration from NTCA countries (and from elsewhere) needs to be decided based on an accurate representation of reality. Dangerous and xenophobic prejudices against immigrants should have no place in American political discourse, and should certainty not dictate U.S. policy on the matter. The thousands of people risking their lives traveling from NTCA countries do it to secure a better future for them and their families, and to escape vast poverty and violence. That is a struggle that should be familiar to most Americans, whose families came to this country under similar circumstances.

In fact, according to Pew Research, a vast majority of U.S. citizens support measures to improve the living conditions of asylum seekers at the U.S. border and to increase assistance to NTCA countries. Perhaps most surprisingly given the current political environment, 72 percent of Americans (and a majority of Republican voters) believe undocumented immigrants should be allowed to stay in the U.S., provided that they meet certain conditions. This is encouraging, and suggests that there is vast public support for a bipartisan consensus on immigration reform.

The United States has had a significant role in Central American history. In order to have a positive impact on this region's future, the U.S. needs to remember its own history and enact an immigration policy that is humane and pragmatic.

U.S. President Donald Trump shakes hands with a member of the US Customs and Border patrol during a roundtable on immigration and border security at the US Border Patrol Calexico Station in Calexico, California, April 5, 2019. (SAUL LOEB/AFP/GETTY IMAGES)

discussion questions

1. President Trump has declared a national emergency at the southern border, deployed military forces to support U.S. immigration and customs officials, and diverted appropriated defense funds from infrastructure projects to improve physical barriers along the border. How great a threat to U.S. national security is the situation in the Northern Triangle and along the U.S.-Mexico border?

2. Consider the duration and the importance of U.S. foreign relations with the countries in the Northern Triangle. Do you regard these challenges to be immediate, more mid-term (three to six years), or long-term (seven years or more)? How would you judge the area's importance to U.S. foreign policy goals?

3. Which U.S. foreign policy instruments are most applicable to addressing these challenges? Consider diplomacy, information, military, and economic measures.

4. Given the importance you have ascribed to the region, consider the three principal factors the author suggests are driving immigration from the Northern Triangle to the U.S.:
•The lack of economic opportunity in the NCTA countries.
•The desire of immigrants to reunite with their family members.
•The widespread violence and criminality in the Northern Triangle.

5. Reflect on your policy choices. Did your group reach consensus on which factor is most important, and which instruments are likely to be most effective?

6. The author concludes that current U.S. immigration policy is "ineffective, morally wrong, and contrary to U.S. interests." Do you agree? If so, how will your recommendations improve the situation in the Northern Triangle and along the southern border of the U.S.?

suggested readings

Guadarrama, Irma N. **In the Shadow of the Half Moon: Struggles of Women From Central America in Search of a New Life**. 181 pp. Scotts Valley, CA: CreateSpace Publishing, 2018. Why do women from the Northern Triangle countries of Central America risk their lives along with their children's, traversing through the treacherous, dangerous Mexican corridor, full of chaos and not knowing if they will live another day, if delinquents will steal their last peso, hurt them, or kill them?

Kinzer, Stephen. **Blood of Brothers: Life and War in Nicaragua.** 450 pp. Cambridge, MA: Harvard University Press, 2007. *Blood of Brothers* is Kinzer's dramatic story of the centuries-old power struggle that burst into the headlines in 1979 with the overthrow of the Somoza dictatorship. It is a vibrant portrait of the Nicaraguan people and their volcanic land, a cultural history rich in poetry and bloodshed, baseball and insurrection.

McCullough, David. **The Path Between the Seas: The Creation of the Panama Canal.**. 698 pp. New York, NY: Simon and Schuster, 1978. From the Pulitzer Prize–winning author of Truman, here is the national bestselling epic chronicle of the creation of the Panama Canal. In *The Path Between the Seas*, acclaimed historian David McCullough delivers a first-rate drama of the sweeping human undertaking that led to the creation of this grand enterprise.

Martinez, Oscar. **A History of Violence: Living and Dying in Central America.** 288 pp. Brooklyn, NY: Verso Books, 2017. Martínez travels to Nicaraguan fishing towns, southern Mexican brothels where Central American women are trafficked, isolated Guatemalan jungle villages, and crime-ridden Salvadoran slums. With his precise and empathetic reporting, he explores the underbelly of these troubled places.

Arnson, Cynthia J. **In The Wake of War**. 320 pp. Palo Alto, CA: Stanford University Press, 2012. *In the Wake of War* assesses the consequences of civil war for democratization in Latin America, focusing on questions of state capacity. Contributors focus on seven countries Colombia, El Salvador, Guatemala, Haiti, Mexico, Nicaragua, and Peru where state weakness fostered conflict and the task of state reconstruction presents multiple challenges.

Mayers, Steven. **Solito, Solita: Crossing Borders with Young Refugees from Central American.** 336 pp. Chicago, IL: Haymarket Books, 2019. They are a mass migration of thousands, yet each one travels alone. Solito, Solita, ("Alone, Alone"), is a Voice of Witness collection of oral histories that tell the stories of youth refugees fleeing their home countries and traveling for hundreds of miles seeking safety and protection in the United States.

Don't forget: Ballots start on page 98!!!!

To access web links to these readings, as well as links to additional, shorter readings and suggested web sites,

GO TO www.fpa.org/great_decisions

and click on the topic under Resources, on the right-hand side of the page.

China and Latin America
by Margaret Myers

This photo taken on August 6, 2018 shows a truck unloading animal feed made from soybeans, which are imported from Brazil, at a port in Nantong in China's eastern Jiangsu province. (AFP VIA GETTY IMAGES)

C hina seemingly leaped onto the stage in Latin America in the past two decades, establishing a remarkable presence across countries and sectors in a matter of a few years. Chinese involvement in Latin America has of course dated back centuries, to at least the mid-1800s, when Chinese indentured laborers were shipped to Latin America build railroads and work on plantations. Others have pointed as far back as the 16th century as the genesis of the relationship, noting that the Manila Galleon trade routes established commercial contact between the Philippines, Mexico, and Macao, now a Chinese Special Administrative Region. A considerable degree of political engagement was also evident in the mid-20th century, during the Mao Zedong era, when the Chinese Communist Party (CCP) engaged with

MARGARET MYERS *is director of the Asia & Latin America Program at the Inter-American Dialogue, where she has published extensively on China's relations with the Latin America and Caribbean region.* The Political Economy of China-Latin America Relations *and* The Changing Currents of Trans-Pacific Integration: China, the TPP, and Beyond, *her co-edited volumes with Dr. Carol Wise and Dr. Adrian Hearn, respectively, were released in 2016. Myers has also testified before the House Committee on Foreign Affairs on the China-Latin America relationship and is regularly featured in major domestic and international media. Myers previously worked as a Latin America analyst and China analyst for the U.S. Department of Defense, during which time she was deployed with the U.S. Navy in support of Partnership of the Americas. Myers is a Council on Foreign Relations term member. She was the recipient of a Freeman fellowship for China studies and a Fulbright Specialist grant to research China-Colombia relations in Bogotá. In 2018, she was identified by Global Americans as one of the "new generation" of public intellectuals.*

like-minded governments throughout the region. But the expansive commercial activity and investment characteristic of the current China-Latin America relationship is a relatively new phenomenon, and one that has been transformative for the region.

The recent boom in Chinese overseas engagement is generally associated with the implementation of China's "going-out strategy" in 1999. Part of China's broader process of "reform and opening-up," the policy promoted overseas engagement, mostly by Chinese state-owned enterprises, to promote the export of Chinese goods and services, supplement China's supply of natural resources, and foster the development of Chinese multinational companies. In their initial ventures abroad, most Chinese companies headed closer to home, to Asia or even Africa, but a number of companies made initial inroads in Latin America in the late 1990s and early 2000s. Some of China's earliest activity in the region included China National Petroleum Corporation's (CNPC) exploration project in Peru in 1994 and the company's sizable oil concession in Venezuela in 1997.

Many of China's overtures in Latin America over the past two decades have broadly supported the tenets of the going-out strategy. Through the efforts of Chinese companies, the region has become a valuable export destination for Chinese goods—trade grew from about $2 billion in 2000 to nearly $149 billion in 2018. China-Latin America trade ties intensified in the aftermath of the 2008 global financial crisis, as China faced decreasing demand from Europe and the United States for its exports. Chinese offerings in Latin America have also quickly expanded from mostly low-skill manufactures to a growing range of high-tech goods and services, including high-speed rail, 5G telecom-

munications infrastructure, and ultra-high-voltage electricity transmission.

Latin America—especially South America—has also been a critical source of natural resources for China ever since Chinese firms first engaged the region. Chinese demand is increasingly concentrated in four Latin American commodities: soy, crude oil, iron, and copper. These four commodities accounted for 59.2% of all Chinese imports from Latin America from 2013–17, as Boston University's Rebecca Ray has demonstrated. High rates of Chinese demand for the region's minerals are linked to China's own model infrastructure-led economic growth. Periods of massive infrastructure investment across China, including as part of the country's fiscal stimulus after the Global Financial Crisis, have meant surging demand for construction materials, including Latin American iron and copper. Brazilian and Argentine trade in soy has also boomed alongside Chinese demand for animal feed, the result of an agricultural trade policy that prioritizes importation of soy and a rapidly expanding middle class that consumes more meat.

In addition to trade, Chinese investment in Latin American raw materials also gained momentum in the 2000s. For China's leadership, the 2008 global food price crisis highlighted the country's considerable dependence on foreign markets and companies for supply of agricultural goods. As they grappled with soaring food prices, Chinese policymakers formulated new guidelines for both overseas investment and domestic production. Chinese companies have since grown their presence across Latin American and other regions' agro-industrial supply chains to better control supply and pricing. In Latin America, this effort was led by COFCO, China's main grains trader, through targeted acquisitions in processing, storage, and trading. Chongqing Grain Group, Sanhe, China National Heavy Machinery Corporation and many others have also invested in factories, pressing plants, mills, and other agricultural infrastructure in Latin America. Chinese mining invest-

ment in the region is also prolific, but is mostly focused on extraction, rather than across the entire supply chain. Three Chinese companies—Shougang, Chinalco, and MMG—hold sizable and growing mining assets in Peru. Chinese mining activity, including of the illegal variety, is also evident elsewhere in the region, including in Bolivia, Colombia, Guyana, and Venezuela.

The Latin American region is comparatively marginal to China's energy security, supplying around 10% of China's oil and only a fraction of its imported coal and natural gas, but the region still factors into China's efforts to "hedge" its energy acquisition strategies and establish a balanced portfolio of suppliers and assets. Much of China's trade in oil with Latin America has been secured by oil-backed loans from China's "policy banks," China Development Bank and China Export-Import Bank, which has disbursed hundreds of billions in finance to Latin America and other regions since the early 2000s. Oil-backed loan agreements require countries such as Venezuela and Brazil to make all or a portion of loan payments in crude oil.

Although trade in commodities still underpins the economic relationship, the China-Latin America dynamic is also increasingly being shaped by China's efforts to revitalize its slowing economy. China's leadership views overseas engagement, especially through large-scale infrastructure investment, as supportive of certain domestic policy objectives, including economic upgrading, trade facilitation, and employment of excess capacity in steel and other sectors—the result of inefficiencies in some of the country's state-dominated industries.

With all of this and potential profits in mind, Chinese firms have expressed interest in developing about 150 transport infrastructure projects in Latin America and the Caribbean since 2002, including numerous road, rail, port, and other deals. Some of the more sizable proposals, such as the $50 billion Bioceanic Railway, stretching between ports in Peru and Brazil, would aim to transport Brazilian soy

Before you read, download the companion **Glossary** that includes definitions, a guide to acronyms and abbreviations used in the article, and other material. Go to **www. fpa.org/great_decisions** and select a topic in the Resources section. (Top Right)

and other goods to Peru, facilitating trade in key commodities. If backed by Chinese finance, the proposed railway could also provide opportunities for Chinese construction firms and for exportation of rail and other equipment to Latin America. Many of China's loans for infrastructure development in Latin America include procurement clauses requiring the use Chinese contracting firms and the importation of specified quantities of Chinese goods. These stipulations are intended to boost Chinese exports of goods and services, while also putting China's surplus dollar reserves to productive use, and even promoting Chinese currency internationalization in some cases. In Argentina, Brazil, Ecuador, and Venezuela, in particular, Chinese equipment exporters and construction companies have been key beneficiaries of projects backed by Chinese finance.

In the area of transport infrastructure, China has been most successful in negotiating port deals in Latin America, with about 20 port projects either in progress or already completed thus far, according to Inter-American Dialogue analysis. These vary considerably in type and scale, from dredging and expansion deals to construction and/or operation of entire ports. In other cases, Chinese companies have acquired existing port facilities. Two terminals of the Santos port in Brazil were acquired by Chinese shipping firm COFCO in 2014 and 2015, for example, as part of the company's purchases of a majority share in Dutch firm Nidera and all of Hong Kong's Noble Group's soft commodities arm.

In addition to transport infrastructure, China has also pursued a number of high-profile energy infrastructure projects in the region, including numerous dams and electricity transmission projects. Some of these projects were viewed as important opportunities for Chinese infrastructure companies, such as Gezhouba, Sinohydro, and State Grid, to grow their market share in Latin America. In Ecuador alone, former President Rafael Correa and Vice President Jorge Glas signed seven hydropower construction con-

View of the Belo Monte Hydroelectric Power Plant in Altamira, Para State, Brazil on March 11, 2019. (MAURO PIMENTEL/AFP VIA GETTY IMAGES)

tracts with Chinese firms, including for the Coca-Codo, Sopladora, Minas San Francisco, and Quijos dams, in an effort rid the country of power shortages and provide surplus power for export to neighboring countries. Chinese investment in electricity infrastructure is similarly extensive in Brazil. Having already constructed transmission lines from the country's Belo Monte hydroelectric dam to city centers such as Sao Paulo and Rio de Janeiro, Chinese state-owned power company State Grid has noted that it will invest an additional $38 billion in Brazil over the next five years, including in transmission, generation and other power industry segments.

Despite the rapid growth in Chinese trade with and investment in the region over the past two decades, China has also encountered its share of setbacks in Latin America. Latin America is cast as a "land full of vitality and hope" in China's official policy, but Chinese investors have for many years viewed the region's distance from Asia as prohibitive. Others have viewed the region's regulatory environments and bidding processes as exceedingly complex or taxing, especially as relative newcomers to the Latin America investment environments.

The region's perceived complexity is exacerbated by a lack of due diligence on the part of some Chinese

companies in the region, leading to unforeseen conflicts and resulting project delays or cost overruns. In Bolivia, for example, the Rositas Dam project was stalled following protests about a lack of prior consultation with affected communities by the Chinese-Bolivian consortium tasked with the dam's construction. In Ecuador, the seven hydroelectric projects that are either partially or wholly owned by Chinese contractors have faced numerous delays, due in large part to engineering and environmental problems. Corruption allegations have also been problematic for Chinese companies. They led to the cancellation of a Querétaro railway concession in Mexico and inquiries into two hydroelectric dams in Argentina, among other challenges.

Venezuela has also become a regular source of stress for Chinese policymakers and the many banks and companies operating there, even as Beijing maintains strong ties to Nicolás Maduro's government. In 2018, China ended a critical grace period for Venezuela on its debt payments, which was interpreted as a sign of Beijing's growing impatience with Maduro's mismanagement of economic affairs. Chinese oil companies continue their work in the country, however, sometimes in partnership with Venezuelan national oil company PdVSA. National Assembly leader Juan Guaidó's claim to the Vene-

Workers are seen as copper output begins at the Chinese-owned Mirador mining project in Tundayme, Ecuador July 18, 2019. (DANIEL TAPIA/REUTERS)

zuelan presidency presents yet another challenge to Chinese decisionmakers, particularly if a new Venezuelan government were to restructure outstanding debt to China.

Despite its sometimes-rocky entrée into Latin America, and some enduring challenges, China has become a key economic partner for most every country in the region. Two decades since the implementation of the "going-out" strategy, China still looks to the region for markets, resources, and opportunities to compete internationally with global firms. Now, though, China is among the dominant players in in some of the region's most strategic markets. Chinese companies such as Huawei, ZTE, and China Mobile are poised to export far more in the way of goods and services as the region looks to adopt 5G and develop smart cities. Chinese surveillance technologies, though controversial element of China's growing export basket, have also grown in popularity in recent years. Variations of the technology are evident in Bolivia, Guyana, Panama, Uruguay, Venezuela, and other countries in the region.

In terms of raw materials, Brazil has become an increasingly critical market for Chinese soy importers, especially after China placed tariffs on U.S. soy exports as part of the ongoing U.S.-China trade war. In 2018, Brazil exported 66.1 million tons of soybeans to China, far more than the U.S., and will export even more to China in 2019. Chinese investors are also actively expanding their investments in the region's minerals. In addition to copper and gold, Chinese companies have invested extensively in various lithium projects. Chinese company Tianqi Lithium paid more than $4 billion to become the second-largest shareholder in Sociedad Química y Minera (SQM), a Chilean mining company. The deal gives the company control over nearly half the current global production of lithium, a main component in battery manufacturing. In addition, China's Ganfeng Lithium bought SQM's 50% stake in the Cauchari-Olaroz lithium project, located in Argentina's Jujuy Province. Chinese companies will also likely be active in a number of Bolivian lithium projects in the coming years.

China's interest in infrastructure development also continues unabated, especially as the Belt and Road, Xi Jinping's signature, infrastructure-based foreign policy initiative, makes its way to Latin America. China's over $110 billion in cumulative foreign direct investment in the region through 2018 has focused extensively on infrastructure development. Newly articulated agreements, including Chinese participation in the construction of the Bogotá metro, suggest continued interest in transport and other infrastructure projects. Companies have also demonstrated interest in moving beyond short-term construction contracts toward equity investments in Latin America, meaning longer-term interests in projects beyond the initial construction phase, to include in project operation and maintenance.

The volume of Chinese activity in Latin America in the coming years will largely depend on China's own economic health. China's economic

Trucks are seen as copper output began at the Chinese-owned Mirador mining project in Tundayme, Ecuador July 18, 2019. (DANIEL TAPIA/REUTERS)

Chinese Policy toward Latin America and the Caribbean

China's most recent strides in Latin America are due in large part to a series of carefully crafted policies that advance China's own interests while addressing some of Latin America's development priorities. China's 2016 Policy Paper on Latin America and the Caribbean—an upgrade to the 2008 version—highlights the various ways in which China intends to cooperate with the region (e.g., on financial integration, space cooperation, and educational exchange), while also casting China and Latin America as critical partners in a shifting global order. The policy calls for alternative approaches to global governance, in which the countries of the Global South feature more prominently, and proposes cooperation with Latin America on a wide variety of both region-specific and global challenges, including climate change and trade protectionism.

Other policies, such as the "1+3+6 cooperation framework"—first announced during President Xi Jinping's trip to Fortaleza, Brazil, for the 2014 BRICS (Brazil, Russia, India, China, and South Africa) Summit—were crafted in response to calls for diversification of Chinese trade and investment. The "1" in the title means one plan, referring to the China-CELAC Cooperation Plan (2015–19), which was published after the China-CELAC ministerial meeting in Beijing in January 2015. The "3" refers to the economic "engines"—trade, investment, and financial cooperation—that will drive China's relations with the region in the coming years. And the "6" in this framework refers to the six industries in which China plans to focus its attention: energy and resources, infrastructure construction, agriculture, manufacturing, scientific and technological innovation, and information technologies.

Though less frequently cited by Chinese officials, Premier Li Keqiang also introduced another numerical policy—the "3×3" model for Sino-Latin America economic cooperation—during his visit to the region in 2014. This policy proposes cooperation between Chinese and Latin American enterprises, societies, and governments (3) in logistics, power generation, and information technology (3). Li simultaneously proposed a $30 billion special fund to develop production capacity in these and other industries.

China's numerical policies for Latin America aren't promoting of a fundamental shift in Chinese engagement, considering that Chinese entities are already active in all of the above-mentioned sectors, to varying degrees. They are instead intended to communicate China's commitment to more and increasingly diversified engagement and to a "systematic upgrading of the relationship," as Zhu Qingqiao, director general of the LAC division at the Chinese MOFA, explained during a 2014 meeting at the Inter-American Dialogue in Washington, DC. As China contends with economic shifts at home, these frameworks also pave the way for China's top communications, infrastructure, IT, and other high-tech firms to establish new markets, contracts, and partnerships in Latin America—a goal clearly articulated in China's overseas investment policies.

China's has demonstrated some commitment to alternative forms of global governance, as articulated in its 2016 policy paper, by creating the Asian Infrastructure Investment Bank (AIIB) and other fora for multilateral cooperation. Brazil is a founding member of the AIIB and several other Latin American governments are in the process of seeking membership. Cooperation on climate change and other global issues is less apparent, despite China's interest in positioning itself distinct from the United States on these matters.

challenges, which Beijing attributes to a structural deleveraging after years of debt-intensive growth, will make it difficult for China to achieve 6% economic growth in the coming months, according to Chinese Premier Li Keqiang. This situation will only be exacerbated by a protracted U.S.-China trade war. If China's growth slows considerably, Latin America should expect some tapering of Chinese interest in certain sectors. Mergers and acquisitions and greenfield projects already dropped from a record level of $17.5 billion in 2017 to just $7.6 billion in 2018. China's policy banks have also issued comparatively low levels of finance to Latin American governments over the past two years, although other Chinese financial actors (e.g., commercial banks and regional private equity funds) are also increasing their activity in the region to a certain extent.

Regardless of Beijing's GDP growth projections, it would be reasonable to expect a more focused approach to investment from Chinese companies and banks in the coming years—with investment and finance funneled toward those industries that are most supportive of China's domestic policy objectives. These include strategic sectors such as telecommunications and electricity transmission, where China has demonstrated considerable competitive advantage. As China continues to grapple with its food and energy security challenges, trade will also remain concentrated in primary commodities, with limited interest from China in importing more expensive, processed or refined variations. Amidst mounting economic uncertainties at home or abroad, Chinese construction and other companies may begin to take reputational and financial risk more seriously when selecting projects in Latin America, leading to a possible tapering of overall infrastructure investment in the region.

The Belt and Road Initiative

Backed by the Silk Road Fund, China's policy banks, and the Asian Infrastructure Investment Bank (AIIB), the Belt and Road Initiative (BRI) is the signature foreign policy initiative of Chinese President Xi Jinping, and one with wide-ranging economic, diplomatic, and geopolitical aims. When initially conceived in 2013, the Initiative imagined the development of a multi-trillion dollar web of infrastructure and other projects across Eurasia, to promote trade and other forms of connectivity while improving prospects for economic development among partner nations. The BRI was described at the time as supporting five avenues (*wu tong*) for cooperation, including on policy, finance, trade, infrastructure, and people-to people exchanges.

Over the past six years, the project has evolved from two specific geographical routes—an overland Silk Road Economic Belt and a sea-based 21st-century Maritime Silk Road—toward an increasingly global ambit. Latin America was officially included in the BRI in 2018, following China's inclusion of the Arctic region. Prior to that, Chinese officials had highlighted a few Latin American countries as likely participants in the BRI. Mexico was singled out as an "important node" in the Initiative's extension during the September 2017 BRICS Summit, for example. Panama became a "natural extension" of the BRI during Chinese Foreign Minister Wang Yi's visit to the Central American nation that same year.

Though not well understood in Latin America, and subject to varying definitions even in China, the BRI and the opportunities it represents have been attractive to Latin American governments. As a result, 19 countries in the region have signed bilateral Belt and Road Cooperation Agreements with China since 2017. Panama, which broke ties with Taiwan in 2017, was the first country in the region to sign one of these agreements, which are in the form of a memorandum of understanding. As former president of Panama Juan Carlos Varela indicated in a speech in Hong Kong in 2019, the BRI is "all about connectivity and Panama is one of the most connected countries in the region." He added that his country saw a "big opportunity" in the BRI.

Now that the China-backed Belt and Road Initiative has taken root in the Latin American and Caribbean region, hopes are high that Chinese investment

Unpacking China

Of importance when analyzing China's approach to the region is an understanding that China is not a monolithic presence in Latin America, but instead consists of multiple actors with diverse interests and motivations. It is important, as political scientist Ariel Armony has written, "to unpack the idea of the Chinese state." There are indeed occasions when China acts as a unitary state, with very clear national goals. But there are also instances when China acts in a seemingly fractured and divergent manner. Although China upholds a centralized hierarchy, variations in interpretation and implementation among different institutions and at different levels of Chinese government have led to wide-ranging outcomes in China's overseas activity.

The interests and motivations of Chinese companies also vary considerably depending on their size and ties to the Chinese government. For example, Chinese investors in Latin American agriculture range from massive state-owned enterprises, such as COFCO, which has invested extensively in Latin American agro-industry with support from the Chinese state to small firms, such as Zhejiang Fudi, which was created by 50 farmers from Huafeng village in China's Zhejiang province. Faced with land limitations at home, the villagers explored the possibility of pooling their individual financial resources to buy Brazilian land for soy production. After establish-ing Zhejiang Fudi Agriculture Group, they purchased 16,800 hectares in Rio Grande do Sul and Tocatins for the production of soy.

Whether directly supportive of China's national interests or not, the cast of Chinese characters is also changing somewhat in Latin America. An increasingly diverse group of Chinese firms, lenders, and investors is now engaging with the region. China's commercial banks, such as ICBC and Bank of China, are playing a more prominent role in the region, for example. They are in some cases issuing more credit to Latin America than China's major policy banks, China Development Bank and China Export-Import Bank.

Chinese companies and funds are also increasingly active in Latin American private equity. Chinese firm Didi's acquisition of 99, the Brazilian ride-share company, is one such example. As China becomes increasingly active in the tech space, a wide variety of Chinese technology companies are also looking to invest in the region, including in information and communications technologies (ICT). Chinese ICT investment in Latin America would presumably provide opportunities not only for providers of ICT services and infrastructure, but also for the development of increasingly advanced technologies (e.g., artificial intelligence platforms and applications) that are catered to local populations.

will address some of the region's most pressing transportation and other infrastructure needs. So far at least, China-backed infrastructure deals are indeed in the works throughout the region, including in the three countries that recently established diplomatic ties with China. China bid on and won a number of construction contracts in Panama over the past year and a half, and has also discussed a possible railway with Panamanian officials, which would run from Panama City to the border of Costa Rica. The railway, for which an initial feasibility study was recently completed, was among the first ventures in the region to be officially affiliated with the BRI.

The political dimension

When China began investing more extensively in the region in the early 2000s, the Chinese government sought support from Latin American governments for a handful of fairly straightforward foreign policy objectives, including recognition of China's "market economy" status and support on questions of territorial integrity (e.g., China's views on Taiwan, Tibet, the South China Sea, and Xinjiang).

Taiwan, in particular, has been a prominent factor in China's political dealings with the region for a number of decades, dating back to the establishment of the People's Republic of China (mainland China) in 1949. After many years of diplomatic competition with China and numerous, often controversial, examples of "checkbook diplomacy," Taiwan had achieved 15 diplomatic allies in Latin America and the Caribbean at the end of 2008, including Paraguay, some Caribbean nations, and most of the countries in Central America. That same year Taiwan's newly elected president, Ma Ying-Jeou, proposed a "diplomatic truce" with China, effectively halting the practice of providing financial assistance to small nations in exchange for diplomatic recognition. For the next eight years, China and Taiwan largely refrained from grandiose diplomatic gestures.

Competition quickly reignited following the May 2016 election of Democratic Progressive Party candidate Tsai Ing-wen, however, and concerns in China about her perceived pro-independence agenda. Since President Tsai's election, Chinese officials have been increasingly active in those countries that continue to support Taiwan, touting the economic benefit of stronger ties with China. As a result, over the past two years alone, three countries in the region—the Dominican

Members of the military and journalists (R) gather on the dock as the 'Feng Chia' (L-1115) and 'Ming Chuan' (C-1112) navy frigates are pictured during a ceremony to commission the two Perry-class guided missile frigates from the US into the Taiwan Navy, in the southern port of Kaohsiung on November 8, 2018. - President Tsai Ing-wen vowed on November 8 that Taiwan would not "concede one step" in defending itself as she inaugurated two frigates bought from the US aimed at boosting the island's naval capabilities against China threats. (CHRIS STOWERS/AFP VIA GETTY IMAGES)

Republic, El Salvador, and Panama—shifted their diplomatic recognition from Taiwan to China.

China reportedly offered the Dominican Republic a package worth $3 billion in exchange for diplomatic recognition, over half of which was destined for infrastructure projects. The Dominican Republic is also in the process of securing a $600 million loan from China's Export-Import Bank to upgrade its power distribution systems, and Dominican President Danilo Medina has flagged additional projects for possible Chinese support, including the modernization of the Port of Arroyo Barril. El Salvador's former ruling Farabundo Martí National Liberation Front (FMLN) tentatively negotiated at least two major projects with China—renovation of the

La Union port and a possible special economic zone, which would account for about 14% of Salvadoran territory and much of the country's coastline—before siding diplomatically with Beijing. These proposals are currently under review by El Salvador's new government. Panama is the process of negotiating a free trade agreement with China and has negotiated a number of infrastructure deals with the Asian nation, including the development of two port facilities.

As the Dominican Republic, El Salvador, and Panama navigate their new ties with China, Taiwan's remaining allies in the Latin American and Caribbean region—Haiti, Guatemala, Honduras, Nicaragua, Saint Kitts and Nevis, Saint Lucia, and Saint Vincent and the Grenadines—are no doubt weighing their options. Some may fear that cutting ties with Taiwan would lead to retaliation from the U.S. U.S. senators have indicated a strong preference that Guatemala and Honduras remain steadfast in their diplomatic support for Taiwan. In September 2019, the Senate Foreign Relations Committee passed the Taiwan Allies International Protection and Enhancement Initiative (TAIPEI) Act to engage more extensively with governments that support Taiwan's diplomatic recognition while downgrading ties with countries that do not, and possibly suspending or altering U.S. foreign assistance to the latter.

In addition to Taiwan, South-South cooperation is another enduring feature of Chinese foreign policy in the region, and one that is consistent with China's long-standing self-identification as a developing country. China's grants and concessional lending in Latin America and the Caribbean, in addition to factoring in China-Taiwan competition, can also be interpreted as a function of Beijing's South-South policy. China's support for developing country interests in international climate and trade forums are also supportive of the China's South-South agenda. Though a top polluter itself, China called on rich countries to "pay their debts" on climate change during the COP24 meet-

ings in December 2018, for example, criticizing developed countries for not doing enough to reduce greenhouse gas emissions and provide finance to help poor countries do the same.

Beyond these decades-old features of Chinese foreign policy is an increasingly complex political and diplomatic agenda. Beijing has focused extensively on the power of diplomacy since the Mao Zedong era, but China has focused with greater intensity on the development of soft power under the leadership of Xi Jinping. In 2014, at the beginning of his presidency, Xi proclaimed a need to "increase China's soft power, give a good Chinese narrative, and better communicate China's message to the world." More recently, during the 2017 19th Party Congress, Xi called on China to expand its "capacity for engaging in international communication so as to tell China's stories well, present a true, multi-dimensional and panoramic view of China, and enhance our country's soft power."

In response to these calls, and as part of broader BRI-related, people-to-people diplomatic efforts, China has employed an array of actors to improve China's image and advance its interests abroad. These range from Confucius Institutes and International Department delegations to foreign language media outlets, think tank missions, and

cultural troupes, for instance. As Chinese scholars Zhao Kejin and Gao Xin have noted, "Diplomacy is no longer confined to the domain of foreign affairs, but it has become a multiplayer, multi-task undertaking for China—transformed from a mere governmental function under the control of the Ministry of Foreign Affairs to one that includes the work of the Party, the government, the National People's Congress, the Chinese People's Political Consultative Conference, the People's Liberation Army (PLA) and so forth."

China has also sought to develop productive relationships within Latin American regional organizations for a number of years, including by establishing observer status at the Organization of American States, becoming a member of the Inter-American Development Bank, engaging with IDBInvest and CAF-Development Bank of Latin America, and working at times with the Santiago-based United Nations Economic Commission for Latin America and the Caribbean (ECLAC). China also established the China-CELAC Forum in 2015, utilizing the nearly defunct Community of Latin American and Caribbean States (CELAC), established by Venezuelan President Hugo Chavez in 2011, as a vehicle for the new China-led regional platform. The Forum has since been used to articulate Chinese policy toward the region, including on the Belt and Road Initiative, and to develop a five-year plan for China-Latin America cooperation.

Another important dimension of the political relationship is the effect of Chinese economic engagement on regional politics and democratic governance. China maintains a strict policy of non-interference in the domestic affairs of sovereign nations, but even a strictly economic agenda in Latin America can have political and governance-related implications for the region. There are concerns, for example, that Chinese engagement may be facilitating corruption in certain countries. China's policy banks have often extended finance though credit lines with no publicly specified purpose, limiting the availability of infor-

Minister of Foreign Affairs and State Counselor of the People's Republic of China, Wang Yi (R) and the Dominican Republic Foreign Minister Miguel Vargas Maldonado (L), uncover the inauguration plaque during the inauguration ceremony of the Chinese Embassy in Santo Domingo, on September 21, 2018. (ERIKA SANTELICES/AFP VIA GETTY IMAGES)

mation for domestic constituencies and for corruption prevention. In Venezuela, for example, these arrangements have stoked allegations that Chinese funds have essentially disappeared, without much benefit to the Venezuelan population.

China also continues to rely on the project preferences of individual governments when considering infrastructure projects. This occasionally has led to the selection of national leaders' "pet" or "prestige" projects, such as the Nestor Kirchner and Jorge Cepernic dams in Argentina, which were thought to have benefited former President Cristina Kirchner and her associates, but were deemed of low relative priority for energy sector development in studies conducted by the Argentine Energy Ministry. Other national development finance institutions operating abroad, including Brazil's BNDES, have also tended to rely on government "wish lists," but as indicated by the BNDES-linked *lava jato* scandal, this approach is often linked to corruption in Latin America.

The extent to which China exerts any influence over election outcomes in the region is less clear, but China has certainly been accused, especially by the U.S. government, of "propping up a failed regime" in Venezuela through the extension of multi-billion-dollar lines of credit. In other cases, China's influence is less direct. The decision by El Salvador's former government to cut ties with Taiwan came just months ahead of that country's presidential elections. The FMLN may have hoped that China's two large-scale offerings—renovation of the La Union port and a massive special economic zone— would boost their standing in the polls, but the party was voted out of office in February 2019.

As China becomes a dominant economic partner for many countries in the region, whether in terms of trade or as a source of investment or finance, Chinese entities are increasingly capable of influencing host country decision-making, whether they do so intentionally or not. The same is of course true of the region's other major economic partners and there

Members of the Chinese Confucius institute take part in a Lunar New Year celebration in Vina del Mar city, about 121 km (75 miles) northwest of Santiago, February 3, 2011. The Lunar New Year begins on Thursday and marks the start of the Year of the Rabbit, according to the Chinese zodiac. (ELISEO FERNANDEZ/REUTERS)

is no shortage of examples of U.S. and other external influence on the region's politics, for example. China's effect on regulatory and other decision-making is likely to be increasingly pronounced in the coming years, however. Extensive investment in some of the region's most critical economic sectors has already led some governments in Latin America to change investment-related regulations to promote continued Chinese engage-

ment. China also hopes for broad-based support in international organizations for a series of agenda items, including in global debates on internet governance. In addition Chinese company efforts to engage more extensively in the tech space in Latin America, including through grants for smart cities and surveillance equipment, will give China growing influence over the region's broader tech-related decisionmaking.

A "win-win" relationship?

China is an increasingly critical partner for the Latin American region. The country is South America's top trade partner and comes in second to the U.S. for the rest of the region. Chinese finance and investment has also been transformative, especially in specific countries and sectors. But the nature of Chinese engagement—especially a trade relationship based on the extensive import of specific primary commodities from the region and export of increasingly high-value-added manufactured goods—is thought to be problematic for the region from a development perspective. Although commodity production is not inherently inferior in terms of value-added potential, as World Bank and other economists have indicated, weak diversification of exports exposes the region

to price and demand shocks. For South America's resource rich economies in particular, China-Latin America trade dynamics have resurrected development debates from the 1960s abut "unequal exchange," the "resource curse," and heightened "dependency." Indeed, South American countries' reliance on exports of certain primary commodities left some in difficult circumstances when global commodity prices dropped in 2014.

China has also been linked to decreases in market share for some of the region's manufacturers. Industries in Brazil, Colombia, and Mexico all face competition from China in their own markets. According to a study from the United Nations Economic Commission on Latin America and the Caribbean (ECLAC), Mexico in particular has faced sizeable growth in consumption of imports from China—from 3.3% to 6.4% between 2005 and 2010. The most affected sectors in Mexico were the textile and apparel industry, auto parts, industrial machinery and equipment, and metals and derivatives. Sectors such as industrial machinery and equipment, office machinery, electrical equipment and metal products in Argentina, Brazil, Colombia, and Mexico have also faced considerable competition in third markets.

Controversy has also surrounded the presence of low to mid-skilled Chinese workers in Latin America and the Caribbean, centered on a perception that low-skill Chinese laborers are being employed instead of capable local labor. One prominent example was China's investment in the Baha Mar hotel in the Bahamas. China Construction Americas signed a contract that allowed for the employment of up to 7,000 Chinese workers over a specified period of time, although fewer actually arrived. The Bahamian Contractors' Association objected to the use of Chinese construction workers, indicating that they were not consulted about opportunities for highly experienced Bahamian. Tensions generated by the use of Chinese labor have also surfaced elsewhere in the Caribbean, as well as in Central America, Venezuela, Guyana, and Suriname, among other countries. Chinese companies have tended to limit their use of Chinese low-skill labor in recent years, perhaps in response to negative reactions from local populations.

The environmental effects of Chinese engagement are also of growing concern. China is heavily invested in infrastructure and extractives—sectors with outsize environmental impact. China-backed infrastructure projects are in some cases transforming the region's delicate ecosystems. Sinohydro's dredging project in Peru will reportedly alter the dynamics of the affected rivers and their capacity to sustain lakes in natural parks like the Pacaya Samiria. Chinese companies have also sometimes struggled to meet the region's ambitious environ-

mental and social standards, leading to social conflict or environmental damage. This is especially common where enforcement has been lacking from national governments in Latin America. Moreover, of China's pipeline of proposed transport and other infrastructure projects, many are located in especially biodiverse parts of the region. Future development could therefore further degrade the region's ecosystems.

China's effect on job growth, social inequality, and on a wide variety of other development issues have been studied to a degree, but are not yet well understood. Progress toward sustainable development in the region will require enhanced commitment from the Chinese ministries, embassies, banks, and companies to sustainable development goals and international standards on corporate social responsibility. Some Chinese companies and institutions are making strides in this respect,

but others still lag behind their peers.

The extent to which China's engagement is promoting of the development interests of Latin America will depend to an even greater degree on the actions of Latin American governments and stakeholders. Research suggests that the performance of Chinese companies comes down to the political will of local governments to maintain hard-fought standards and ensure accountability, whether on labor issues, environmental matters, prior consultation, or in other areas. Pervasive Sino-Latin American trade imbalances also demand creative policy responses from Latin American governments and trade blocs. New thinking on this issue will be critical not only to balance relations with China, but also to enhance competitiveness and strengthen the region's economic standing as it competes in what is now a very different economic order, with new markets and expanding sources of competition.

The U.S.-China-Latin America "triangular" relations

Over the past two years, the United States has sought a more direct role in shaping the evolution of China-Latin America relations. At the beginning of 2018, then Secretary of State Rex Tillerson voiced his—and presumably the broader Trump administration's—concerns about China's rise in the region. Tillerson warned Latin America about its ties to China, stating, "China's offers always come at a price," and describing Beijing's ambitions as imperialistic. When current U.S. Secretary of State Mike Pompeo assumed the position, he took a similar message to the region. During a trip to Mexico City Pompeo stated, "China has invested in ways that have left countries worse off." While in Chile he noted that Chinese deals in Latin America generally introduce corrosive capital or generate corruption. Warnings about the perils of engaging with China were also delivered by U.S. officials in Argentina, Chile, and other countries, referencing China's effect on

Latin American governance, security, corruption, regulatory capacity, and financial stability, and in a range of other areas.

While some of the U.S.'s articulated concerns certainly resonate with Latin American audiences, the Trump administration's efforts to portray China as a relative bogeyman in Latin America have generally been criticized or countered by scholars and officials in the region. Peru's foreign trade minister, Eduardo Ferreyros, responded to Secretary Tillerson's initial comments, noting that China is a "good trade partner" and that Peru is "careful with all of its trade relations." U.S. scholars and policy professionals have also lobbied for a more productive response to China's rapid growth in Latin America and other regions.

Although it has been the most vocal on the topic, the Trump administration isn't the first to fret over China's rise in the region. In fact, the U.S. government has been taking stock of Chinese interests in Latin America and the Caribbean since the 1990s. Concerns surfaced around 1998 about Hong Kong firm Hutchinson Whampoa's involvements in the Panama Canal. Chinese billionaire Wang Jing's canal adventures in Nicaragua were also closely monitored in Washington starting in 2013. And China's interests in Venezuela, including Chinese financial support for the governments of Hugo Chavez and Nicolas Maduro, continue to aggravate U.S. officials. The U.S. has also pointed to possible dual (civilian-military) use infrastructure investment as an example of China's broader strategic interests in Latin America, and as a possible response to U.S. engagement in the South China Sea. Among other areas of concern are China's growing cyber operations in the region, which have been in place for a number of years in an effort to increase positive sentiment toward China in the region, often in support of economic objectives, but are increasingly sophisticated.

Behind all of this is a broader—possibly warranted—concern that the U.S. risks losing influence, competitiveness, and control in Latin America as China grows its presence in the region. According to the Pew Research Center's Global Attitudes Survey, nearly all of the region's top economies now have a more favorable view of China than the United States. Some, such as Brazil, have favored China for a number of years, whereas Mexico and Peru began viewing China more positively in 2017. U.S. companies are also going head to head with increasingly experienced and capable Chinese firms in Latin America, including in areas such as tech, finance, and agriculture, where U.S. firms have been active for many decades.

To "level the playing field" in Latin America and other regions, the Trump administration has engaged in a year-and-a-half-long trade war with China, and a so-called "tech war," wherein the U.S. has sought to limit China's access to American technology and markets. Both "wars" will have prolonged economic consequences for China and the U.S., certainly, by unraveling long-

This photo taken on May 23, 2019 shows workers checking aerosol in a factory which produces for export to Brazil, Argentina, Chile, Egypt, India and other countries, in Dongyang, in China's eastern Zhejiang province. (AFP VIA GETTY IMAGES)

established supply chains. But Latin America and other regions are expected to fair badly as well. Brazil benefitted in 2019 from a boost in soy exports to China—the result of tariffs placed on U.S. soy. Mexico has seen some benefits, too, as international companies relocate their production from China to cut mounting costs from the trade war. But protracted U.S.-China tensions are expected to have lasting negative effects on the global economy. The IMF estimates slowing global growth in 2019, including in third markets, based in large part on U.S.-China trade tensions. Ongoing economic uncertainty could also weaken Latin American currencies if populations there invest in U.S. dollars to avoid the effects of local currency devaluation. A decoupling of the tech sector will also affect options and prices for tech consumers across the globe.

U.S. concerns about China have increasingly "real world" implications for Latin American countries, whether in terms of rising prices for the region's consumers, or as regional governments are encouraged to avoid engagement with China in favor of partnership with the U.S. and other traditional allies. There are indeed

some drawbacks associated with the Chinese model, including evidence of a continued lack of due diligence in certain China-financed infrastructure projects, for example. China's environmental impact is also sizable given the extent of Chinese trade and investment in extractives and infrastructure. But U.S. pressure to limit the region's economic options and partnerships could also have unfortunate consequences for Latin America's economic growth and well-being.

U.S. interests in Latin America—including vis-à-vis China—are best served by strengthening U.S.-Latin America ties rather than highlighting China's flaws. As China approaches the region with extensive investments and attractive, cooperation-based policy, the U.S. must take a similar approach to the region, focusing on areas in which the U.S. can make a real and "mutually beneficial" difference while working with the region to ensure that procurement and other processes are fair and transparent. Despite the geographic distance, China recognizes the appeal of inclusive rhetoric and development-oriented policy to Latin American governments—maybe better than the U.S. at this juncture.

discussion questions

1.The U.S. has a long and sometimes troubled relationship with Latin America. In what ways does China's engagement with the region differ from that of the U.S.? Is China likely to be viewed as an imperialist or hegemonic power in the region?

2. How might China's economic partnerships in South America affect China's relations with the U.S., especially amidst ongoing trade negotiations? In what ways will shifting trade patterns affect U.S. ties to the region?

3. Huawei is well positioned to sell 5G and other technology to many countries in Latin America and the Caribbean. The company is unlikely to be banned from forthcoming 5G roll-outs despite U.S. warnings about the security implications of Chinese telecommunications technologies. Are there any realistic measure that the U.S. could use to limit the sale of Chinese 5G infrastructure in the region? Should it use those measures?

4. As China's economic engagement deepens Latin America, Beijing's potential influence over regional affairs is likely to expand. To what extent has China already affected political outcomes in the region? Should China be held accountable for economic and political turmoil in Venezuela?

5. To what extent does Chinese economic engagement result in support for China's interests in international organizations, such as the United Nations?

6. China maintains a policy of non-interference in the domestic affairs of sovereign nations. This extends to the provision of credit to Latin American governments. China's loans have few policy conditions in comparison to loans from major international financial institutions. Chinese state banks have also lent extensively to countries in the region with limited access to international financial markets. To what extent is China's model of lending beneficial to Latin American governments? Is China responsible for high rates of sovereign debt in Latin America?

suggested readings

Myers, Margaret and Wise, Carol. **The Political Economy of China-Latin America Relations in the New Millennium.** 302pp. London, UK: Routledge, 2016. In this book, China-Latin America relations experts Margaret Myers and Carol Wise examine the political and economic forces that have underpinned Chinese engagement in the region, as well as the ways in which these forces have shaped economic sectors and policy-making in Latin America.

Jenkins, Rhys. **How China is Reshaping the Global Economy: Development Impacts in Africa and Latin America.**. 432 pp. Oxford, UK: Oxford University Press, 2019. *How China is Reshaping the Global Economy* looks at the factors which led to rapid economic growth in China and the way in which this has affected global manufacturing, commodity markets, the international presence of Chinese companies, and financial glows.

Gallagher, Kevin P.. **The China Triangle: Latin America's China Boom and the Fate of the Washington Consensus.** 256 pp. Oxford, UK: Oxford University Press, 2016. In *The China Triangle*, Kevin P. Gallagher traces the development of the China-Latin America trade over time and covers how it has affected the centuries-old (and highly unequal) U.S.-Latin American relationship.

Denoon, David B. H. **China, The United States, and the Future of Latin America: U.S- China Relations Volumn III.** 432 pp. New York, NY: NYU Press, 2017. This volume draws upon a variety of policy experts, focusing on the viewpoints of South American and Caribbean scholars as well as scholars from outside states. China's new global reach and its ambitions, as well as the U.S. response, are analyzed in detail.

Ray, Rebecca, Gallagher, Kevin and Lopez, Andres. **China and Sustainable Devlopment in Latin America: The Social and Environmental Dimension.** 382 pp. New York, NY: Anthem Press, 2017. *China and Sustainable Development in Latin America* documents the social and environmental impact of the China-led commodity boom in the region.

Roett, Riordan and Paz, Guadalupe. **Latin America and the Asian Giants: Evolving Ties with China and India.** Washington, D.C.: Brookings Institution Press, 2016. In the years since China has adopted a "going global" strategy to promote its overseas investment, expand export markets, and gain much-needed access to natural resources abroad, Sino–Latin American relations have both deepened and broadened at an unexpectedly rapid pace.

Don't forget: Ballots start on page 98!!!!

To access web links to these readings, as well as links to additional, shorter readings and suggested web sites,
GO TO www.fpa.org/great_decisions
and click on the topic under Resources, on the right-hand side of the page.

The Philippines and the U.S.: change with continuity?

by Julio S. Amador III and Deryk Baladjay

Philippines President Rodrigo Duterte (C) and Chinese President Xi Jinping review the guard of honors as they attend a welcoming ceremony at the Great Hall of the People in Beijing on October 20, 2016. (THOMAS PETER/AFP/GETTY IMAGES)

From colonial rule, to commonwealth, and finally ally, the relationship of the Philippines and the United States is enduring but oftentimes quixotic. For the Philippines, there seems to be no other country that can hold it in thrall like the United States. The relationship between the United States and the Philippines goes back more than a century. The two countries have shared a long history of military, political, and economic ties, despite the geographical distance between them. Both countries addressed the communist threat during the Cold War in the 1960s, and their relationship with one another became even closer during the Reagan era, when the Kirkpatrick doctrine (named for UN Ambassador Jean Kirkpatrick) complemented the rise of

authoritarianism in the Philippines during the late 1970s—a period marked by an increase in U.S. economic and military aid transfers. Moreover, transfer of military support from

JULIO S. AMADOR III *is Executive Director of the Philippine-American Educational Foundation, Fellow at the Asia-Pacific Pathways to Progress Foundation, and Senior Research Fellow at the Ateneo Policy Center of the Ateneo School of Government. His research and policy interests are in Philippine foreign policy and national security, U.S.-Philippines relations, and ASEAN.*

DERYK BALADJAY *is an MA candidate at the De La Salle University-Manila. He specializes in security, conflict and peace studies in and around East and Southeast Asia*

the United States to the Philippines during the late 1990s also increased when both countries brokered an addendum of a visiting forces agreement to the pre-existing mutual defense treaty. This relationship carried over to the 21st century when both countries expressed support for one another in the war against terrorism beginning in 2001 and, decades later, when both countries saw to the enhancement of their respective armed forces' interoperability within the Asia Pacific region. Since the early 20th century, the Philippines' foreign policy tradition has been emblematic of a close association with the United States. Then the introduction of Rodrigo Duterte changed the U.S.-Philippine bilateral relationship and challenged the status quo. Or did it, really?

The election of Rodrigo Roa Duterte as the new commander in chief of the Philippines in 2016 was a game-changer. Rodrigo Duterte represented many firsts, including being the first president to have come from the southern island of Mindanao and being the first president to have come from a mayoral position (he served as the Mayor of Davao city for over 22 years). His election as president effectively placed southern voices into the fore of the national agenda. This was important because the central bureaucracy is heavily criticized for the overconcentration of its delivery of public services in the capital and its provincial peripheries. Rodrigo Duterte is also a metaphorical game-changer because he was the manifestation of the rise and legitimation of populism in Philippine democratic politics. During his campaign for the presidency, Duterte made 30 promises, including to address social issues like corruption and drug addiction within a timetable of some 3 months up to 6 years. These promises were received by applause but also doubts from civil society.

Before you read, download the companion **Glossary** that includes definitions, a guide to acronyms and abbreviations used in the article, and other material. Go to **www. fpa.org/great_decisions** and select a topic in the Resources section. (Top Right)

During the long history between the countries, the U.S.-Philippine bilateral relationship has been subject to various domestic and foreign pressures. During his campaign, Duterte's populist rhetoric was directed against then U.S. President Barack Obama. Critics of the U.S.-Philippine bilateral relations have labeled the mutual friendship as having imperialistic undertones and have, on multiple occasions, actively protested it. One prominent challenge to this ebbing relationship is Duterte's foreign policy calibration when, four months into office, he announced a pivot to China and a relative distancing from the United States. This was a great departure from the Philippine foreign policy tradition of his predecessors who largely believed in the critical role that the United States played in the country and in the region.

This pivot to China further exacerbated the already tumultuous situation in the West Philippine Sea (the Philippines officially calls parts of the South China Sea up to its 200-nautical-mile exclusive economic zone the West Philippine Sea) when China's nine-dash line claim provided it impetus for military build-up in the region. Since 2012 China has tried to claim maritime domain in the large expanse of the West Philippine Sea and has also been encroaching on the exclusive economic zones of neighboring Southeast Asian states. This development constantly challenges the principle of freedom of navigation as Chinese maritime and naval forces have, on multiple occasions, threatened the use of force in enforcing its illegal claims over the disputed regions.

These pressing geopolitical developments have tested U.S. military commitment to its historical ally. All these contributed to Duterte's pragmatic rebalancing. But to understand the logic of Duterte's foreign policy initiatives, a look at the history of U.S.-Philippine relations is essential.

A complicated history

U.S.-Philippine relations can be traced as far back as the 1898 Spanish-American War. The United States, which had engaged militarily with the Spanish forces based in Cuba, declared war against Spain on February 15, 1898, and deployed its armed forces to Cuba, Puerto Rico, and the Philippines which, coincidentally, was also undergoing its social revolution against the Spanish colonizers. When the Malolos Republic of the Philippines announced its independence from Spanish rule on June 12, neither the United States nor Spain, the two belligerents of the 1898 Spanish-American War, recognized it. A peace protocol was reached between the two war belligerents on August 12, 1898, followed by the Treaty of Paris, agreed to within the same year. The Treaty of Paris formalized Spain's ceding of territories to the United States, including Cuba, Puerto Rico, and the Philippine archipelago. In the case of the Philippine exchange, Spain was paid the sum of $20 million. Problems erupted when

Felipe Agoncillo, the Filipino lawyer who was supposed to represent the First Philippine Republic in the Paris Treaty signing, was denied participation in the negotiation. Having learned of the America's betrayal of trust, President Emilio Aguinaldo formally declared war against the United States on February 5, 1899.

The U.S.-Philippine War would go on for three years, only to falter on March 1901 with Emilio Aguinaldo's capture. US President William McKinley (1897–1901) pursued a policy of benevolent assimilation actively superseding and undermining Spanish colonial elements at the time. In spite of its imperfections, the United States' colonization of the Philippines presented itself as an opportunity for national reimagination. Thanks to the three pillars of American colonial statecraft, social policies took form and were jumpstarted in the archipelago: introduction of the public education system, competent civil service recruitment, and the replacement of the Spanish guardia civil

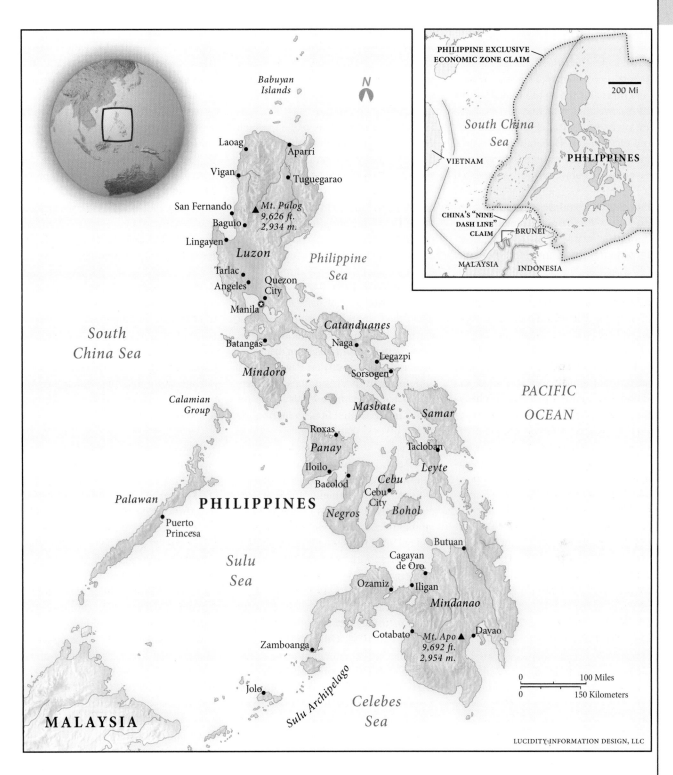

with the Philippine Constabulary in 1901. Newly inaugurated US President Theodore Roosevelt (1901–09) officially ended the Philippine insurrection on July 1902, despite lingering sporadic guerilla resistance in the archipelago. While the touted pillars of American colonial statecraft provided the initial framework for the early Philippine so-

ciety, it was not without failures. Land redistribution policies that were enacted lacked support mechanisms and only perpetuated ownership within the American and Filipino business class who had vested interests in land and natural resources. Instituted tax policies that replaced the Spanish taxation system remained burdensome as well.

Moreover, governance in the southern island of Mindanao had become more militaristic than that in Luzon, the largest and most populous island in the Philippines.

A significant contribution of the American colonization period was the contour of an early Philippine government. Much like the American system, the early form of a Philippine government employed the distribution of powers that greatly favored the smaller provincial constituents. This was in conjunction with the transactional merits of American patrons that post-colonial Filipinos took after. The first municipal elections of December 1901 and, later on, the first provincial governor elections of February 1902, segmented a Philippine Assembly that embodied this transactional dynamic. More importantly, the formation of the early national elite and ruling class was patterned after this transaction dynamic. Nevertheless, the institutional reforms ensured that the Philippine Assembly would take on representative features.

Republican presidents McKinley, Roosevelt and William Howard Taft (1909–13) argued that the benevolent assimilation of the Philippines would take long periods of time and therefore require a piecemeal, guided approach to the administration of the archipelago. But this was not shared by democrat President Woodrow Wilson (1913–21), who sought the immedi-

"Take Your Choice", William McKinley raising U.S. flag in the Philippines, and William Jennings Bryan chopping it down, with U.S. flags flying over Puerto Rico and Cuba, as Uncle Sam and another man watch from U.S. soil, (ARTWORK BY F. VICTOR GILLAM, JUDGE MAGAZINE, MAY 12, 1900; CREDIT: JT VINTAGE/GLASSHOUSE/ ZUMA WIRE/NEWSCOM)

ate democratization of the Philippines. Alongside Wilson's Philippine counterpart, Manuel Quezon, the move for the filipinization and democratization of the colonial government gained momentum. On March 1934, the Tydings-McDuffie Act was passed, which would provide the Philippines with a decades' worth of preparation for a scheduled 1946 independence declaration. A constitutional plebiscite was also held on May 1934 for the approval of the 1935 Constitution. With the election of Manuel Luis Quezon (1935–44) as the second Philippine president, the Commonwealth of the Philippines was inaugurated in 1935.

The period of relative peace enjoyed under the Commonwealth government came to an abrupt halt when Imperial Japan launched air raids from the island of Formosa (Taiwan) on Pearl Harbor and on some of Philippines' military facilities on December 7, 1941. This resulted in the United States entering the Second World War. The Japanese invasion of the Philippines and of Southeast Asia challenged Western colonial rule and further sparked nationalist anticolonial movements for independence. Imperial Japan declared Philippine independence on October 1943 and installed the Second Republic with José Paciano Laurel (1943–45) as the new president. Widespread fighting by the U.S. Armed Forces in the Far East against the Imperial Japanese Army was sustained throughout 1943 and toward late 1944. Only one organized resistance group—the Hukbong Bayan Laban sa Hapon (colloquially known as HUKBALAHAP or HUKs, literally translated as, "People's Army against the Japanese")–was able to sustain an insurgent revolution against the Japanese. On October 20, 1944, General MacArthur landed on Samar and began the military operations that eventually liberated the Philippines from Japanese occupation. The Republic of the Philippines was inaugurated as scheduled on July 4, 1946, fulfilling the decade-old Tydings-McDuffie Act. The inauguration also marked the start of the Third Republic of the Philippines.

Military relations between the two

countries had improved during the Japanese invasion of the Philippines. It was under Philippine President Sergio Osmeña (1944–46) that the earliest attempt to broker a military base agreement between the two governments took place. The agreed mandate between presidents Osmeña and Harry S. Truman (1945–53) called for the territorial integrity of the Philippines, the mutual protection of both the United States and the Philippines and the maintenance of peace in the Pacific region. After all hostilities against Japan ceased, President Truman signed the Philippine Military Assistance Act, which saw to the training of Philippine military and naval personnel and the transfer and maintenance of military equipment. President Roxas shifted his foreign policy toward a stronger alliance with the United States. This move was strengthened when the Military Bases Agreement of 1947 was reached.

The aftermath of the Second World War saw the persistence of Communist elements in the Philippines and in the rest of East and Southeast Asia. The HUKs that were once determined to overthrow Imperial Japan's colonial efforts now took on Communist, anti-imperialist and anti-colonial elements. President Truman and Philippine President Elpidio Quirino (1948–53) brokered the Mutual Defense Treaty on August 30, 1951—the quintessential military treaty that guided the U.S.-Philippine bilateral relations up to the 21st century. The United States maintained close rapport with the Philippine government by offering military support against the Communist insurgency of the HUKs. The first official signs of dissatisfaction with U.S.-Philippine bilateral relations were hinted at under President Diosdado Macapagal's (1961–65) administration when the Philippines War Damage Claims Bill was rejected by the on May 1962. The Macapagal administration retaliated by cancelling an official visit in 1963. Moreover, the administration's Proclamation No. 28 saw the transfer of Independence celebration from the 4th of July (as per the Tydings-McDuffie Act) to June 12 (as per the Malolos Republic's 1898 independence declaration).

Beginning in the 1960s, Philippines' domestic concerns were complicated by international financial institutions. The Philippine economy was unsustainable, especially because its export revenue could not finance debt repayment. Philippine exports were driven by raw materials. From 1967 to 1971, sugar, coconut, and forestry products made up 70% of Philippine exports. Also, American development assistance had drastically declined in the late 1960s. The entrance of the World Bank and the International Monetary Fund into the fray offered hope for salvation but did not, in any manner, guarantee it. In particular, the presence of the World Bank had become massive in the Philippines from 1970 to 1982—spanning the leaderships of presidents Nixon, Ford, Carter and Reagan. To implement and satisfy the radical stabilization measures needed to enforce the structural adjustments set forth by the international financial institutions, President Ferdinand Marcos (1965–86) declared martial law on September 21, 1972. Within a year of declaring martial law, President Marcos won increased American military support, which jumped from $18.5 million to $45.3 million in 1973, and was accompanied by an increase in the supply of war materiel along with capacity and personnel training by the United States to combat Communist and Muslim insurgencies. Speculations suggest that the Marcos administration exploited these security concerns to ensure the continuation of American military and economic aid to the Philippines. Adding fuel to the fire, during the Marcos years' public spending was fueled by public debt. The military and economic aid from the Nixon, Ford and Carter administrations to the Philippines were minimal, but continued the trend of doling out foreign assistance in spite of human rights violations.

During the Carter administration (1977–81), a thin line was drawn between economic and military assistance after the signing of the Arms Export Control Act of 1976. The U.S.-Phil-

President Reagan and Philippine President Ferdinand Marcos, along with First Ladies Imelda Marcos and Nancy Reagan, walk into the White House after the arrival ceremonies on the South Lawn September 16, 1982. (BETTMANN/GETTY IMAGES)

ippine Military Bases Agreement was renewed on 1979 with the promise of $500 million in U.S. foreign aid to the Marcos administration. The line drawn between economic and military aid was erased under the Reagan administration. Under Ronald Reagan (1981–89), the U.S. government bundled foreign aid, inluding both economic and military. The Communist threat, which had been the rallying cry of the governments of the United States and the Philippines during the onset of the Cold War, played a large role in the U.S.-Philippine bilateral relations. This was especially highlighted when U.S. Secretary of Defense Caspar Weinberger visited Manila in April 1982 and affirmed the role of U.S. military bases in quelling the Communist threat. During this period President Reagan's foreign policy had increased support for repressive right-wing regimes throughout the developing and underdeveloped countries, dubbed chiefly as the Kirkpatrick Doctrine.

Corazon Aquino and the EDSA "People Power" Revolution (named after the Epifanio de los Santos Avenue, a major Philippine thoroughfare) overthrew the Marcos dictatorship—characterized as aberrant in the latter years of its lifespan. Under the first Aquino administration the U.S.

government was assured that all military and security commitments and financial obligations would be honored. The Philippine government was keen not to over-borrow in the late 1980s due to domestic developments: domestic debt of some $12.3 billion that comprised some 40–50% of the national budget; natural disasters, an earthquake in 1990 and the eruption of Mt. Pinatubo in 1991; and the Gulf

Corazon Aquino in Manila, Philippines, on January 31, 1987. (ERIC BOUVET/GAMMA-RAPHO/ GETTY IMAGES)

Filipino soldiers participate in the Amphibious Landing training as part of the 2018 Balika-tan exercises between the Philippines and the United States in Zambales Province, the Philippines, on May 9, 2018.(XINHUA/ROUELLE UMALI/GETTY IMAGES)

personnel visiting the United States.

President Benigno Aquino III's (2010–16) foreign relations with China were conflict-ridden due to boundary spats in the West Philippine Sea. Although China had long been known to engage in maritime disputes, territorial disputes worsened under the second Aquino administration when in 2012, Philippine and Chinese vessels engaged in a stand-off in the Reed and Scarborough shoals—maritime areas located within the Philippines' exclusive economic zone. On January 22, 2013, the Aquino administration filed a landmark case in The Hague and an Arbitral Tribunal under Annex VII of the United Nations Convention on the Law of the Sea (UNCLOS) was constituted. In 2016, the tribunal ruled that China's expansive claim to sovereignty over the waters of the South China Sea had no legal basis. However, there is no mechanism for enforcing the decision. Coupled with this separation from China, President Aquino III intensified relations with the United States. In 2014, the governments of the United States and the Philippines brokered the Enhanced Defense Cooperation Agreement (EDCA) on April 28, after eight months of negotiations.

war that impeded and reduced Filipino remittances. But by this time, support for the renewal of the U.S.-Philippine Military Bases Agreement had declined. The military bases agreement was not renewed by the Philippine Senate on September 1991 by a slim margin and the bilateral relations of the United States and the Philippines hit an all-time low.

During the administration of President Fidel Ramos (1992–98) the Philippines and other East Asian countries, especially its treaty allies Japan, Taiwan, South Korea, Thailand and, quasi-ally Singapore, still saw the United States as the prime guarantor of security against an emerging China. All are strategically situated along the peripheries of China. The Status of Forces Agreement, a precursor to the 1999 Visiting Forces Agreement, was reached by the U.S. and the Philippine governments but was not put into effect due to growing anti-U.S. sentiments in the Philippines. The 1993 East Asian Miracle confirmed the market-governed economy approach of Japan, South Korea, Hong Kong, Singapore, Malaysia, Indonesia and Thailand. But then the 1997 Asian financial crisis hit most of the Asian countries, sowing the seeds for populist governance. Despite losing

foreign investments in the process, the Philippines was largely resilient throughout the crisis.

It was only under President Joseph Estrada (1998–2001) that the Visiting Forces Agreement was revisited, resulting in two agreements that came into force in May 1999, outlining parameters for U.S. Armed Forces visiting the Philippines and for Filipino

Current issues besetting U.S.-Philippine relations

Contemporary U.S.-Philippine relations is beset with challenges. A key domestic issue that strikes at the heart of bilateral relations is the prevailing human rights crisis brought about by President Duterte's war on drugs. As of August 2017, the Philippine National Police were responsible for some 9,000 drug-related killings, although human rights watchdogs say the figure is closer to 14,000. Based on officially reported statistics, the poor were noted to have been the number one victims of the drug war. While the United States could have responded through its 1997 Leahy Law, which limits or prevents the U.S. government from transferring foreign assistance to countries with gross human rights violations, this has not happened. During

the 31st ASEAN Summit on November 2017, held in Manila, there was no discussion of human rights as President Donald Trump expressed his full support of the Philippine government's war on drugs.

What may come as a shock is the prevailing paradox of Duterte's sustained high approval ratings in spite of the drug killings. There are two plausible explanations. First, Duterte positioned himself as the repudiating demagogue, casting himself as an anti-establishment populist. His promotion of radical social response to the drug problem strategically positions himself as a man of action—something that appeals to Filipinos. His administration has also effectively managed the mass discontent with the previous administration's supposed inaction on social issues. The Duterte administration has also strategically deployed the politics of fear. This return to national "bossism" on the local level and the use of executive policing powers have spurred possible state-sanctioned violence. President Duterte's popularity was not because of a revolt of the poor masses but rather a protest of the new middle class that had failed to reap the benefits of good governance of the previous administration. In an attempt to quell the criticisms of the drug war, the Duterte administration has named Philippine Vice President Leni Robredo, staunch critic of the government's drug war program, to be anti-drug czar after she accepted Duterte's offer to lead and co-chair the Philippines' Inter-Agency Committee on Anti-Illegal Drugs (ICAD).

Another issue that strikes at the heart of the U.S.-Philippine bilateral relation is the Duterte administration's pivot to China and Russia, paralleled with a proactive distancing from the United States. President Duterte manipulated the fragile public perception of the Filipinos on the historical atrocities committed by the United States in the Philippines and, through his angry remarks, galvanized support for his foreign policy preference. President Duterte's attempts at loosening the ties with the United States is a postcolonial repudiation of America; to liberate the Philippines from its status as some sort of neocolonial ward.

Duterte's pivot away from the U.S. need not be construed as complete severance of ties, but rather as a recalibration of interests. Despite the hints of historical revenge, the Philippines' defense posture in the region is optimally maintained. The Duterte administration's acceptance of the 2014 EDCA, which affirms mutual cooperation to promote peace and security in the region, is indicative of the government's policy response to the uncertainties posed by China's regional preponderance. Nevertheless, the recent Philippine policy approach to China (which some label as appeasement) is straining U.S.-Philippine relations. But this policy is not ill-informed, at least on the part of the Philippine government. The Philippine government's inaction on the Arbitral ruling on the West Philippine Sea is attributed to one particular circumstance. According to the Philippine national government, the inaction on the ruling can be attributed to the country's attempts to gain soft Chinese material inducements, especially in the advent of China's Belt and Road Initiative coupled with its foreign loans en masse. The visit of U.S. State Secretary John Kerry on July 26, 2016, in fact, played a critical role in the Duterte administration's foreign policy strategy. Secretary Kerry advised lessening the emphasis on the Arbitral ruling when dealing with maritime disputes, further suggesting that a more strategic approach toward China is afoot. While the Philippines' relationship with the United States is strained, it does not mean that the latter will abandon the former. While U.S. Asian alliances maintain concerns of security risks, the United States remains the prime guarantor of security to its peripheral allies. This is especially true for a long-time treaty ally like the Philippines.

A third challenge to the U.S.-Philippine bilateral relations is the Philippines' withdrawal from the International Criminal Court (ICC). In conjunction with the drug war that Duterte initiated in the latter half of 2016, the international community took notice of the drastic handling of drug prevalence and the subsequent decline of human rights conditions in the Philippines. President Duterte's vocal protests, some spanning sovereignty concerns and political independence of public administration, have been met with harsh criticism from the international community as the death toll of the drug war kept rising. On March 17, 2018, the Philippines submitted a written notification to the United Nations of an intent to withdraw from the Rome Statute (the treaty that established the ICC) to which it had been a party since 2011. The ICC was notified a day later. The Duterte administration's withdrawal from the Rome Statute followed a preliminary examination launched by the ICC—a course of action to warrant whether an investigation is needed—on the Duterte administration's drug war. As of March 17, 2019, the Philippines is officially no longer a party to said statute. The United States is not a party to the statute, either.

A fourth challenge to the bilateral relationship is the diminishing presence of the United States in the West Philippine Sea primarily due to mari-

Protesters burn an image of President Rodrigo Duterte near the Philippine Congress on July 22, 2019, in Manila, Philippines. (JES AZNAR/GETTY IMAGES)

time disputes with China, the regional giant. 74,000 U.S. troops are currently deployed in the Asia Pacific across five treaty allies of the United States: Australia, Japan, South Korea, Thailand and the Philippines. Aside from the number of troops deployed, the United States has maintained minimal associations with any maritime disputes. To this effect, China has reinforced its territorial claims in the region alongside its bolstering of economic and financial assertions in the Asia Pacific. For example, China's Belt and Road Initiative seeks to boost economic connectivity and infrastructure along the old Silk Road and throughout the Eurasian region. The China-Pakistan Economic Corridor alone could amass some $62 billion worth of revenue in investments. This is further reified by the Regional Comprehensive Economic Partnership between China and the rest of Asia, to which the United States is not a party. In 2015, the creation of the Asia Infrastructure Investment Bank (or AIIB) effectively challenged the West-affiliated regional international financial institutions like the Asian Development Bank and the Japan International Cooperation Agency. Despite the Philippine government's clamor for intervention in the West Philippine Sea debacle, the United States has limited its stance and its position on the matter—one loosely based on verbal agreements reached by the former Obama administration and Xi Jinping's administration. These mutually agreed upon limits serve as constraints to the United States' intervention in the West Philippine Sea, effectively restricting its actions to freedom of navigation initiatives and freedom from maritime coercion, intimidation and threats. A shared coexistence between the United States and China was initially envisioned by both presidents Barack Obama and Xi Jinping on the matter of China's rise. The United States will allow such for as long as it is peaceful, prosperous, stable, and responsible. But this was effectively reversed under U.S. President Donald Trump.

Lastly, and perhaps the more exigent one, is the challenge of legal ambiguity and equity in the military agreements between the United States and the Philippines. When Philippine National Defense Secretary Delfin Lorenzana called for the review of the 1951 Mutual Defense Treaty in December 2018, the United States took great measure in ensuring continued commitments and support for the transfer of military personnel in the Philippines. But this assurance was thinly veiled with the same undertone of maintaining legal ambiguity in the Mutual Defense Treaty, which drew the concern of Secretary Lorenzana. Secretary Lorenzana went so far as to suggest that legal ambiguity in military agreements can lead to confusion and doubt especially when mutual defense obligations are triggered. This active concern is only logical as China aggressively projects its dominance even within the Philippines' exclusive economic zone. Moreover, a comparison of the two agreements from 2014—U.S. defense cooperation with Japan and with that of the Philippines—suggests that there exists a disparity in legal specifications and clarifications in the defense obligations between the United States and the Philippines. Secretary Lorenzana's concern remains on point through and through: Ambiguity in military agreements is perilous considering Chinese regional preponderance and territorial aggression. The Philippine government's concerns were quelled when, on March 1, 2019, U.S. Secretary of State Mike Pompeo assured the Duterte administration that any armed attack in the West Philippine Sea will trigger defense obligations outlined in the Article 4 of the 1951 Mutual Defense Treaty. While Secretary Pompeo's opportune and timely comment may abate the Philippines' lingering doubts on U.S. commitment in maritime disputes for now, manifestations of the U.S.'s obligations to the treaty remains to be seen.

Policy options

In spite of China's meteoric rise in the region over the past decades, the United States remains as the Philippines' single most credible and trustworthy security partner. The second Obama administration had maintained a strategic posture with the Philippines due to vested key interests in the bilateral relationship, particularly in the maintenance of external (disputed territories as flashpoints for conflict escalation) and internal security (peaceable resolution to the separatist insurgency) within the Philippines and throughout the Southeast Asian region. The entrance of Rodrigo Duterte definitely shook the U.S.-Philippine bilateral relations to the core. Despite the Obama administration's enormous strides in maintaining strategic relations with the Philippine government, it remained critical of the latter's gross human rights violation in the conduct of its drug war. The Trump administration's appeasement of Duterte's policy agenda, on the other hand, may be a strategic response to the Philippines' rebalancing toward China and Russia. The United States' Asia Reassurance Initiative Act of 2018 alone is indicative of "the United States' continued commitment to the region" despite the encroaching threats to democratic institutions in Asia. This, in part, also complements the Trump administration's "Free and Open Indo-Pacific" strategy/framework in Asia.

Rodrigo Duterte currently serves as the single most important factor for the U.S.-Philippine bilateral relations. Under his executive watch, the bilateral relations of the United States and the Philippines may either come out stronger in the end or wither, stagnate even, in the process. But this does not in any way preclude the influence of domestic and international forces. As a matter of fact, the strengthening of U.S.-Philippine relations is anchored on how the United States will respond to the Philippines' recalibration and rebalancing.

Building good-will. One unorthodox process, at least in this case, would be building good-will. Whenever President Duterte invokes instances of American colonial excess, the governments' ties with one another tend to take a beating. One possible way of building good-will is providing for historical reparations. A recent example is the return of the Balangiga bells last December 11, 2018. (the Balangiga massacre took place in 1901 during the Philippine-American war. American forces took three church bells as trophies of war.) The bells were particularly important for President Duterte as a symbol of colonial oppression by the United States; that unless the church bells of Balangiga were not on Philippine soil, the unjustified massacre of Balangiga remains an affront to U.S.-Philippine relations. This was remedied when U.S. Ambassador to the Philippines Sung Kim and other American political leaders endeavored to arrange the return of the church bells to the Philippines.

Defense cooperation. Like fostering socio-political good-will, the maintenance of a comprehensive defense cooperation in the region, and with the country, is necessary. This may pertain to drafting succinct, timely and relevant defense cooperation guidelines between the United States and the Philippines. But the instance of the 2014 EDCA indicate that this is not the case. In contrast to the 2014 U.S.-Japan Defense Cooperation, the 2014 EDCA serves more as logistical transfer and jurisdictional parameter agreements on military equipment and its use. The former, on the other hand, outlines comprehensive defense guidelines under invasion scenarios coupled with bilateral cooperation mechanisms allowing for the similar logistical concerns that makes up the Philippines' 2014 EDCA. To contextualize the Philippines' 2014 EDCA, China's aggressive military build-up in the West Philippine Sea is now allegedly capable of launching missiles in the region alarming both the Philippines' Department of National Defense and the United States' Pentagon. Moreover, an updated VIIRS (Visual Infrared Imaging Radiometer Suite) satellite imagery released by the Philippines' Karagatan Patrol (Sea Patrol) shows that foreign vessels from Vietnam, Taiwan and China are within the exclusive economic zones along the western Philippine coastline, with speculation that Chinese vessels, commercial and non-commercial alike, comprise a majority of these.

Philippine President Rodrigo Duterte (R) and U.S. President Donald Trump (L) hold a bilateral meeting on the sidelines of the 31st Association of Southeast Asian Nations (ASEAN) Summit at the Philippine International Convention Center in Manila on November 13, 2017. (ROLEX DELA PENA/AFP VIA GETTY IMAGES)

Implementing the 2016 Arbitral Tribunal ruling. When the arbitral tribunal ruling against Chinese expansion in the South China Sea was released on July 12, 2016, it was a remarkable foreign policy victory for the outgoing Aquino administration. It was, however, Rodrigo Duterte's administration that inherited the success. Pursuing the arbitral tribunal ruling is now incumbent on the new government; however, President Duterte's rhetoric indicates that the government will not be pursuing the implementation of the ruling for two reasons: a risk-assessment of conflict escalation with China and Duterte's choice of amicable dispute settlement with China through verbal agreements. President Duterte still maintains his firm position on matters of the Philippines' sovereignty and territorial integrity, as he elaborated in his recent State of the Nation Address last July 22, 2019. This has been a source of concern for many of the critics of Duterte administration. Figures like retired Senior Associate Justice Antonio Carpio of the Supreme Court of the Philippines have been forthright about the necessity of protecting the West Philippine Sea as a global common from China's grand thievery.

Pivoting to ASEAN. The ASEAN bloc approach is also the best means of maintaining security and order within and around the West Philippine Sea. Experiences with the ASEAN bloc indicate that it is a good counterbalance to Chinese territorial aggression. All ASEAN countries are within China's peripheral sphere of influence. Each vary in their experiences and relationship with China. But structuralizing an ASEAN bloc as counterbalancing entity against China is not an easy feat especially because the regional bloc is more a convening body than an enforcing one. In 2017, ASEAN was most outspoken in pointing out the controversial missile testing of North Korea, invoking administrative action from countries like Japan and the United States to ensure that Kim Jong-un's government was held accountable. While the preponderant China posits a different case, a viable option remains: for the Philippines (and the United States) to turn to ASEAN countries for a pooling of security capacity. The U.S. and the Philippine governments need not look far from the ASEAN region. It is also important for the Philippines to actively ensure its fellow Asian neighbors that this strategic turn to ASEAN does not go in contravention to their claims in the disputed regions.

discussion questions

1. Under present United States' foreign policy, do the Philippines have a good reason to be suspicious of U.S. assurances given the ambiguities of the Mutual Defense Treaty and the verbal reassurances of the Secretary of State? What factors do you think might cause the United States to hesitate to respond in contravention of the treaty mandates?

2. China's expansion into the South China Sea has not been significantly challenged by the United States. What suggestions would you propose to counter China's expansionist activities in implementing the Belt and Road program which would reassure the Philippines of our commitment to them?

3. Duterte's authoritarian policies share a lot in common with other authoritarian leaders around the world. The United States policy has been to not condemn these policies. In the case of the Philippines, should the United States use more assertive diplomacy to try to deter increasing assertion of authoritarian rule? If so, what suggestions would you make to the State department?

4. Corruption has been wide spread under the Duterte administration, as has increased use of violence. How much should these conditions impact our relationship with the Philippines? What policies would you suggest given the fact that these are domestic Philippine issues?

5. Human rights, the rule of law and constitutionalism are bedrock principles for democratic nations. Duterte's withdrawal from the Rome Statute opens the door to increased contravention of those principles in his country. What possible strategies could the US develop to persuade the Duterte government to change course?

6. America's past colonial history in the Philippines has not been forgotten by them, especially the middle class and is reflected in part by Duterte's "pivot" to China and Russia. What policies would you propose to promote better U.S. relations with the Philippine people?

suggested readings

Abinales, Patricio N. and Amoroso, Donna J . **State and Society in the Philippines.** 464 pp. Lanham, MD: Rowman & Littlefield, 2017. This clear and nuanced introduction explores the Philippines' ongoing and deeply charged dilemma of state-society relations through a historical treatment of state formation and the corresponding conflicts and collaboration between government leaders and social forces.

Karnow, Stanley. **In Our Image: America's Empire in the Philippines.** 536 pp. New York, NY: Ballantine Books, 1990. Stanley Karnow won the Pulitzer Prize for this account of America's imperial experience in the Philippines. In a swiftly paced, brilliantly vivid narrative, Karnow focuses on the relationship that has existed between the two nations since the United States acquired the country from Spain in 1898, examining how we have sought to remake the Philippines "in our image," an experiment marked from the outset by blundering, ignorance, and mutual misunderstanding.

Hamilton-Paterson, James. **America's Boy: The Marcoses and the Philippines.** 502 pp. London, England: Faber and Faber, 1998. James Hamilton-Paterson, who knew the Philippines well having lived there for some years, resolved in *America's Boy* to examine the Marcoses more closely - not to exonerate them but, rather, to explain the political and social roots of their regime, sustained for so long by support from Washington.

Bartholomew, Rafe. **Pacific Rims: Beermen Ballin' in Flip-Flops and the Philippines' Unlikely Love Affair with Basketball.** 416 pp. New York, NY: Berkley Books, 2011. In *Pacific Rims*, Rafe Bartholemew, journalist, New Yorker, and veteran baller, ventures through the Philippines to investigate the country's love of basketball.

Wolff, Leon. **Little Brown Brother: How the United States Purchased and Pacified the Philippines**. 418 pp. Oxford, England: Oxford University Press, 1992. First published in 1960, *Little Brown Brother* won the Francis Parkman Prize from the Society of American Historians in 1962 as the book which "best combined serious historical scholarship and literary distinction." Available again, this book looks at a long history of Filipino struggle for independence.

Miller, Jonathan. **Rodrigo Duterte: fire and fury in the Philippines.** 352 pp. New York, NY: Scribe, 2018. Through interviews with Duterte himself, his sister, daughter and son, two former presidents, old friends, death squad hitmen, and relatives of his victims, Channel 4 News' Asia Correspondent Jonathan Miller shows that far from the media cartoon of The Godfather, John Wayne, Hugo Chavez, and Donald Trump rolled into one, Duterte is a sinister, dangerous man, who should not be taken lightly.

Don't forget: Ballots start on page 98!!!!

To access web links to these readings, as well as links to additional, shorter readings and suggested web sites,

go to www.fpa.org/great_decisions

and click on the topic under Resources, on the right-hand side of the page.

America's uneven approach to AI and its consequences
by Susan Ariel Aaronson

A man looks at a demonstration of human motion analysis software at the stall of the artificial intelligence solutions maker Horizon Robotics during the Security China 2018 exhibition on public safety and security in Beijing, China, October 24, 2018. (THOMAS PETER/REUTERS)

The world's oceans are in trouble. Global warming is causing sea levels to rise and reducing the supply of food in the oceans. The ecological balance of the ocean has been disturbed by invasive species and cholera. Many pesticides and nutrients used in agriculture end up in the coastal waters, resulting in oxygen depletion that kills marine plants and shellfish. Meanwhile the supply of fish is declining due to overfishing. Yet to flourish, humankind requires healthy oceans; the oceans generate half of the oxygen we breathe, and, at any given moment, they contain more than 97% of the world's water. Oceans provide at least a sixth of the animal protein people eat. Living oceans absorb carbon dioxide from the atmosphere and reduce climate change impacts.

Many civil society groups (NGOs) are trying to protect this shared resource. As example, OceanMind uses satellite data and artificial intelligence (AI) to analyze the movements of vessels and compare their activities to historical patterns. The NGO can thus identify damaging behavior such as overfishing.

SUSAN ARIEL AARONSON *is Research Professor of International Affairs and Director of the Digital Trade and Data Governance Hub. Aaronson conceived of and directs the Hub, which aims to educate policymakers, the press and the public about domestic and international data governance issues from digital trade to public data governance. Aaronson is also a Cross-Disciplinary Fellow at GWU and a Senior Fellow at the think tank Center for International Governance Innovation (GIGI) in Canada. Aaronson's research focuses on data governance and trade, human rights, and governance of new technologies.*

8

The decline of the world's oceans is what scholars call a wicked problem—one so complex that it will require innovative, cost effective, and global solutions. Many executives, business leaders, and policymakers, among others, hope that AI such as that utilized by OceanMind could provide insights and, ultimately, solutions to such difficult problems.

One can describe AI as a "global public good" because of its potential to help humankind address such problems. Global public goods are goods with **benefits and/or costs** that potentially extend to all countries, people, and generations. Although most AI is provided by private firms, market mechanisms alone cannot distribute AI (or AI capacity) equally throughout the world. AI is far from a perfect technology: current variants of AI can be biased or incorrect. Moreover, humans may become too trusting of AI. Given these problems, AI is most likely to meet its potential as a public good if data is as diverse and correct as possible, and if researchers from around the world compete to develop and produce to AI.

As of October 2019, some 30 industrialized and middle-income countries have developed plans, incentives, and policies to stimulate national, rather than international, AI research and adoption. In general these countries have firms developing AI systems as well as rules governing the use of some types of data such as personal data. (See Table 1) But most countries are in the early stages of learning how to govern data, let alone data-driven technologies. Nonetheless, the people of the world won't be able to reap the benefits of AI unless policymakers work at the national and international levels to create an effective enabling and regulatory environment for AI.

Nations differ as to what an effective enabling environment should include, but in general, Western nations

are calling for ethical AI, internationally shared AI research, an internationally accepted system of norms to govern both data and AI, and the adoption of policies to discourage unethical and anti-competitive behaviour by firms providing/using AI services. Meanwhile, governments such as India and South Africa are less willing to share their citizens' data until they firm up strategies to utilize and govern data. As example, in March 2019, India issued a draft national e-commerce policy that said that India should be the prime beneficiary of the data of Indians. These national perspectives make it hard to find a unified approach to developing and governing AI.

The U.S. should play a major role in encouraging international development and dissemination of AI because it has so much at stake: it holds the largest

Table 1
G-20 AI plans
as of August 2019

Argentina	No strategy
Australia	No strategy
Brazil	No strategy
Canada	2017
China	2017
France	2018
Germany	2019
India	2018
Indonesia	No strategy
Italy	2018
Japan	2017
Mexico	2018
Rep. of Korea	2017
South Africa	No strategy
Russia	No strategy
Saudi Arabia	No strategy
Turkey	No strategy
UK	2018
U.S.	2019
EU	2018

SOURCE: THOMAS STRUETT, DIGITAL TRADE AND DATA GOVERNANCE HUB, GWU

share of the global market for AI services. Moreover, if integrated properly, AI would not only benefit the U.S. economy but also government operations and, thereby, citizen/taxpayer welfare.

But the U.S. is sending mixed signals about how it views AI as well as its willingness to work with other states to govern AI. American policymakers recognize that AI is a general purpose technology—one that can contribute to productivity and economic growth in many other sectors. As example, Lt. General Jack Shanahan, who directs the Joint AI Center at the U.S. Department of Defense noted, "A.I. is an enabler, much more like electricity than a gadget, a widget or a weapons system."

General purpose technologies tend to yield economic and social turbulence, as society and jobs adapt to their direct and indirect effects on employment, on society, and on democracy. These technologies often have social, political and economic spillovers that transcend borders. Accordingly, nations **must** cooperate to address these effects.

On one hand, the U.S. has cooperated with other countries in building AI. In its 2017 National Security Strategy, the Trump administration promised, "We will nurture a healthy innovation economy that collaborates with allies." On the other hand, the Trump administration has also made it clear that it intends to develop strategies that will allow the U.S. economy to dominate global AI markets. In the same National Security Strategy cited above, the Trump administration stated that, "To maintain our competitive advantage, the United States will prioritize emerging technologies critical to economic growth and security such as data science, encryption, autonomous technologies…and artificial intelligence. Moreover, because AI is an essential component of tools such as drones and robotics relied upon by the U.S. military, U.S. policymakers have concluded that the U.S. must maintain a competitive edge in AI for national security reasons. As a result, the Trump administration has taken a nationalistic, protectionist, and insular approach to AI. It has proposed export

Before you read, download the companion **Glossary** that includes definitions, a guide to acronyms and abbreviations used in the article, and other material. Go to **www.fpa.org/great_decisions** and select a topic in the Resources section. (Top Right)

controls on AI, dramatically limited work and educational visas, and alienated close scientific partners such as Canada, France, and Japan. With these policies, the U.S. could slow the progress of AI as a tool to address some of the world's problems.

If policymakers want American AI to be effective, rooted in trust, and produced and utilized internationally, they should think about AI as a global public good. The Trump administration has put forward an approach to AI with some thoughtful components, but its approach could also undermine AI because it reduces the openness needed to attract the best researchers and produce the most effective AI systems.

Definitions and consequences

AI is a broad term that is used to describe computer systems that can sense their environment, think, learn, and act in ways that humans do. Organizations use AI in digital assistants such as Apple's Siri, chatbots such as H&M's chat bot assistant, and machine learning applications such as Waze, which can direct users through traffic jams. Governments also increasingly rely on AI to save time, money, and find new solutions. The U.S. military has used AI to predict component failure on tanks, while Kansas City developed a machine learning algorithm to help forecast when potholes will form on city streets. AI applications use computational analysis of data to uncover patterns and draw inferences. These applications in turn depend on machine learning technologies that must ingest huge volumes of data.

Effective AI requires high-quality, up-to-date, complete and correct data to ensure accurate predictions and avoid discrimination and bias. To build AI or machine learning systems, engineers need lots of data (data volume), variety of data (data variety), and good data that is correct (data quality and veracity). AI systems are not able to distinguish between reliable and unreliable data. If the algorithms are built on incorrect, unreliable data, these systems will come up with incorrect,

discriminatory, unethical, or misleading results.

Because training data must be broad, high-quality, and correct, most AI firms require lots of data. And because these applications require lots of data – and that demand may change over time as applications and training strategies evolve – no nation alone can govern AI, or any other data driven sector. Policymakers will need to develop internationally accepted, interoperable principles, rules, and strategies to govern AI. Most have focused on using trade agreements to advance the free flow of data and to create large pools or sources of data.

But not every AI firm or government has access to lots of data because the data-driven economy is built on information asymmetries. Firms that have significant computing power are better positioned to extract and utilize data to create new products and services than firms that do not have such computing access. In addition, because data-driven firms must make large capital investments to exploit big datasets, information asymmetry also applies across firms. These big firms (such as Google, Amazon, Alibaba, and Tencent) already have an advantage. The more data they have, the more easily they can use algorithms to transform raw data into new value-added data products. They can then sell these products along with existing products. Moreover, these new products and services generate even more data, which, in turn, further perpetuates the market power of these firms.

Information asymmetry also applies across countries. Of the 30 largest internet companies by market capitalization, the U.S. has 18; China has 6; Australia, Argentina, Canada and Japan have 1 each; and the EU has none. In its 2016 annual development report, the World Bank stated that, despite the widespread dissemination of digital technologies, many countries, including many middle-income and developing countries have not yet been able to benefit. To a great extent, developing countries do not have the expertise, capital, or infrastructure to

nurture data-driven firms. Most of the firms transitioning to this new data-driven economy are in middle-income and wealthy countries. While there is no clear data on firms developing and selling AI services, most of these firms have operations in a few nations (Australia, Canada, China, France, Germany, India, Israel, the U.S.). These nations have excellent universities, significant AI expertise, and access to a broad and growing supply of data to consistently improve AI.

Moreover, according to Jack Clark, Policy Director for Open AI, many types of AI are still in an early phase of development. These relatively early-stage AI systems have achieved good enough results to inspire a large number of actors (business and government) to invest. However, these early-stage AI systems are not always accurate (e.g. they can lead to discrimination or imperfect solutions). He warns, "we can expect the technical weakness of AI systems to 'scale up' with the amount of computational power poured into them unless we develop smarter algorithms and better systems of governance," for the organizations both developing and deploying them. These AI systems could make major mistakes with significant social consequences, another reason why governance of AI is so important.

Finally, the research sphere, like the internet and the world's oceans, is a "commons"—a place where many people share resources and services. Individual users could destroy the commons if they act only according to their own self-interest. But the commons can thrive if it is governed effectively, by individuals, firms, and governments.

Thus, if we want to improve AI, we should want to encourage international research collaborations and competition. Research in sectors such as AI is likely to be more effective with an international feedback loop, where many people at many different levels contribute to research. Scientists need a free and open environment to provide such feedback. Yet, the U.S. Government is increasingly taking steps to shelter and isolate U.S.-made AI instead of fostering multinational collaborations.

The U.S. Approach to AI

America has long been a leader in AI. According to Michael Kratsios, Chief Technology Officer and Deputy Assistant to the President at the White House Office of Science and Technology Policy, "America has roughly 2,000 AI companies, more than double our closest global competitor. We boast more AI unicorns, those being startups valued over $1 billion, than any other nation. Of the 32 AI unicorns, the United States has 17." Kratsios is asserting that the U.S. is dominating AI. Other analysts agree that the U.S. leads in talent, research, development and hardware related to AI. Many even contend that the U.S. has significant comparative advantage in AI.

But Kratsios is clearly nervous about America's ability to continue its dominance of AI research and markets for AI. In that same September 2019 speech described above, Kratsios noted, "the uniquely American ecosystem must do everything in its collective power to keep America's lead in the AI race and build on our successes . . . for the benefit of the American people. We start from a position of great strength, and we have a plan to keep winning."

Kratsios is not alone--policymakers, business leaders and others see that advantage as under threat from Chinese competition. They argue that China uses government funds to subsidize its AI companies and it mandates close cooperation between tech firms and government. I argue that while Chinese innovation may reduce America's lead, it also invigorates American researchers.

Trump administration steps that could promote AI as a global public good

a. Plans and ethics

The Obama administration first articulated a National Artificial Intelligence Research and Development Strategic Plan in 2016. The Research and Development Strategic Plan promised that the U.S. Government would make long-term investments in AI research, develop effective methods for human-AI collaboration, understand and address the ethical, legal and societal implications of AI, ensure the safety and security of AI systems, develop shared public datasets and environments for AI training, and test, measure and evaluate AI technologies through standards and benchmarks.

The Trump administration expanded on that plan, when President Trump launched the American AI Initiative in February 2019. The Executive Order that contained the Initiative made it clear that as under Obama, AI research would be a priority. But the Trump administration AI strategy had a more select audience—business. The administration would help businesses and educators develop an AI-ready workforce. The Order claimed that Trump administration officials were ready to engage with researchers, businesses, and governments in other countries. But by engagement, the Trump administration did not always mean cooperation.

Like previous administrations, the Trump administration sought public comment on America's AI strategy. However, the administration did not involve civil society groups in the development of these AI plans. The American AI Initiative had a section on AI and workers and another on AI and ethics, but it did not invite ethicists or workers associations to the AI outreach events. As example, in May 2019, The White House hosted the Artificial Intelligence for American Industry Summit to discuss both the promise of AI and the policies needed to maintain U.S. leadership in the age of AI. Not surprisingly, some observers have condemned the administration for focusing too much on business needs and involvement and ignoring the broader research potential of AI.

To its credit, the administration has taken several steps to build an international consensus on the ethical use of AI. In May 2019, the U.S. joined with 41 other countries at the OECD to announce an international agreement for building trustworthy artificial intelligence. Moreover, the Department of State has asked the public to comment as to whether computer systems that can be used for the monitoring, interception, collection, preservation and/or retention of information can be freely exported or should be tightly controlled. These technologies include many built on AI, including: non-co-

Michael Kratsios, CTO of The United States, on center stage during the final day of Web Summit 2019 at the Altice Arena in Lisbon, Portugal, November 7, 2019. (SAM BARNES/ SPORTSFILE FOR WEB SUMMIT/GETTY IMAGES)

operative location tracking (products that can be used for ongoing tracking of individuals' locations without their knowledge and consent), drones and unmanned aerial vehicles, facial recognition software, automated biometric systems, social media analytics software, and gait analysis software. The U.S. has taken a leadership role in deciding which uses of AI are not ethical and which countries should benefit from open access to certain AI systems. But the U.S. did not engage with other nations on the export question regarding these types of AI.

b. Approach to research

The Trump administration has taken other important steps to facilitate the development of AI for the world at large. Despite its general inclination to cut non-defense budgets, it proposed increasing taxpayer funding for AI research. It sought to continue the leading research organization—the National Science Foundation's work on AI. NSF is also encouraging and coordinating AI research and adoption among other USG agencies.

But as noted above, the Trump administration wants taxpayer dollars to yield applied research by focusing on public-private partnerships. For example, the National Science Foundation (NSF) created an NSF-Amazon collaboration on fairness in AI. That program calls for an initial $7.6 million to be awarded to researchers in the form of three-year grants ranging from $750,000 to $1.2 million. Amazon provided half the money for the grants but has no say in which research projects get the money.

c. Competition policy and the regulation of business

Trump administration officials are caught in a conundrum. On one hand, they want to maintain and even strengthen America's data giants to facilitate global competition in AI. On the other hand, these same officials are under significant domestic and global pressure to rein in the predatory practices of some of the largest American firms that research, utilize and sell AI

services, specifically Amazon, Alphabet (Google), and Facebook. But if the U.S. government regulates how these firms operate, their costs will rise and over time, they could have less funding and expertise to compete with firms from other countries on AI services.

Despite a wide range of scandals involving these firms, USG officials moved slowly to investigate the business practices of the data-giants. As public sentiment in the U.S. has become more supportive of breaking up or regulating these data giants, members of Congress and regulators have become more determined to build an effective antitrust case. Federal officials are examining if any of the big data firms engaged in anti-competitive practices, and the Federasl Trade Commission (FTC) has imposed fines against some of these firms.

Meanwhile, the U.S. is taking other steps to ensure that markets for AI are competitive. Increasingly AI firms make their algorithms open source so individuals can comment on and improve them. But many also patent their AI. In 2019, the U.S. Patent Office called for public comment on whether AI should be patentable. U.S. laws state that an invention must contain patent-eligible subject matter in order to receive patent protection. Abstract ideas, laws of nature, and natural phenomena are excluded from patentable subject matter. Moreover, only a human can hold a patent. But the patent official has already received applications generated by AI, with human and computer systems contributions.

d. Domestic and international data governance

Without direct intent, the Trump administration has promoted AI as an international public good. It has led efforts at the domestic and international levels to make public data more useable for data analytics. Trump officials followed Obama administration policy designed to ensure that Federal public data (data collected and held by government) be provided openly online and where possible available in a form computer systems can easily utilize

(machine readable format). The U.S. government sought public comment on a Federal Data Strategy to govern and leverage the Federal Government's data and in so doing improve the use of data for decisionmaking and accountability for the U.S. Government, including for policymaking, innovation, oversight, and learning.

The Trump administration was also the first nation to place language on public data in trade agreements. Trade policymakers have included language in the U.S./Mexico/ Canada trade agreement and the U.S./Japan digital economy agreement signed in October 2019 to encourage both the free flow of data and to encourage policymakers to provide public data in a machine-readable format. The trade agreement language is voluntary. In U.S.-Japan, it states, "to the extent that a Party chooses to make government information available to the public, it shall endeavor to ensure that the government information is in a machine-readable and open format and can be searched, retrieved, used, reused, and redistributed." But the motivation is clear—researchers in business and government will benefit if they can use data from public, proprietary and personal sources to solve problems or provide more effective services.

e. Some support for the protection of personal data in trade agreements

Researchers need lots of data to make AI effective. Firms can obtain access to that data through internationally accepted rules governing cross-border data flows. Its most recent trade agreement, between the U.S. and Japan, states, "Each Party shall adopt or maintain a legal framework that provides for the protection of the personal information of the users of digital trade." This language is binding, but it does not require that personal data be protected, only that countries have a framework. Moreover, the U.S. does not require that regimes among signatories be interoperable. Instead it encourages interoperability with language noting "Recognizing that the Parties may take different legal approaches to protecting personal information, each Party should encourage the development of mechanisms to promote interoperability between these different regimes." Thus, while the U.S. says its approach to AI is designed to build trust, its approach to personal data protection provides a floor, which may be insufficient to sustain trust in AI.

Steps designed to advance AI that could undermine AI as a global public good.

While taking important steps that advance AI for the world, the Trump administration has also taken many steps that undermine an international approach to AI.

a. A view of AI as essential to national security and a military technology

The U.S. has promoted a nationalist conception of AI, over-emphasizing its role as a military technology and its importance to national security . As of 2019, almost every branch of the U.S. military has an AI arm. The head of the Joint Artificial Intelligence Center for the military, Lt. General Shanahan noted that the military needs AI to better understand the world it operates in, and it needs to excel at AI if it is to have influence. He also sees a competition among nations to advance AI. "At its core, we are in a contest for the character of the international order in the digital age. Along with our allies and partners, we want to lead and ensure that that character reflects the values and interests of free and democratic societies. I do not see China or Russia placing the same kind of emphasis in these areas."

b. Limiting foreign investment in U.S. AI and proposing AI export controls

The U.S. has long supported an open climate for investment, except when such investment could impair national security. But receptiveness to international investment has changed in the wake of fears of Chinese competition in high tech sectors such as AI. In 2018, Congress passed a law, the Foreign In-

vestment Risk Review Modernization Act, which expanded the power of a committee of senior government officials to block transactions on national security grounds; these proposals reflect such concerns. The Committee would look for "red flags," where transactions involve critical technology or companies that collect sensitive personal data.

These officials took other steps that could undermine rather than encourage U.S. AI competitiveness. In January 2019, the Commerce Department asked for public comment on export controls related to emerging technologies such as AI. Should the administration adopt such controls, firms would find it harder to work with firms in other countries. They could also increase costs, and thereby make it harder for U.S. firms to compete overseas. Finally, such controls, if adopted, could reduce U.S. interaction and competition with other firms, which could affect the pace of innovation in AI. Firms have already reduced their willingness to sell sensitive technologies overseas.

Moreover, the Department of Commerce bypassed traditional strategies for developing regulations in the U.S. Most of the time, policymakers devise such export controls under a regular public notice and comment process and then, depending on such comments, additional sectors could be added to lists of goods that have both civilian and military uses that are agreed upon by larger groups of countries. However, in September 2019, Commerce Department officials said that some of the export restrictions will be developed under a regulation that allows controls to be applied on an emergency basis and bypasses a public comment process. The strategy appears to contradict America's commitment to democratic governance of AI.

c. Restricting immigration and the AI talent pool

The Trump administration has also restricted work and student visas, reducing the already limited pool of AI researchers in the U.S. Restricting foreign students could undermine

America's tech system and reduce employment. America's AI talent pool includes not only individuals born within the 50 states and territories, but also individuals who choose to study and then to work in the U.S. The number of foreign students attending U.S. universities have been declining over the last few years for a multitude of reasons. However, potential students increasingly feel unwelcome in the U.S.

Meanwhile, Trump officials have warned universities that they could lose research funding if they work with foreign students or benefit from foreign funding. In May 2019, the White House Office of Science and Technology Policy (OSTP) launched through the National Science and Technology Council the Joint Committee on Research Environments (JCORE) to bring a "whole of government" approach to address the most pressing challenges facing the U.S. research and scientific community. It created a Subcommittee on Research Security "to protect America's researchers from undue foreign influence without compromising our values or our ability to maintain the openness and integrity of our innovation ecosystem." Researchers and universities are finding themselves in between a rock and a hard place—choosing between U.S. and international investment.

China has responded with anger in response to these strategies. Chinese scientists have warned that new U.S. research restrictions will hinder collaboration and threaten Chinese funding for joint projects. If these policies continue, they could gradually and collectively undermine the basic research necessary to facilitate AI competitiveness, reducing the public good nature of AI. Finally, they could also prod China to focus more on its own innovation.

d. Alienating Chinese research partners

The U.S. is also punishing Chinese AI companies, accusing them of selling technologies that enable Chinese repression of minorities and human rights activists. Human rights groups and journalists have reported that the Chinese government has detained more than a million ethic Uighurs, Turkish-speaking Muslims, in reeducation camps in China. Chinese officials deny that the Uighurs are imprisoned in these camps and maintain that what they call vocational training centers do not infringe on Uighurs' human rights. No foreign journalists or government officials have been allowed to visit the camps. Instead of working with U.S. allies on a unified strategy, in October 2019, the Trump administration blacklisted (which means Americans can't work with) eight companies that allegedly used AI services to monitor Uighurs within China. The firms blacklisted included: Megvii, an image recognition software developer sometimes referred to as being the world's most valuable AI start-up; iFlytek, a voice recognition specialist; Hikvision , one of the world's biggest CCTV systems manufacturers; SenseTime, a start-up that makes AI services for use in smart city, transport and education applications; and Yitu, a developer of machine vision and voice recognition tools. These firms are reliant on U.S.-based know-how, but U.S. firms are also reliant on these companies as customers and competitors. Several of these companies work closely with U.S. AI companies and universities, including MIT.

With this action the U.S. became the first nation to punish Chinese companies for misuse of AI, a reiteration of its commitment to human rights. But in doing so, the U.S. also signaled that it was not willing to encourage and possibly allow international collaboration on variants of AI using facial recognition. There are positive uses of such technologies. Moreover, the step could inspire China to devote more resources to separating its firms from U.S. firms, researchers, and capital. Almost every data giant has an AI research lab in China. The *Wall Street Journal* reported that many of these firms not only collaborate on research with U.S. universities but are dependent on advanced U.S. chips: "In the long term, the move could spell an end to partnerships with U.S. companies and institutions that go back years and limit access to top overseas talent, experts said."

(From L) EU Commission President Jean-Claude Juncker, Britain's Prime Minister Theresa May, Norway's Prime Minister Erna Solberg, Senegal's President Macky Sall, New Zealand's Prime Minister Jacinda Ardern and French President Emmanuel Macron attend a launching ceremony for the 'Christchurch call' in Paris, on May 15, 2019. (CHARLES PLATIAU/AFP/GETTY IMAGES)

e. Alienating allies by not addressing disinformation and hate speech

Meanwhile, the administration has not cooperated consistently with its traditional allies on several issues that concern democratic nations: online terrorism and hateful speech, misinformation and disinformation, and protection of personal data.

While citizens and policymakers alike have long promulgated hateful speech, lies and propaganda, the sheer volume of such speech has made it a threat to democracy. AI and social media platforms play a leading role in perpetuating this threat, as governments and individuals use bots powered by AI to disseminate disinformation. AI systems could also mitigate the threat by monitoring dissemination online.

The Trump administration has done little to regulate social media platforms that use AI to determine content and to remove untruthful, fake, or malicious content. The U.S. has moved slowly for two reasons: first, America's longstanding commitment to freedom of expression, and second, because of a key U.S. law, Section 230 of the Communications Decency Act. In the early days of the internet, Congress decided that the internet could not thrive without protecting content providers. It delineated

that these firms are not publishers and should not be held to account for what users place on their platforms. Democrats and Republicans alike have long seen this law as essential to the success of the American internet.

Moreover, the Trump administration has also tried to encourage other countries to adopt a similar approach. In the U.S./Mexico/Canada FTA (USMCA or NAFTA 2.0) says, "no Party shall adopt or maintain measures that treat a supplier or user of an interactive computer service as an information content provider in determining liability for harms related to information stored, processed, transmitted, distributed, or made available by the service, except to the extent the supplier or user has, in whole or in part, created, or developed the information." While this language does not inhibit the ability of a signatory to regulate such services, the U.S. is signaling that these protections are essential for social platforms. Others may read these signals as saying that such protections are more essential than protecting the public from harmful content. Interestingly, in October 2019, some Republican members of Congress criticized the inclusion of section 230-like language, noting it was an issue under debate in the U.S.

Moreover, citing first Amendment

concerns, the Trump administration has refused to sign the Christchurch Call, a commitment by 17 governments, the EU, and tech companies to take steps to eliminate terrorist and violent extremist content online. The call acknowledges that "respect for freedom of expression is fundamental. However, no one has the right to create and share terrorist and violent extremist content online." Content moderation is hard; yet, the U.S. has so far has taken no steps to punish companies that carry such content.

f. Regulation of personal and public data

Some argue that America's failure to enact an online data protection law is not only a problem for the U.S.; it puts the data protection of citizens of other countries at risk. Because of the huge amounts of data needed for AI and the dominance of U.S. companies in providing AI services, strong data protection is essential to the provision of AI so people feel safe using and relying on these services. But, the U.S. does not have a unified data protection law, although 3 states (most importantly California) have passed such laws and 12 are considering as of June 2019. Critics such as Access (an international NGO working on digital rights) noted that the U.S. regulatory agency, the FTC, has barely instituted cases or demanded sizeable fines. Hence, they argue that U.S. data protection is ineffective not just for Americans but the world's people. As evidence that America's approach is ineffective, the FTC fined Facebook only $5 billion for the Cambridge Analytica Scandal, where this data analytics company harvested the personal data of millions of peoples' Facebook profiles without their consent and used it for political targeting. Analysts saw the fine as too small to prod the company to actually do an effective job of protecting personal data.

Taken in sum, the U.S. has put forward a comprehensive AI strategy that advances AI in the U.S. and internationally. However, it is also acting in ways that undermine AI as a global public good.

What is the EU doing?

The EU has made clear it wants global leadership in "developing and deploying cutting-edge, ethical and secure AI." Policymakers in the EU insist that AI can be developed and utilized in an ethical manner that is respectful of human rights.

Like the U.S., the EU has also put forward a detailed plan for ethical AI, which the EU terms "trustworthy and human-centric AI." The 27 nations of the EU have increased funding and published a roadmap to achieve trustworthy AI. But as in the United States, EU policymakers struggle to regulate AI and data effectively.

Some EU member states, such as the UK, Germany, France, and Spain, have many competitive AI firms. Yet these firms are much smaller than their U.S. counterparts and do not have access to the large data pools of the U.S. or Chinese data giants. EU ministries have challenged some of the practices of the large data firms such as Facebook, Google and Amazon. European agencies have levied heavy fines against firms that engage in uncompetitive business practices and individual EU member states, particularly France and Germany, have worked hard to counter disinformation. European policymakers have also focused on the costs of disinformation and hate speech to democracy. In October 2019, Europe's highest court, the European Court of Justice, ruled that it could require Facebook and other social platforms to take down hateful speech and disinformation. But human rights groups noted that the decision raised significant questions about how companies should behave if hateful speech was legal in one nation but not another. Moreover, the court did not explain how Facebook and other such companies can delete posts, without going through the posts of all its users, a significant violation of their online privacy. Finally, it raised questions of how to reconcile this ruling with freedom of expression, another human right.

The EU, like the U.S., uses trade agreements to promote the free flow of data, which allows its researchers and firms to gain access to larger pools of personal and public data. But the EU approach rests on its commitment to strong regulation of the General Data Protection Regulation (GDPR), which protects personal data of EU citizens. Perhaps most importantly, the EU adopted regulations that grant users greater control over their data and ban firms from using AI as a sole decisionmaker in choices that can undermine human rights and freedoms.

The EU's approach to protecting personal data used in AI and other data services has gained international converts. Other countries, including Brazil, Mexico, Thailand, India, Indonesia, and Hong Kong have built on the EU model. Meanwhile, the EU has recognized 12 countries as having equivalent (adequate) levels of personal data protection, and many more are striving to become adequate so that they can freely trade data with and from EU citizens.

Most recently, the EU has designed a senior official, the former Commissioner for Competition, Margrethe Vestager, as Executive Vice President-designate of a Europe fit for the Digital Age. If she is approved by the EU Parliament, her job would be to coordinate tax, competition and industrial policies related to data-driven sectors. Her elevation reveals that the EU views trust and competitive markets as equally important as innovation.

The EU has been more open than the U.S. to foreign investment in AI and to allowing collaborative research in AI. As example, France and Canada have established a panel to support and guide the responsible development of artificial intelligence that is grounded in human rights, inclusion, diversity, innovation, and economic growth.

Nonetheless, the EU approach is

not without problems. Several EU laws such as the Copyright Directive, designed to advance some human rights undermine others, such as freedom of expression. EU efforts to prevent disinformation may also give firms powers to regulate content that governments should maintain. Meanwhile, the EU also wants to encourage innovation, but it is also raising costs to innovators through regulation such as GDPR, which mandates that firms make AI algorithms explainable if an individual believes an algorithm was used in a discriminatory manner.

Taken in sum, the EU wants AI to benefit European economic growth, but it is also working to ensure that AI benefits the broader public. Like the U.S., it struggles to balance public demands for regulation with the need to innovate. But in contrast with the U.S., the EU is open to international collaboration.

Findings and recommendations

AI has great potential. By combining and analyzing big datasets, policymakers could make economies more efficient and government more effective. Moreover, researchers could use AI to address complex problems. But the Trump administration has not developed coherent policies that could advance AI globally. While it has many thoughtful aspects, the Trump administration has also put forward strategies on immigration, work visas, export controls, access to public data, encryption, and competition policy that will reduce the competitiveness of U.S. firms and the credibility and flexibility of U.S. AI research. These policies could also alienate longstanding research allies and trade partners.

Recommendation 1: The U.S. should limit restrictions on AI research collaboration only to those areas that pose an identified threat to national security.

As the world's AI leader, the U.S. should rethink its AI strategy, building out from the concept that AI is a global public good. Moreover, U.S. (and international) policymakers should stop thinking of AI development as a race or a zero-sum game, where only one country (and its firms) lead. Instead the U.S. should do more to disseminate AI and data governance expertise so that AI can meet its potential.

Recommendation 2: The U.S. should demand greater transparency from the companies that provide us with AI regarding how they use data, when they use AI and provide

AI services to consumers, and how they invest in AI.

America needs to adopt a different approach to its data behemoths. These companies hoard the data we give them, mixing them over time to build new innovative services. These firms require huge computing resources, lots of capital, thousands of computer chips, and tons of energy to power their mammoth servers. The data giants may be crowding out these assets and making them too expensive for smaller companies as well as universities. Mandated transparency offers a way to hold the data giants to account without depriving them of significant funds to innovate.

With greater transparency, we will have a greater ability to effectively regulate the data giants (and the AI they produce). Moreover, the public will be better informed about how often they interact with AI.

Recommendation 3: The U.S. should work with international organizations such as the World Bank, ITU, UNCTAD, the OECD and others to encourage states to develop plans for the regulation and exchange of different types of data.

The U.S. needs to do more to help developing countries produce and utilize AI. The U.S. government should help other nationsd develop a strategy for how public and personal data is to be used and exchanged across borders (a national data plan). The plan should focus on ensuring that public data is open and personal data, especially personally identifiable data is adequately

protected. Personally identifiable information is information that can be used to identify, contact or locate a single person, or to identify an individual in context.

Such a plan should address issues of ownership, control, portability, equity (is the data developed and analyzed in an even-handed manner?) and monetization of data (who can earn money for data and how). Policy makers will also have to address issues related to the cloud and data transfer — how a country can control the transfer of data that might include personally identifiable information or data that is important for national security. Such plans should also address how firms can mix various types of data while protecting personal data and metadata, as well as address questions of what entities can monetize the results of the mixture of personal, proprietary and public data. Each country will need to evolve strategies that allow policy makers to maintain trust online consistent with their norms for governance.

But developing countries do not have data-driven sectors (such as AI) and may struggle to regulate data. Moreover, they must choose between devoting resources to governing data and investing in public health or education. The U.S. has a responsibility to help these nations.

Conclusion

These days the U.S. is building walls rather than bridges. But if policymakers want AI to reach its potential, the U.S. should help other countries use this technology to address some of the problems that bedevil the world's people.

discussion questions

1.If the U.S. closes itself off from the world—is it stronger and safer or weaker and more prone to hacking?

2. Will the advance of AI have as profound an effect on the economy as the computer revolution?

3. AI is more about Big Data. Is it a stretch to expect a global agreement on Ethics and AI? What might a unified data protection law include? What exactly needs to be regulated and how?

4. What is the level of privacy an individual can expect living in a modern society? Is privacy, as a concpet, going to become alien in the future?

5. If AI is a "global public good" than what are it's associated negative "externalities"? (Such as the weakening of democracy, the rise of populism and the loss of privacy.)

6. Should the U.S. hold big data companies accountable for spreading users personal information? (Similar to how the EU has gone after Facebook and Google.) Would that have a negative effect on the growth of AI?

suggested readings

Coleman, Flynn. **A Human Algorithm: How Artificial Intelligence is Redefining Who We Are.** 335 pp. Berkeley, CA: Counterpoint, 2019. *A Human Algorithm: How Artificial Intelligence Is Redefining Who We Are* examines the immense impact intelligent technology will have on humanity. These machines, while challenging our personal beliefs and our socioeconomic world order, also have the potential to transform our health and well-being, alleviate poverty and suffering, and reveal the mysteries of intelligence and consciousness.

Furst, Keith and Wagner, Daniel. **AI Supremacy: Winning in the Era of Machine Learning.**. 524 pp. Scott Valley, CA: CreateSpace, 2018. Artificial Intelligence (AI) is having a profound impact on individuals, businesses, and governments, but what is required to get ahead and stay ahead of the curve AI is not well understood.

Lee, Kai-Fu. **AI Super Powers: China, Silicon Valley and the New World Order.** 272 pp. Boston,MA: Houghton Mifflin Harcourt, 2018. In *AI Superpowers*, Kai-fu Lee argues powerfully that because of these unprecedented developments in AI, dramatic changes will be happening much sooner than many of us expected.

Borders, Max. **The Social Singularity.** 208 pp. CMM Institute for Personal and Social Evolution, 2018. Although the technological singularity fast approaches, Borders argues, a parallel process of human reorganization will allow us to reap enormous benefits. The paradox? Our billion little acts of subversion will help us lead richer, healthier lives—and avoid the robot apocalypse.

O'Neil, Cathy. **Weapons of Math Destruction: How Big Data Increases Inequality and Threatens Democracy.** 288 pp. New York, NY: Broadway Books, 2017. Tracing the arc of a person's life, O'Neil exposes the black box models that shape our future, both as individuals and as a society. These "weapons of math destruction" score teachers and students, sort résumés, grant (or deny) loans, evaluate workers, target voters, set parole, and monitor our health.

Stephens-Davidowitz, Seth. **Everybody Lies: Big Data, New Data, and What the Internet Can Tell Us About Who We Really Are.** New York, NY: Dey Street Books, 2018. *Everybody Lies* offers fascinating, surprising, and sometimes laugh-out-loud insights into everything from economics to ethics to sports to race to sex, gender and more, all drawn from the world of big data.

Don't forget: Ballots start on page 98!!!!

To access web links to these readings, as well as links to additional, shorter readings and suggested web sites,
GO TO www.fpa.org/great_decisions
and click on the topic under Resources, on the right-hand side of the page.

About the balloting process...

Dear Great Decisions Participants,

As you may already know, my name is Dr. Lauren Prather and I have been working with the Foreign Policy Association (FPA) for the last five years on the National Opinion Ballot (NOB). A version of this letter has appeared in previous briefing books, so I'm only writing a quick hello this year.

My research is primarily focused on international relations. I am a faculty member at the School of Global Policy and Strategy at the University of California, San Diego (UCSD) and have research projects on a range of public opinion topics, from foreign aid to climate change to national security issues. I also teach a class on public opinion and foreign policy for my university.

One of the key difficulties in my research is that the public is often uniformed or misinformed about the topics. This is where you come in! The Great Decisions participants continue to be some of the most informed Americans about foreign policy issues, and the NOB is the perfect opportunity to voice those opinions.

The NOB is also one of the only public opinion surveys in the United States that attempts to gather the opinions of the educated public. Thus, it has great value to researchers and policymakers alike. Some of the questions in which researchers are interested include the following:

- Are the opinions of the educated public significantly different from those of the average American?
- How does public opinion about foreign policy change over time?
- How does public opinion on one foreign policy issue relate to public opinion on other foreign policy issues? For example, are people who support U.S. government policies to mitigate climate change more or less willing to support drilling in the Arctic?
- How do different segments of the population, men or women, liberals or conservatives, view foreign policy choices?

In order to answer the types of questions researchers are interested in, such as how do people's opinions change over time, the NOB needs to have certain attributes. We need to have a way to organize the ballots by participant across all topics. That way, we know, for example, how participant #47 responded to the question about climate change mitigation and how he or she responded to the question about drilling, even if those were in different topics in the NOB. Your random ID number is the **only thing** connected to your responses and **never** your e-mail address. In fact, as a researcher, I must receive the approval of my Institutional Review Board by demonstrating that your data will be protected at all times, and that your responses will be both confidential and anonymous.

If you have any questions or comments, I am always happy to respond via e-mail at LPrather@ucsd.edu. To learn more about my research and teaching, you can visit my website at www.laurenprather.org.

Thank you again to everyone who has participated in the NOB over the years. I have learned a tremendous amount about your foreign policy views and it has greatly informed my own research. In the future, I hope to communicate to the scholarly world and policy communities how the educated American public thinks about foreign policy.

Sincerely,
Lauren Prather

2020 National Opinion Ballot

First, we'd like to ask you for some information about your participation in the Great Decisions program. If you are not currently a Great Decisions program member, please skip to the "background" section.

How long have you participated in the Great Decisions program (i.e., attended one or more discussion sessions)?

❏ This is the first year I have participated

❏ I participated in one previous year

❏ I participated in more than one previous year

How did you learn about the Great Decisions Program?

❏ Word of mouth

❏ Local library

❏ Foreign Policy Association website

❏ Promotional brochure

❏ Other organization _____

Where does your Great Decisions group meet?

❏ Private home

❏ Library

❏ Community center

❏ Learning in retirement

❏ Other _____

How many hours, on average, do you spend reading one *Great Decisions* chapter?

❏ Less than 1 hour

❏ 1–2 hours

❏ 3–4 hours

❏ More than 4 hours

Would you say you have or have not changed your opinion in a fairly significant way as a result of taking part in the Great Decisions program?

❏ Have

❏ Have not

❏ Not sure

Background Section: Next, we'd like to ask you some information about your background.

How strongly do you agree or disagree with the following statement? Although the media often reports about national and international events and developments, this news is seldom as interesting as the things that happen directly in our own community and neighborhood.

❏ Agree strongly

❏ Agree somewhat

❏ Neither agree nor disagree

❏ Disagree somewhat

❏ Disagree strongly

Generally speaking, how interested are you in politics?

❏ Very much interested

❏ Somewhat interested

❏ Not too interested

❏ Not interested at all

Do you think it is best for the future of the United States if the U.S. takes an active role in world affairs or stays out of world affairs?

❏ Takes an active role in world affairs

❏ Stays out of world affairs

How often are you asked for your opinion on foreign policy?

❏ Often

❏ Sometimes

❏ Never

Have you been abroad during the last two years?

❏ Yes

❏ No

Do you know, or are you learning, a foreign language?

❏ Yes

❏ No

Do you have any close friends or family that live in other countries?

❏ Yes

❏ No

Do you donate to any charities that help the poor in other countries?

❏ Yes

❏ No

Generally speaking, do you usually think of yourself as a Republican, a Democrat, an Independent or something else?

❏ Republican

❏ Democrat

❏ Independent

❏ Other _____

With which gender do you most identify?

❏ Male

❏ Female

❏ Transgender male

❏ Transgender female

❏ Gender variant/non-conforming

❏ Other _____

❏ Prefer not to answer

What race do you consider yourself?

❏ White/Caucasian

❏ Black/African American

❏ Hispanic/Latino

❏ Asian American

❏ Native American

❏ Other _____

❏ Prefer not to answer

Were you born in the United States or another country?

❏ United States

❏ Another country

Are you a citizen of the United States, another country, or are you a citizen of both the United States and another country?

❏ United States

❏ Another country

❏ United States and another country

How important is religion in your life?

❏ Very important

❏ Somewhat important

❏ Not too important

❏ Not at all important

What is your age? _____

Are you currently employed?

❏ Full-time employee

❏ Part-time employee

❏ Self-employed

❏ Unemployed

❏ Retired

❏ Student

❏ Homemaker

What are the first three digits of your zip code? (This will allow us to do a state-by-state breakdown of results.)

_____ _____ _____

Can you give us an estimate of your household income in 2018 before taxes?

❏ Below $30,000

❏ $30,000–$50,000

❏ $50,000–$75,000

❏ $75,000–$100,000

❏ $100,000–$150,000

❏ Over $150,000

❏ Not sure

❏ Prefer not to say

What is the highest level of education you have completed?

❏ Did not graduate from high school

❏ High school graduate

❏ Some college, but no degree (yet)

❏ 2-year college degree

❏ 4-year college degree

❏ Some postgraduate work, but no degree (yet)

❏ Post-graduate degree (MA, MBA, MD, JD, PhD, etc.)

Now we would like to ask you some ballot questions from previous years:

1. From 2016's "Climate Geopolitics": All else equal, would you like the next president to be someone who favors government action to address climate change, or someone who opposes such action?

❏ The next president should be someone who favors government action to address climate change

❏ The next president should be someone who opposes government action to address climate change

2. From Great Decisions 2014 "Food and Climate" : To deal with the problem of climate change, do you think the U.S. government is doing too much, not enough, or about the right amount?

❏ Too much
❏ Not enough
❏ About the right amount

3. From Great Decisions 2015 "India Changes Course": To what extent do you see tensions between India and Pakistan as a possible threat to the vital interests of the United States in the next 10 years?

❏ Critical threat
❏ An important, but not critical threat
❏ Not an important threat at all
❏ Not sure

4. From Great Decisions 2017 "Prospects for Afghanistan and Pakistan": Do you approve or disapprove of the United States conducting missile strikes from pilotless aircraft, called "drones", to target extremists in countries such as Pakistan and Afghanistan?

❏ Approve strongly
❏ Approve somewhat
❏ Disapprove somewhat
❏ Disapprove strongly

5. From Great Decisions 2017 "U.S. foreign policy and petroleum": How threatening to U.S. national security do you think America's dependence on foreign oil is?

❏ Very threatening
❏ Somewhat threatening
❏ Not too threatening
❏ Not thretening at all

6. From Great Decisions 2015 "Human Trafficking": Do you think the U.S. government should increase, keep the same or decrease the amount of money it gives other countries to fight human trafficking?

❏ Increase
❏ Keep the same
❏ Decrease
❏ Not sure

7. From Great Decisions 2016 "International Migration": How likely is it that Congress will pass immigration reform legislation?

❏ Very likely
❏ Somewhat likely
❏ Not too likely
❏ Not at all likely

8. From Great Decisions 2014 "China's foreign policy": In dealing with a rising China, do you think the U.S. should…

❏ Undertake friendly cooperation and engagement with China
❏ Actively work to limit the growth of China's power

9. From Great Decisions 2017 "Latin America's political pendulum": In your view, is the temperature of U.S.-Latin America relations likely to get better, get worse, or remain about the same over the next five years?

❏ It will get better
❏ It will get worse
❏ It will remain the same

10. From Great Decisions 2008 "Foreign Aid": Should a donor country use foreign aid to promote a political agenda?

❏ Yes
❏ No
❏ Maybe

11. From Great Decisions 2015 "Privacy in the digital age": How concerned are you personally about the privacy of personal information you give out on the Internet, as well as privacy regarding what you do on the Internet?

❏ Very concerned
❏ Somewhat concerned.
❏ Not at all concerned
❏ Not sure

12. From Great Decisions 2012 "Cybersecurity": What party or parties is best equipped to lead in the global governance of cyberspace?

❏ a multilateral body, like the UN, where all countries have a say
❏ Liberal democracies, such as the U.S., that have a commitment to open networks
❏ A collaboration between the public and private sectors
❏ The private sector alone

Topic 1. Climate Change and the Global Order

1. Have you engaged in any of the following activities related to the "Climate Change and the Global Order" topic? Mark all that you have done or mark none of the above.

- ❏ Read the article on climate change in the 2020 Great Decisions briefing book
- ❏ Discussed the article on climate change with a Great Decisions discussion group
- ❏ Discussed the article on climate change with friends and family
- ❏ Followed news related to climate change
- ❏ Taken a class in which you learned about issues related to climate change
- ❏ Have or had a job related to climate change
- ❏ None of the above

2. How interested would you say you are in issues related to climate change?

- ❏ Very interested
- ❏ Somewhat interested
- ❏ Not too interested
- ❏ Not at all interested

3. To what extent do you think climate change has changed as a threat in the last six years or so?

- ❏ Much worse
- ❏ Somewhat worse
- ❏ About the same
- ❏ Somewhat better
- ❏ Much better

4. Should climate change be the "top priority" for the President and Congress?

- ❏ Yes
- ❏ No
- ❏ Unsure

5. Generally, most policies that are developed to help combat or reduce the effects of global climate change…

- ❏ Do more good than harm
- ❏ Do more harm than good
- ❏ Make no difference

6. Which organizations do you think should take the lead in promoting climate change reform?

- ❏ Individual governments
- ❏ Multinational organizations
- ❏ NGOs
- ❏ Civil society

7. Which aspect of climate change concerns you the most?

- ❏ Rising sea levels
- ❏ Global warming
- ❏ Deforestation/Desertification
- ❏ Displaced peoples
- ❏ Climate change does not concern me

8. To the best of your knowledge, how much does human activity effect global climate change?

- ❏ A lot
- ❏ Somewhat
- ❏ Not that much
- ❏ Not at all
- ❏ I don't know

9. Would you like to share any other thoughts with us about climate change? If so, please use the space below.

. . . .

. . . .

. . . .

. . . .

. . . .

. . . .

. . . .

Enter your answers online at
www.fpa.org/ballot

Topic 2. India and Pakistan

1. Have you engaged in any of the following activities related to the "India and Pakistan" topic? Mark all that you have done or mark none of the above

- ❑ Read the article on India and Pakistan in the 2020 Great Decisions briefing book
- ❑ Discussed the article on India and Pakistan with a Great Decisions discussion group
- ❑ Discussed the article on India and Pakistan with friends and family
- ❑ Followed news related to India and Pakistan
- ❑ Taken a class in which you learned about issues related to India and Pakistan
- ❑ Have or had a job related to India and Pakistan
- ❑ Traveled to India and/or Pakistan
- ❑ None of the above

2. How interested would you say you are in issues related to India and Pakistan?

- ❑ Very interested
- ❑ Somewhat interested
- ❑ Not too interested
- ❑ Not at all interested

3. In your opinion, India is more of a…

- ❑ Partner
- ❑ Enemy
- ❑ Neither
- ❑ Don't know

4. In your opinion, Pakistan is more of a…

- ❑ Partner
- ❑ Enemy
- ❑ Neither
- ❑ Don't know

5. With regards to the Jammu-Kashmir dispute between India and Pakistan, the United States should…

- ❑ Support India
- ❑ Support Pakistan
- ❑ Support Jammu-Kashmir self-determination
- ❑ The U.S. should stay out of the dispute

6a. Which do you think is a more likely outcome in the dispute between India and Pakistan over Jammu-Kashmir?

- ❑ War between India and Pakistan
- ❑ Diplomatic agreement between India and Pakistan

6b. In your opinion, what is the most likely outcome of the Jammu-Kashmir dispute?

- ❑ India dominated Jammu-Kashmir region
- ❑ Pakistan dominated Jammu-Kashmir region
- ❑ Return to autonomous region
- ❑ Not sure

7. How important is the India and Pakistan dispute in global affairs?

- ❑ Very important
- ❑ Somewhat important
- ❑ Not too important
- ❑ Not at all important

9. Would you like to share any other thoughts with us about India and Pakistan? If so, please use the space below.

. . . .
. . . .
. . . .
. . . .
. . . .

Topic 3. Red Sea Security

1. Have you engaged in any of the following activities related to the "Red Sea Security" topic? Mark all that you have done or mark none of the above.

- ❏ Read the article on "Red Sea Security" in the 2020 Great Decisions briefing book
- ❏ Discussed the article on "Red Sea Security" with a Great Decisions discussion group
- ❏ Discussed the article on "Red Sea Security" with friends and family
- ❏ Followed news related to "Red Sea Security"
- ❏ Taken a class in which you learned about issues related to "Red Sea Security"
- ❏ Have or had a job related to "Red Sea Security"
- ❏ Traveled to the Red Sea area
- ❏ None of the above

2. How interested would you say you are in issues related to "Red Sea Security?"

- ❏ Very interested
- ❏ Somewhat interested
- ❏ Not too interested
- ❏ Not at all interested

3. Should the U.S. be concerned about the growing presence that China has in the Red Sea region?

- ❏ Very concerned
- ❏ Somewhat concerned
- ❏ Not too concerned
- ❏ Not at all concerned

4. How should the U.S. react to issues of aggression by other nations in the Red Sea?

- ❏ Naval/Military response
- ❏ Economic sanctions
- ❏ Increase patrols in the region
- ❏ Diplomatic sanctions
- ❏ U.S. should not react to issues of aggression in the region

5. Do you think that the foreign countries that have bases/ports in the Red Sea region are responsible for domestic issues in the region?

- ❏ Foreign nations should strive to help solve domestic issues
- ❏ Foreign nations should have no say in domestic issues in the region
- ❏ Not sure

6. In your opinion, what is the biggest roadblock to development in the Red Sea region?

- ❏ Saudi/Yemen conflict
- ❏ Reliance on oil trade
- ❏ Saudi/Iran conflict
- ❏ Local regional conflicts
- ❏ Piracy/Terrorism
- ❏ Not sure

7. In your opinion, should the United States combat the litany of terrorist organizations within the Red Sea region?

- ❏ Yes, with military force
- ❏ Yes, by arming/training local resistance groups
- ❏ No, the United States should not combat terrorist groups in the Red Sea region

8. Would you like to share any other thoughts with us about "Red Sea Security?" If so, please use the space below.

. . . .

. . . .

. . . .

. . . .

. . . .

. . . .

. . . .

Topic 4. Modern Slavery and Human Trafficking

1. Have you engaged in any of the following activities related to the "Modern Slavery and Human Trafficking" topic? Mark all that you have done or mark none of the above.

- ❏ Read the article on human trafficking in the 2020 Great Decisions briefing book
- ❏ Discussed the article on human trafficking with a Great Decisions discussion group
- ❏ Discussed the article on human trafficking with friends and family
- ❏ Followed news related to human trafficking
- ❏ Taken a class in which you learned about issues related to human trafficking
- ❏ None of the above

2. How interested would you say you are in issues related to modern slavery and human trafficking?

- ❏ Very interested
- ❏ Somewhat interested
- ❏ Not too interested
- ❏ Not at all interested

3. Do you think the United States government is doing enough to combat human trafficking?

- ❏ Yes, they are doing enough
- ❏ No, they are not doing enough
- ❏ Not sure

4. How should the United States handle victims of human trafficking who are found in the United States? (Please select one)

- ❏ Resettle them in the U.S.
- ❏ Return them to their country of origin
- ❏ Turn them over to NGO/Rescue group
- ❏ Allow them to file for asylum
- ❏ Other _____

5. In your opinion, to what extent would legalizing prostitution in the U.S. help to alleviate the prevalence of sex trafficking?
- ❏ Alleviate a great deal
- ❏ Alleviate somewhat
- ❏ Neither alleviate nor worsen
- ❏ Worsen somewhat
- ❏ Worsen a great deal
- ❏ Unsure

6. How should the U.S. act with regard to trading with nations where slave labor is used? (Please select one)

- ❏ <u>Limit trade</u> from nations that use slave labor to products that are certified to be made by paid workers
- ❏ <u>Enact sanctions</u> against nations that use slave labor
- ❏ <u>End all trade relations</u> with nations where slave labor is used
- ❏ <u>Cut all ties</u> with nations where slave labor is used
- ❏ Other_____

7. How likely do you think it is that the next Presidential administration will make alleviating human trafficking and modern slavery a priority?

- ❏ Very likely
- ❏ Somewhat likely
- ❏ Not too likely
- ❏ Not likely at all

8. In your opinion, does the U.S. have a moral obligation to combat human trafficking and slavery around the globe?

- ❏ Yes, the U.S. has a moral obligation
- ❏ No, the U.S. does not have a moral obligation
- ❏ Not sure

9. Would you like to share any other thoughts with us about human trafficking and slavery? If so, please use the space below.

. . . .

. . . .

. . . .

. . . .

. . . .

. . . .

. . . .

Topic 5. U.S. Relations with the Northern Triangle

1. Have you engaged in any of the following activities related to the "U.S. Relations with the Northern Triangle" topic? Mark all that you have done or mark none of the above.

- ❏ Read the article on the Northern Triangle in the 2020 Great Decisions briefing book
- ❏ Discussed the article on the Northern Triangle with a Great Decisions discussion group
- ❏ Discussed the article on the Northern Triangle with friends and family
- ❏ Followed news related to the Northern Triangle
- ❏ Taken a class in which you learned about issues related to the Northern Triangle
- ❏ Have or had a job related to the Northern Triangle
- ❏ Traveled to a Northern Triangle country (El Salvador, Guatemala, Honduras)
- ❏ None of the above

2. How interested would you say you are in issues related to the Northern Triangle?

- ❏ Very interested
- ❏ Somewhat interested
- ❏ Not too interested
- ❏ Not at all interested

3. On March 30, 2019, President Donald Trump announced that the U.S. would be cutting off all foreign aid to the Northern Triangle nations. To what extent do you agree with President Donald Trump's decision to cut foreign aid to the Northern Triangle?

- ❏ Very much agree
- ❏ Somewhat agree
- ❏ Neither agree nor disagree
- ❏ Somewhat disagree
- ❏ Very much disagree

4. Do you think President Trump's cutting of foreign aid will have a positive, negative, or no effect on the Northern Triangle nations' ability to curtail migration?

- ❏ Very positive effect
- ❏ Somewhat positive effect
- ❏ No effect
- ❏ Somewhat negative effect
- ❏ Very negative effect

5. Which of the following in your opinion is the biggest cause for the instability in the Northern Triangle? (Please select one)

- ❏ U.S. interference
- ❏ Gang violence

- ❏ The drug trade
- ❏ Corrupt local governments
- ❏ Other _____

6a. In your opinion, should individuals living in the Northern Triangle be able to apply for refugee status in the United States?

- ❏ Yes
- ❏ No
- ❏ Unsure

6b. In your opinion, should migrants who travel from the Northern Triangle to the United States be able to apply for asylum status at the U.S. border?

- ❏ Yes
- ❏ No
- ❏ Unsure

7. Do you think that decriminalizing drug use in the United States will increase, decrease, or not affect the power of drug gangs in the Northern Triangle?

- ❏ Increase
- ❏ Decrease
- ❏ No effect

8. Which of the following in your opinion is the most effect policy to curtail migration from the Northern Triangle? (Please select one)

- ❏ U.S. foreign aid
- ❏ Economic/Political sanctions
- ❏ Military intervention
- ❏ Border wall
- ❏ The U.S. should not try to curtail migration from the Northern Triangle.
- ❏ Other _____

9. Would you like to share any other thoughts with us about the Northern Triangle? If so, please use the space below.

. . . .

. . . .

. . . .

. . . .

Topic 6. China's Road into Latin America

1. Have you engaged in any of the following activities related to the "China's Road into Latin America" topic? Mark all that you have done or mark none of the above.

- ❏ Read the article on China in Latin America in the 2020 Great Decisions briefing book
- ❏ Discussed the article on China in Latin America with a Great Decisions discussion group
- ❏ Discussed the article on China in Latin America with friends and family
- ❏ Followed news related to China in Latin America
- ❏ Taken a class in which you learned about issues related to China in Latin America
- ❏ Travelled to a Latin American country
- ❏ None of the above

2. How interested would you say you are in issues related to China in Latin America?

- ❏ Very interested
- ❏ Somewhat interested
- ❏ Not too interested
- ❏ Not at all interested

3. Do you believe that the growing relationship between China and Latin America is a "win-win?"

- ❏ Yes, I think both China and Latin America will benefit
- ❏ No, I think only China will benefit
- ❏ No, I think only Latin American countries will benefit
- ❏ No, I don't think either China or Latin America will benefit
- ❏ Unsure

4a. How concerned are you regarding the inroads that China has made into Latin America for <u>U.S. national security?</u>

- ❏ Very concerned
- ❏ Somewhat concerned
- ❏ Not too concerned
- ❏ Not at all concerned

4b. How concerned are you regarding the inroads that China has made into Latin America for <u>U.S. economic power?</u>

- ❏ Very concerned
- ❏ Somewhat concerned
- ❏ Not too concerned
- ❏ Not at all concerned

5. How positive or negative do you feel about the Chinese "One Belt, One Road" initiative

- ❏ Mostly positive
- ❏ Somewhat positive
- ❏ Somewhat negative
- ❏ Mostly negative

6. In your opinion, are Latin American nations "better off" taking economic assistance from China than from the U.S?

- ❏ Yes, Latin American countries are better off with China
- ❏ No, Latin American countries are better off with the U.S.
- ❏ Latin American nations are better off left on their own

7. To what extent do you agree with the following statement: The United States should convert to a form of State capitalism (similar to China's) in order to compete with China's Belt and Road initiative?

- ❏ Strongly agree
- ❏ Somewhat agree
- ❏ Somewhat disagree
- ❏ Strongly disagree

8. Would you like to share any other thoughts with us about U.S. global engagement and the military? If so, please use the space below.

. . . .

. . . .

. . . .

. . . .

Topic 7. The Philippines and the U.S.

1. Have you engaged in any of the following activities related to the "The Philippines and the U.S." topic? Mark all that you have done or mark none of the above.

- ❏ Read the article on "The Philippines and the U.S." in the 2020 Great Decisions briefing book
- ❏ Discussed the article on "The Philippines and the U.S." with a Great Decisions discussion group
- ❏ Discussed the article on "The Philippines and the U.S." with friends and family
- ❏ Followed news related to "The Philippines and the U.S."
- ❏ Taken a class in which you learned about issues related to the "The Philippines and the U.S."
- ❏ Have or had a job related to the "The Philippines and the U.S."
- ❏ Traveled to the Philippines
- ❏ None of the above

2. How interested would you say you are in issues related to the U.S. and the Philippines?

- ❏ Very interested
- ❏ Somewhat interested
- ❏ Not too interested
- ❏ Not at all interested

3. Should the United States commit to positive relations with allies, even if those allies have less than reputable leaders in charge?

- ❏ Yes, the U.S. should support allies regardless of who leads them
- ❏ No, the U.S. should only support allies with strong, democratically elected leaders
- ❏ Unsure

4. In your opinion, should the United States offer reparations to the Philippines for their years of colonial rule?

- ❏ Strongly agree
- ❏ Somewhat agree
- ❏ Somewhat disagree
- ❏ Strongly disagree

5. Would you support U.S. military intervention in the South China Sea if China continues to encroach on Philippine naval territory?

- ❏ Strongly support
- ❏ Somewhat support
- ❏ Somewhat oppose
- ❏ Strongly oppose

6. The 2019 midterm elections in the Philippines has seen Rodrigo Duterte and his HNP party consolidate their power over the government. Are you concerned that Duterte will recompose the Philippine government to a single party state?

- ❏ Very concerned
- ❏ Somewhat concerned
- ❏ Not too concerned
- ❏ Not concerned at all

7. Would you like to share any other thoughts with us about the U.S. and the Philippines? If so, please use the space below.

. . . .

. . . .

. . . .

. . . .

. . . .

. . . .

. . . .

. . . .

Topic 8. Artificial Intelligence and Data

1. Have you engaged in any of the following activities related to the "Artificial Intelligence and Data" topic? Mark all that you have done or mark none of the above.

- ❏ Read the article on AI and data in the 2020 Great Decisions briefing book
- ❏ Discussed the article on AI and data with a Great Decisions discussion group
- ❏ Discussed the article on AI and data with friends and family
- ❏ Followed news related to AI and data
- ❏ Taken a class in which you learned about issues related to AI and data
- ❏ Have or had a job related to AI and data
- ❏ None of the above

2. How interested would you say you are in issues related to AI and data?

- ❏ Very interested
- ❏ Somewhat interested
- ❏ Not too interested
- ❏ Not at all interested

3. Which of these, if any, are your largest source of concern with regards to artificial intelligence?

- ❏ Surveillance systems
- ❏ Potential job loss
- ❏ Autonomous weapons
- ❏ Spreading of disinformation
- ❏ Other _____

4. Are you in favor of the United States government regulating personal and public data?

- ❏ Very much in favor
- ❏ Somewhat in favor
- ❏ Neither in favor or oppose
- ❏ Somewhat oppose
- ❏ Very much oppose

5. In your opinion, should the United States government invest in AI firms, or should it remain in the private sector?

- ❏ Yes, the U.S. government should invest in AI firms
- ❏ No, AI firms should remain in the private sector only
- ❏ Unsure

6. Do you trust AI firms with your data?

- ❏ Trust completely
- ❏ Trust somewhat
- ❏ Neither trust nor distrust
- ❏ Distrust somewhat
- ❏ Distrust completely

7. In your opinion, do technology/AI companies hold too much, about the right amount, or not enough influence over the U.S. economy?

- ❏ Too much
- ❏ About the right amount
- ❏ Not enough

8. In your opinion, do technology/AI companies hold too much, about the right amount, or not enough influence over the U.S. government?

- ❏ Too much
- ❏ About the right amount
- ❏ Not enough

9. Would you like to share any other thoughts with us about AI and data? If so, please use the space below.

. . . .

. . . .

. . . .

. . . .

. . . .

. . . .

Global Discussion Questions

No decision in foreign policy is made in a vacuum, and the repercussions of any single decision have far-reaching effects across the range of strategic interests on the U.S. policy agenda. This GREAT DECISIONS feature is intended to facilitate the discussion of this year's topics in a global context, to discuss the linkages between the topics and to encourage consideration of the broader impact of decision-making.

1. Consider "Climate Change and the Global Order" in the context of "Red Sea Security." The Red Sea is one of the global hubs for the oil trade. What would a global shift away from greenhouse gas emitting fossil fuels do to the region both economically, and politically? Would the region still be able to grow? Is there any way that turmoil could be avoided?

2. Consider "U.S. Relations with the Northern Triangle" in the context of "China's Road into Latin America." The United States has a complicated relationship with Central and South American countries. As China moves into the region, what can the U.S. do to restore good relations with their southern neighbors? Should the U.S. consider cooperating on some projects with China?

3. Consider "Climate Change and the Global Order" in the context of "Modern Slavery and Human Trafficking." As both authors point out, climate change could lead to a new generation of migrants and refugees looking for a new home. Should people who are displaced due to climate change be granted refugee status? Do countries that contribute more to greenhouse gas emission have a responsibility to relocate these people?

4. Consider "The Philippines and the U.S." in the context of "China's Road into Latin America." As the United States begins to pull itself back from its allies and neighbors, China is stepping into the void. Should the U.S. be more concerned about China's inroads into allies' governments? Is the pull of China due in part to mistakes of past U.S. administrations, and if so, how can the U.S. seek to remedy these past grievances?

5. Consider "India and Pakistan" in the context of "The Philippines and the U.S." After the revocation of Article 370, Jammu-Kashmir has been inundated with reports of human rights abuses and general strife among the populace. Similar reports have been coming out of the Philippines, where Rodrigo Duterte's war on drugs has had devastating consequences. Does the U.S. have an obligation to step into these nations to prevent these human rights abuses? What role does the UN have, if any?

6. Consider "Artificial Intelligence and Data" in the context of "Modern Slavery and Human Trafficking." As AI systems advance, countries like China has turned to the technology for surveillance purposes. Should the U.S. consider these kinds of surveillance technology to monitor the border? Would this technology be used to prevent all migration, or just to help catch smugglers and traffickers? Does the use of surveillance technology go against the constitution?

7. Consider "China's Road into Latin America" in the context of "Red Sea Security." As China continues to open up and expand their global influence, should the U.S. actively inhibit this growth? What would the world look like with China as the dominant superpower? Will China's global "Belt and Road" initiative push the U.S. out of global prominence, or has the U.S. taken itself out? Should the U.S. try to curtail or limit China's growth?

8. Consider "U.S. Relations with the Northern Triangle" in the context of "Modern Slavery and Human Trafficking." Most of the economic migrants and refugees to the United States come from the Northern Triangle region. How can the U.S. stem the tide of migrants from the region? How has the political climate in the region helped traffickers? Are there solutions that could benefit both the U.S. and Northern Triangle?

9. Consider "India and Pakistan" in the context of "The Philippines and the U.S." Both President Duterte of the Philippines and President Modi of India and their political parties were reelected to their positions with overwhelming majorities. What makes these leaders so popular? Are there any similarities between the two? Are the two countries similar in any other ways? (Economic downturn, Rural vs. Urban split?)

10. Consider "Artificial Intelligence and Data" in the context of "Climate Change and the Global Order." After reading the two articles, which of the two topics do you think will have the most significant effect on global affairs in the next decade? Why is there a fear regarding both AI and Climate Change? Are the coming changes from both inevitable?

For glossaries, additional readings and more, visit
www.fpa.org/great_decisions

Become a Member

For nearly a century, members of the Association have played key roles in government, think tanks, academia and the private sector.

As an active participant in the FPA's Great Decisions program, we encourage you to join the community today's foreign policy thought leaders.

Member—$250

Benefits:
- Free admission to all Associate events (includes member's family)
- Discounted admission for all other guests to Associate events
- Complimentary **GREAT DECISIONS** briefing book
- Complimentary issue of FPA's annual ***National Opinion Ballot Report***

Visit us online at

www.fpa.org/membership

Make a Donation

Your support helps the FOREIGN POLICY ASSOCIATION's programs dedicated to global affairs education.

Make a fully tax-deductible contribution to FPA's Annual Fund 2020.

To contribute to the Annual Fund 2020 visit us online at **www.fpa.org** or call the Membership Department at

(800) 628-5754 ext. 333

The generosity of donors who contribute $500 or more is acknowledged in FPA's *Annual Report*.

All financial contributions are tax-deductible to the fullest extent of the law under section 501 (c)(3) of the IRS code.

FPA also offers membership at the SPONSOR MEMBER and PATRON MEMBER levels. To learn more, visit us online at www.fpa.org/membership or call (800) 628-5754 ext. 333.

Return this form by mail to: Foreign Policy Association, 551 Fifth Avenue, Suite 3000, New York, N.Y. 10176

ORDER ONLINE: WWW.FPA.ORG/GREAT_DECISIONS

CALL (800) 477-5836

FAX (212) 481-9275

❑ MR.   ❑ MRS.   ❑ MS.   ❑ DR.   ❑ PROF.

NAME _____

ADDRESS _____

_____**APT/FLOOR** _____

CITY _____ **STATE** _____ **ZIP** _____

TEL _____

E-MAIL _____

❑ AMEX   ❑ VISA   ❑ MC   ❑ DISCOVER

❑ CHECK (ENCLOSED)

CHECKS SHOULD BE PAYABLE TO FOREIGN POLICY ASSOCIATION.

CARD NO.

SIGNATURE OF CARDHOLDER

EXP. DATE (MM/YY)

PRODUCT	QTY	PRICE	COST
GREAT DECISIONS 2020 Briefing Book (FPA31692)		$32	
SPECIAL OFFER TEN PACK SPECIAL GREAT DECISIONS 2020 (FPA31699) *Includes 10% discount		$288	
GREAT DECISIONS TELEVISION SERIES GD ON DVD 2020 (FPA31693)		$40	
GREAT DECISIONS 2020 TEACHER'S PACKET (1 Briefing Book, 1 Teacher's Guide and 1 DVD (FPA 31695) E-MAIL: (REQUIRED) _____		$70	
GREAT DECISIONS CLASSROOM-PACKET (1 Teacher's Packet & 30 Briefing Books (FPA31696) E-MAIL: (REQUIRED) _____		$725	
MEMBERSHIP		$250	
ANNUAL FUND 2020 (ANY AMOUNT)			

SUBTOTAL $ _____

plus S & H* $ _____

TOTAL $ _____

For details and shipping charges, call FPA's Sales Department at (800) 477-5836.

Orders mailed to FPA without the shipping charge will be held.